LIFE
SENTENCE

Also by Mark Bowden

Doctor Dealer

Bringing the Heat

Black Hawk Down

Killing Pablo

Finders Keepers

Road Work

Guests of the Ayatollah

The Best Game Ever

Worm

The Finish

The Three Battles of Wanat

Hue 1968

The Last Stone

The Case of the Vanishing Blonde

The Steal

LIFE SENTENCE

The Brief and Tragic Career of
Baltimore's Deadliest Gang Leader

MARK
BOWDEN

Atlantic Monthly Press
New York

FIRST EDITION

Published simultaneously in Canada
Printed in the United States of America

This book was set in 12-pt. Arno Pro by Alpha Design & Composition of Pittsfield, NH.

First Grove Atlantic hardcover edition: April 2023

Library of Congress Cataloging-in-Publication data is available for this title.

ISBN 978-0-8021-6242-7
eISBN 978-0-8021-6243-4

Atlantic Monthly Press
an imprint of Grove Atlantic
154 West 14th Street
New York, NY 10011

Distibuted by Publishers Group West

groveatlantic.com

23 24 25 26   10 9 8 7 6 5 4 3 2 1

For Stan Heuisler, who gave me a shot

Contents

So that in the nature of man, we find three principall causes of quarrel. First, Competition; Secondly, Diffidence [self-defense]; Thirdly, Glory. The first maketh men invade for Gain; the second, for safety, and the third, for Reputation . . . for trifles . . .

—Thomas Hobbes, *Leviathan*

Preface

This book began early in 2021, with an invitation from the US Attorney's office in Baltimore, which was eager to talk about its efforts to combat that city's shocking street violence. The prosecutors I met were rightly proud of the work they were doing to take violent gangs off the street, and I assumed they had invited me in hopes that I might write something about it.

They did have a good story to tell, and when I asked them for a specific example, they told me about Trained to Go, a Sandtown gang run by a young man with the unlikely name Montana Barronette. The gang, mostly teenagers, had terrorized its West Baltimore community throughout the previous decade. TTG had been linked to twenty or more killings and convicted and sentenced, as a group, for ten of them. It was a rich opportunity. I knew that the story of how TTG was investigated, arrested, and prosecuted would be fascinating in itself, and journalists rarely get such willing cooperation from law enforcement, especially federal agencies. But what interested me more was a bigger and more important story.

Who was this Montana Barronette? How did he become who he became—a young man, barely out of his teens, known to the Baltimore police as the city's "number one trigger puller"? I had started my career as a reporter in Baltimore. One of the first major stories I wrote was a series about life in a West Baltimore high-rise housing project, which I lived in, off and on, for a week. I was familiar with Barronette's home turf of Sandtown. It had long been considered one of the worst neighborhoods in the city, an exemplar of intractable urban failure and neglect. It was the backdrop for much of David Simon's series *The Wire*, which had begun airing almost twenty years earlier. Why was it still that way? Why was it so seemingly impossible to change? These questions were bigger than the specifics of this story. There were neighborhoods and characters like Sandtown and Barronette in cities all over America, where rates of homicidal violence are an ongoing national disgrace.

So I set out to find answers, framing this book chapter by chapter as part of the larger story. There was Barronette's greased path into drug dealing and murder, starting with his family and childhood circumstances, which pulled him in a direction that would have been hard to resist—even though most young men born in such circumstances do. There was the long racist history of Baltimore itself, the intentionality with which Sandtown was created. That long story intersected with my own upbringing as part of the privileged baby-boomer white caste in the city's northern suburbs, just ten miles by map but in all other respects a whole world away. I looked into the ambitious, expensive, and ultimately futile effort in the first decades of this century to rebuild and revivify Sandtown, and examined the perverse role played by the internet and social media in cheering on violent gang behavior.

Perhaps the most important discovery was that Barronette and his TTG crew were not, as prosecutors and cops suggested, outliers or dangerous psychopaths. They were essentially normal teenagers in an abnormal environment, one that Baltimore (and other cities) had built and sustained very deliberately over centuries. TTG was perfectly adapted to its habitat. To better understand that story, I read a wider range of books and papers, and interviewed more academic experts, than for any other book I have written. Relevant parts of that research and reporting are cited throughout in the text and in source notes.

Ultimately, this isn't a story about an unusual group of young men. It is the story of young men growing up in a place where murderous violence has become a way of life.

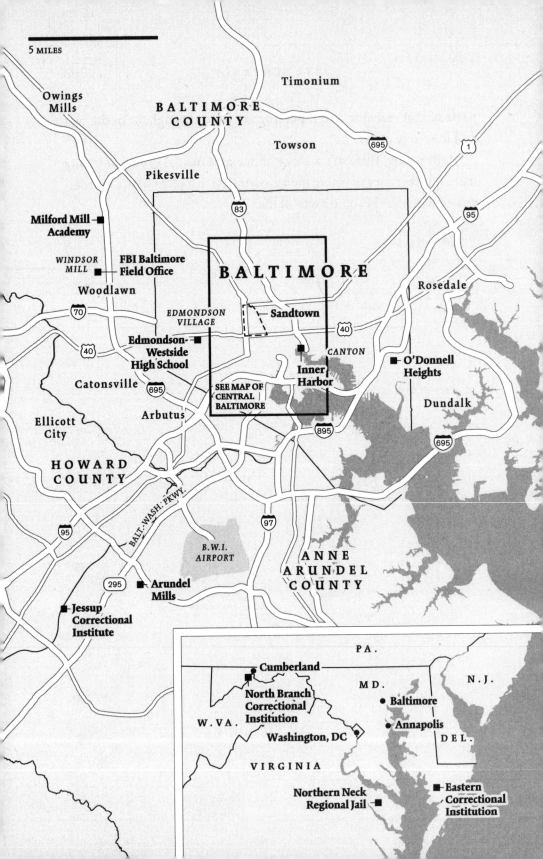

5 MILES

Owings
Mills

Timonium

BALTIMORE
COUNTY

Towson

695

1

Pikesville

Milford Mill
Academy

83

WINDSOR
MILL

FBI Baltimore
Field Office

BALTIMORE

95

Woodlawn

70

Rosedale

EDMONDSON
VILLAGE

Sandtown

Edmondson-
Westside
High School

40

CANTON

O'Donnell
Heights

Catonsville

695

SEE MAP OF
CENTRAL
BALTIMORE

Inner
Harbor

Dundalk

Arbutus

895

695

Ellicott
City

HOWARD
COUNTY

BALT.-WASH. PKWY.

97

95

B.W.I.
AIRPORT

ANNE
ARUNDEL
COUNTY

295

Arundel
Mills

Jessup
Correctional
Institute

PA.

Cumberland

MD.

N.J.

North Branch
Correctional
Institution

Baltimore

W. VA.

Annapolis

DEL.

Washington, DC

VIRGINIA

Northern Neck
Regional Jail

Eastern
Correctional
Institution

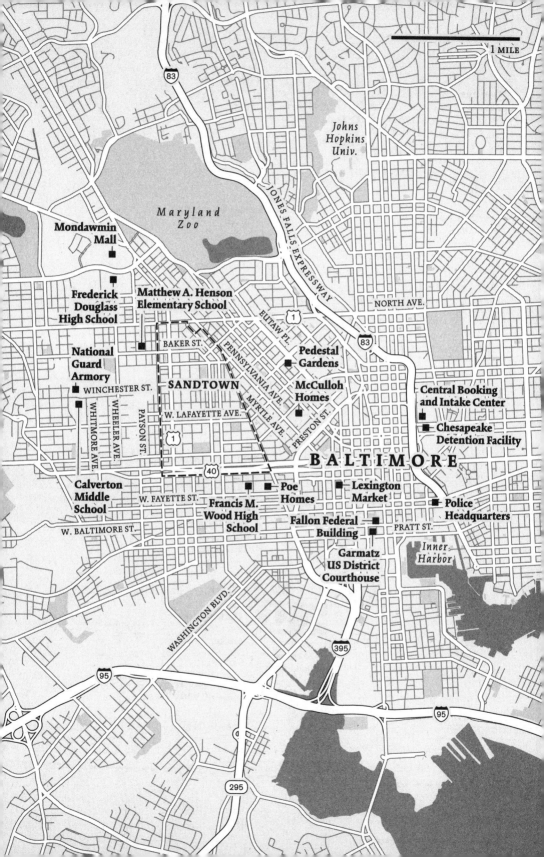

1

The Game
(or, The Greased Path)

Tana with his siblings: left, Shanika, and right, Rell.

*Violence becomes a homing pigeon floating through the ghettos
seeking a black brain in which to roost for a season.*
　　　　　　　　　　　　—Eldridge Cleaver, *Soul on Ice*

When he was a boy, his mother briefly removed him and his baby sister from the apartment in Sandtown where they lived with their grandmother and two older half siblings.

His mother, Annette Burch, brought them to the Poe Homes, a notorious West Baltimore housing project. This would have been in about 2002, when the boy, Montana Barronette, was seven, and his little sister, Sahantana Williams, whom the family called Booda, was two. Less than a mile away, it would have been a sharp change for the children. It took them "over the bridge," south of the sunken, divided Franklin-Mulberry Expressway (US Route 40), a roaring moat that formed the bottom of the world they knew.

The area over the bridge had been long defined by the brick towers of the Lexington Terrace housing projects. Built in the 1950s, in part to house those dislocated by the beginnings of Baltimore's massive modern downtown renewal, the five eleven-story towers were a universally acknowledged disaster. In them were all the ills of the urban poor, compressed. One resident described them as "a living hell." After the buildings were imploded in 1996, their occupants were resettled in the Poe Homes, rows of squat red-brick town houses that filled roughly three large square blocks. This did not resolve the problems of the towers, just spread them horizontally. The neighborhood remained virtually all Black, poor, beset with violence, and a central hub for heroin distribution—a small step down from Sandtown, which was all those things, too.

The removal of Montana and Booda must have seemed a blessing to Annette's mother, Delores, and might have come at her insistence. All four of the children were Annette's. Delores had taken them into her Harlem Avenue apartment one by one, after raising her own brood of five. She worked full-time as a custodian at Baltimore City Hall and had no help from her estranged husband. Annette was always nearby, adrift in the circle of neighborhood drug users, shifting for herself. Eventually her fifth child, James, would come to live with Delores, too. The fathers of these children were truant.

Mother and grandmother were opposite extremes, Annette dissolute, Delores pious and stern. Delores belonged to a local Pentecostal church, and as her daughter delivered child after child, she was trapped by her own sense of responsibility. The children could not be abandoned, or blamed for the sins of their mother or fathers. They had to be taken in, even if this enabled Annette's behavior. So Terrell and Shanika Sivells, Montana Barronette, and Booda and then James Williams were reared on their grandmother's sometimes bitter forbearance. They were not mistreated but felt the bitterness. Because their mother was around, they were caught in a contradiction. At home, Delores dragged them with her to worship so often the neighborhood kids taunted them, calling them "church kids," which they hated. But work kept Delores away often, so they spent a lot of time in the streets with their mother, learning the ins and outs of the corner drug markets. This left them always out of step, teased on the corners, an enemy camp in the Harlem Avenue apartment. "We all went through our own separate hell when we was kids," Shanika would say years later. Annette's decision to take the two youngest with her to Poe Homes may have resulted from an ultimatum or perhaps a fleeting good intention. Whatever the reason, it didn't last.

One morning, not long after the move, the children woke up alone. Montana waited all day, until nightfall, and when their mother failed to return, he left with Booda and flagged down a police car. The officer took them back to Harlem Avenue.

Several things of note about this: It shows the tenor of his upbringing. It shows him to have been poised and capable at age seven. And it also shows him to have been unafraid of the police.

Given the stories told by his older sister, this last is surprising. Shanika grew up in terror of cops. In particular, she remembered a night when police crashed into their apartment, guns drawn, looking for Montana's father, Delroy. Montana was then an infant, named after a paternal Jamaican uncle. Shanika was only three, so her memory is mostly secondhand and probably exaggerated, but there is no doubt that the raid was traumatic. Delroy wasn't there. Annette was nabbed trying to climb out a back window and was taken away. Seeing their mother arrested would be enough to sear the night in the children's memory. For the rest of her childhood, Shanika would blame the raid for her nervous problems and nightmares. Ever after, Delores would shake and pray when she heard a siren. Shanika firmly believed that the police, local and federal, had a vendetta against her family. Delores would say, simply, "I just don't like them."

Yet Montana, at seven, abandoned in a strange place with his baby sister, sought out a cop.

He would have had no memory of the raid. The only police he knew were kindly ones who bought treats at the corner store for neighborhood kids. Montana would sometimes go with other children to the precinct station and beg. For a long time after being abandoned at Poe Homes, he would say that when he grew up, he wanted to be a cop.

It was a dream not destined to last. In Sandtown, cops were seen less as protectors than as an occupying force. The neighborhood might as well have been an adjunct to the Maryland prison system, so many of its men were either locked up or enjoying a brief taste of freedom between jail terms. The neighborhood had the highest incarceration rate not just in Baltimore but in all of Maryland. Nearly everybody knew or loved somebody who had been jailed at one point or another or had been locked up themselves. Like most people convicted of crimes, few felt their punishment was just. Most in the community distrusted police and judges, a rational apprehension with deep historical roots. Such places are a breeding ground for criminals. Writing in an era of lynching and overt Jim Crow restrictions, sociologist W. E. B. Du Bois had noted this more than a century earlier, observing oppressed Black communities in the rural South.

The appearance, therefore, of the Negro criminal was a phenomenon to be awaited; and while it causes anxiety, it should not occasion surprise. . . . When, now, the real Negro criminal appeared, and instead of petty stealing and vagrancy we began to have highway robbery, burglary, murder, and rape, there was a curious effect on both sides the color-line: the Negroes refused to believe the evidence of white witnesses or the fairness of white juries, *so that the greatest deterrent to crime, the public opinion of one's own social caste, was lost,* the criminal was looked upon as crucified rather than hanged. On the other hand, the whites, used to being careless as to the guilt or innocence of accused Negroes, were swept in moments of passion beyond law, reason, and decency. Such a situation is bound to increase crime, and has increased it.

For various reasons, Montana's immediate family had fallen into a condition of petty crime familiar to Sandtown. Delroy was arrested three times in the 1990s. He served at least one prison term and was deported to Jamaica when his son was four. Annette had her share of arrests, and out on the streets she schooled her children in The Game, the ongoing hustle of selling illegal drugs, learning how to work street buys and avoid those who would steal from them or arrest them— sometimes one and the same.

Montana Malik Barronette was born in 1995 in the richest country in the world. Yet by virtue of his race and gender, statistically speaking, he had from his first breath a much smaller chance than most American children of reaching adulthood alive, avoiding prison, or enjoying even modest legitimate success—a college education, say, or a steady job. If he failed to finish high school, he stood a less than fifty-fifty chance of holding a full-time job by the time he was thirty—for white Americans the chances were close to 90 percent. If he did everything right, finished high school or even college and found employment, he would likely earn 20 percent less than a white man. The poverty of Montana's family alone would drag him down, but so would his race—a white child born into a similar situation was three times more likely to escape it. The community around him further reduced his chances; there were few examples of legitimate success and many of failure. In this, he was no different from many other Black American children, particularly those from blighted urban districts and, in Baltimore, even more particularly those from Sandtown. Writing about the neighborhood in his book *Black Baltimore*, published two years before Montana was born, author Harold A. McDougall noted that, in the "virtually all black" district, "unemployment is high, and there are a significant number of female-headed households living at or below the poverty line," and its overall crime rate was the highest in West Baltimore.

Statistics are not destiny, of course, and there are many things that can and do help defeat those odds—good parenting, a strong family and community, good schooling, role models, opportunity, and, not the least, character. Most Black children, by far, do defeat those odds, even those from Sandtown. They not only survive their youth; they avoid the pitfalls on their path and thrive. Kurt Schmoke, the former mayor, estimates that in every high school homeroom class in Baltimore, there is likely one child fully lost to street life. "But in a large school," he says, "that becomes a big number." Without any of the advantages listed above, a child's character, the crucial check on criminal behavior, is strongly tested well before maturity has armed him to resist.

Montana had no advantages. Born poor, he grew up mostly fending for himself. Parents? Selling and using drugs was the family way, one that had brought little beyond misery. Father exiled to Jamaica, mother somewhere in the neighborhood doing her thing. Community? With drug markets openly working the corners, addiction and violence were rampant. There were other hazards. Living in a run-down old town house on Harlem Avenue, the children had a strong chance of being exposed to mentally debilitating lead paint—an enormous problem in Baltimore's poorest neighborhoods. Schools? Harlem Park, the grade school Montana attended, was consistently ranked one of the worst in the state. Opportunity? When he was old enough to look for work, if he chose to look, competition was fierce for the few legitimate jobs, most of which paid only minimum wage.

On the corners, by contrast, The Game paid handsomely.

The pull was gravitational. Montana's path was greased. He was, Shanika would recall, "the baby on the block," running errands for those working the corners, who ridiculed his fondness for the police. Concerned adults, especially late at night, would stop to question him or his siblings. Who did they belong to? What were they doing out by themselves? Montana was a fast learner. Soon he was selling drugs and committing bolder crimes. At nine he was arrested for stealing a car. The police, no longer his friends, took an arrest photo. It shows a frightened slender boy with dark skin, short hair, ears poking out of his small head, big eyes under worried raised brows. He looks younger even than nine, weighing in at all of sixty-five pounds and barely tall enough to see over a steering wheel. By then the street had him.

He was already working for one of the local heroin dealers, Davon Robinson, selling a product labeled "Get Right." It was a complex operation. In little processing and packaging shops, the heroin was cut with any number of white powders—quinine, powdered caffeine, chalk, baking soda, mannitol, crushed pain pills, a substance known as "benita" (said to be "baby laxative"), and so on—reducing the kick but stretching the product and upping the profit. It was delicately apportioned and sealed in gelcaps, which were sold in packs of twenty-five or fifty. The "corner men" directed traffic, dealt with buyers as they drove or walked up, and took their money. Since they were the most visible of the drug shop's workers, out in the open all day and night, they never handled the drugs. A "pack runner" was dispatched to report the sale. The drugs were delivered by "hitters" from the hidden stash—usually in a nearby vacant house—to the buyer. Since this was the overtly criminal part of the exchange, hitters were often the crew's youngest members, who, if arrested, would be charged as juveniles. Both Montana and his half brother Terrell started out as hitters. Industrious and smart, they were soon running their own shop.

When the boys peddled their own product as "Get Right," Robinson complained, and they changed the name to "True Bomb." Besides heroin, they sold fentanyl, cocaine, marijuana, and Percocet, Xanax, and other pills.

Very soon they were making good money. They were Tana and Rell, familiar and feared, players in The Game, part of a strutting, darkly fatalistic street subculture with its own hip style, language, and music. The dead-end nature of the enterprise was part of its attraction. Disputes over status and turf were routinely settled with handguns, readily obtained. This was not, as we tend to think of outlaw behavior, rebellious. Tana simply embraced what he found. Children adapt readily to their environment. His world had been violent from the start, from the beatings meted out by his frustrated grandmother when he misbehaved to those delivered by bullies on the street. And beatings were the least of it. Children in Sandtown learned early to duck and run for cover at the sharp pop of gunfire. They were accustomed to seeing the oily pool of blood on the sidewalk under a victim, its oddly metallic odor, and the sight of spilled viscera or brains. These were not singular traumatic events but as ordinary as ice cream trucks tootling down suburban streets. They were also formative, particularly when the victim was a relative or friend, altering normal expectations for a long life. Fatalism came naturally.

As did contempt for the police. The brothers' rise as Sandtown street dealers coincided with a complete breakdown of law enforcement in Baltimore. The divide between Black communities and police was a given, rooted in a long history of racial injustice and insensitivity, but in Baltimore it was aggravated by the force's futility. Getting away with murder was routine. Citywide, the homicide clearance rate—just arrests, not convictions—was less than one-third, and it was far worse in Black neighborhoods. In 2015, the year Tana and Rell were in full stride, there were sixty-four killings in the Western District, the Baltimore Police Department division comprising Sandtown and several other neighborhoods. By the end of that year, only eighteen culprits had been charged—less than half the citywide rate. This both encouraged shootings and severely discouraged witnesses from helping the cops. Often the killers were well known, but so long as they remained at large, it meant talking to the police—snitching—wasn't just pointless, it was dangerous. So ordinary citizens turned their heads, which, as many cops saw it, made the community itself complicit. Any tenuous bridges between police and community collapsed in April 2015, when a Black twenty-five-year-old named Freddie Gray was arrested in Sandtown and suffered injuries in a police van on the way to lockup that resulted in his death a week later. The arresting cops were accused of first injuring Gray's back and then taking him for a fatally rough ride, unsecured in the back of their vehicle. Protests flamed into riots. Failed attempts to prosecute the arresting officers fed the anger.

And when the mayhem subsided, the police, stung by community antagonism and outraged by efforts to prosecute their brethren, effectively stopped policing Sandtown and other Black neighborhoods. This, predictably, fed still more violence. In a lawless place, people seek their own justice. Shooting or robbery victims exacted their own revenge or were avenged by family and friends. Gun violence took off like a runaway chain reaction. In the first half of the decade the number of murders citywide annually was about 200; in 2015 it was 344, and totals in following years stayed in that vicinity. Sandtown and neighborhoods like it had slipped out of control. All of this would lead to a federal takeover of the city police department in 2017.

This calamitous descent was, for the most part, extraneous to Baltimore's wider white community, where violence was rare and law enforcement more diligent, efficient, and respected. For suburbanites and those whites living in the city's most affluent areas, like nearby Bolton Hill, Roland Park, or Guilford, the shootings were a *Black* thing. This racist assumption formed an inferential loop: if one assumed violence was common in Sandtown because Black people lived there, the more violent it became, the more the assumption seemed true. It had always been thus.

Sandtown was a particularly egregious example, but Baltimore was not the only city plagued by gun violence in Black neighborhoods. During the first eighteen years of the twenty-first century, about 162,000 Black people were murdered in America, notes sociologist Elliott Currie in his 2020 book *A Peculiar Indifference*, citing figures from the Centers for Disease Control and Prevention. Black men between the ages of fifteen and twenty-nine made up more than half of that number. A young Black man has sixteen times the chances of dying from violence as his white counterpart—this in a country whose young white men are, according to Currie, five times more likely to be murdered than young German men and twenty times more likely than young Japanese men. Somehow this is not, and never has been, considered a big deal in white America. On New Year's Day in 2022, Amy Goldberg, a veteran trauma surgeon at Philadelphia's Temple University Hospital, after treating twelve shooting victims, two of whom died, tweeted, "Where is the outrage . . . from everyone?" In an interview with the *Philadelphia Inquirer*, she explained, "I was just so angry, as we all should be. The number of homicides are outrageous, more than ever. I just couldn't understand. We need to be moved. What's it going to take [for] us to be moved to do something?"

But doing something about Black on Black violence has never been a social priority. The epidemic of violent death in Black communities is rarely even mentioned by political candidates, other than those running in afflicted localities. Newspapers and local media typically ignore all but the most shocking incidents. The shooting and killing has become, simply, urban background noise, shrugged off as thugs preying on thugs or, to put a finer point on it, Blacks preying on Blacks. Even though social scientists, beginning with Du Bois, have roundly debunked the idea that Blacks are inherently more violent than whites, this myth is widely, if not always consciously, accepted by whites who do not consider themselves racist, for the same reason that most whites do not see racism in the hugely disproportionate percentage of Black people behind bars. I can remember my grandfather, as we drove through a Black neighborhood in Chicago in the 1950s, telling my brothers and me, "Roll up your windows and lock the car doors. These people are dangerous." He didn't use the word "people." In my early years as a reporter in Philadelphia, I remember asking my white city editor why we weren't writing more stories about the murders happening in the city every night. "It's not news," he said, flatly. "*Those people* are always killing each other." It goes without saying that the violent deaths of 162,000 whites would not be background noise.

In the worst afflicted neighborhoods, murder and maiming by gunfire are so much a fact of life that they have spawned an aberrant subculture. Exiled in their own cities, Black Americans by necessity had always formed separate local societies. In some cities, Baltimore included, these produced a flowering of discrete music, dance, painting, and literature in the early twentieth century. But they also produced a criminal class regarded, as Du Bois pointed out, with a measure of sympathy, if not esteem, by the very communities it preyed upon.

Today, those young Black men who drift away from school— Schmoke's one child per homeroom class—compete for status and success on their neighborhood corners. They war ferociously. In Baltimore, city police have identified 320 distinct local gangs. For each, The Game is lethally serious. Where death is normalized, life is cheapened, especially when it is so little noted by the larger world. Centuries of that disinterest, along with social and economic isolation, have bred violent cultism in places like Sandtown. One of the consequences of being relegated to the lowest caste, Du Bois noted, was "recklessness." This was certainly true for Tana. Discarded by society—in his case by his own family—he embraced his dead-end status, living fast and expecting to die young or to face long imprisonment—which was actually less likely than being felled by a bullet. Who cared? What did it matter? And if his own life meant so little, how much did anyone else's matter?

Delores was overmatched as Annette's children reached their teens. "She was frustrated because she needed help," says Shanika, who as a child chafed under her grandmother's authority, but who would have sympathy for her as a grown woman and a mother herself. Growing up in the twenty-first century, she and Terrell and Montana spurned Delores's old-fashioned and religious ways. The street offered more immediate and tangible rewards. If they saw things they wanted on TV or in movies, or things other children had, the answer at home was always, "Y'all got to learn how to make your own money." So they did. When she was twelve, Shanika once made $100 in one day selling drugs. Terrell, a year older and male, did better than that. Boys were more prized than girls for the street hustle. Girls, as Shanika would learn soon enough, were prized for other things.

As long as she could, Delores stayed in the fight. She found summer jobs for Terrell and Shanika. But the demands of real work, and the low pay, couldn't compete. Shanika was soon drinking alcohol and using some of the drugs she sold. She and Terrell stopped going to school. Shanika was thrown out of the apartment when she was fifteen. Terrell went soon after. They moved across the bridge to stay with their mother. Montana, who looked up to them, especially to Terrell, followed a few years later, around the time Shanika got pregnant, and Delores relented and let her return home until she gave birth.

By 2012, it was just the brothers on the streets hustling. They became notorious. With its outsize stakes, The Game bestowed not just status but glamour. Even suburban white boys adopted Black street lingo and fashion and consumed rap music and videos that celebrated "gangsta" life. Authenticity was prized above all. A rapper might pretend to have street cred and might even enjoy a bump in sales if he was arrested, but Tana and Rell were the real thing. Their business, which in time they chose as much as it chose them, was not just accepted by their family and friends, it was embraced.

For the brothers, homelessness was no hardship. It suited them not to have a fixed address. Escaping the Harlem Avenue apartment meant escaping Delores's disapproval, the last vestige of adult control. They thrived. It was the one avenue for which they had an advantage, having entered The Game when most children were still being sent to bed early. They had money. They roved from place to place, staying with friends. They were popular, admired. They got high and drank and, soon enough, were having sex, often with multiple girlfriends. Tana would father a son and daughter by two different women, Rell three daughters. They were living a teenage dream. To rise above this, Tana would have to have been extraordinary. As it happened, he would prove himself extraordinary not by transcending The Game but by mastering it.

Danger was a big part of the allure. One way to achieve status, especially for the young, is to tempt fate, the more recklessly, the better. For most teens, in most places, the penalty for such behavior might mean a broken bone, a bad hangover, perhaps the occasional misdemeanor arrest. In Sandtown the risk was mortal—which upped the status points accordingly. Street rules made more intuitive sense than Delores's Christianity. The street blessed the bold, not the meek. Someone slaps you, slap back harder. It was about building a hard rep, never backing down, and commanding respect.

There was even a righteous rationale for it. Americans—of every race and social class—craved narcotics. They had to come from somewhere. While suburbanites were not getting busted for recreational drugs stashed in bedroom drawers, those who sold it to them were going to jail. The laws were baldly hypocritical. This was particularly true in Sandtown, where some of the very cops who busted corner crews and seized their product turned around and sold it. When you looked at the hugely disproportionate number of Africans American locked up on drug charges, it was easy to see the whole multibillion-dollar incarceration industry as just the latest face of a time-honored American project, Keeping the Black Man Down. Trapped in the worst neighborhoods with bad schools and few employment opportunities, viewing the relative affluence of the larger white society, it was easy to react with reckless anger and defiance. Du Bois would write, in *The Philadelphia Negro*: "How long can a city say to part of its citizens, 'It is useless to work; it is fruitless to deserve well of men; education will gain you nothing but disappointment and humiliation'? How long can a city teach its black children that the road to success is to have a white face? How long can a city do this and escape the inevitable penalty?" The penalty is street crime and violence. Hustling drugs, making money, enjoying the illicit pleasures of the life was a way to get back, to raise a middle finger to injustice. It was the price Baltimore paid for centuries of inequity. As for Tana, he was all in. Prison or an early grave? *"Fuck all you anyway!"*

Everybody could see that Tana, in particular, was smart. He was also likable, genial, even goofy, singing, cooing his little raps, teasing—his sister thought he could be a real pain in the ass. Rell was often stoned, so spacey and slow that people wondered whether he was all there. On the street, people called him "Smiles." But if older brother was all about maintaining a pleasant buzz, little brother had plans.

His ambition showed in unexpected ways. Even as his earnings and rep grew in the street, Tana carefully preserved his options. Without Delores or anyone else to rouse him up in the morning and point him out the door, and despite the examples of his dropout father, mother, older brother and sister, and most of his friends, Tana continued to show up at Edmondson-Westside High School. He played football and basketball and did well enough to graduate, in 2013—the first person in the family to, as Shanika put it, "walk across that stage."

He told his sister that he was also going to break their family's cycle of poverty and ruin, and that he wanted to be an example to other kids, to show them, he said, "that they don't have to be a street nigger." He applied for a program with State Farm that would train him to drive big trucks, steady work that paid well and came without gunplay—a calm, respectable life with middle-class comforts. So even as he was building his street rep, he preserved this option—another path—of becoming a "worker," the word in Sandtown for those who earned an honest living. Workers were regarded with a mix of pity and respect. You could admire the decency of those who shunned The Game, but for most it led only to a low-wage treadmill of drudge work and dashed hopes. So many things stood in the way of greater legitimate success. In 2015, the year Tana turned twenty, Harvard University researchers ranked one hundred American communities by how easy it was for a child born into poverty to escape. Baltimore placed dead last. Still, Tana kept that chance alive. His acceptance to the trucking program arrived in the mail just days after his own fate was settled for good.

But for him The Game was irresistible. For that he had role models aplenty, like Pony Head, Jan Gray, the reigning corner king in Sandtown, with his new sneakers, gold chains, steamy girlfriends, and the fine leather wallet that swung from a chain on his hip.

2

Shabangbang Shaboing

Pony Head's mug shot.

All my niggas TTG, they Trained to Go, shawty . . .
I got a O-40, wit' like four bodies on it
Twerk, puttin' niggas in the dirt
Enemies necessary, make her work . . .
Trained to go, shawty
—Waka Flocka Flame, "TTG," Flockaveli

It took Pony Head a long time to realize that The Game—*his* game—had changed. And in a very bad way.

The big clue he missed came on the night of May 4, 2014, a pleasantly cool Sunday under the streetlamps at the corner of North Carey Street and Harlem Avenue, when he exchanged taunts with that nineteen-year-old upstart Tana.

Carey and Harlem form a particularly wide intersection because traffic slows where Harlem, running east–west, halts at Carey and then resumes a half block south. The jog divides the neighborhood row houses into full and half-block segments, punctuated by open lots, and creates something like a neighborhood square. People were out, sitting on steps along the sidewalk. There was a pleasant hum of talk and laughter, the air scented with cigarettes and the dusky aroma of weed. Pony Head was in the mix, as usual, keeping an eye on business. This was his world, his neighborhood. He was in the lap of family, friends, money, and women. In this little quarter of West Baltimore, Pony ruled.

It was a dubious distinction. Sandtown, a roughly triangular tract of seventy-two row-house blocks amid Baltimore's larger urban sprawl, was like a sore that would not heal: block after block of row houses in rampant decay, vacant three-story structures with fronts encrusted in years of grime, with peeling paint and faded Formstone, doors and windows either empty or covered with warped, gray plywood, once proud marble stoops stained black, worn at the center from a million footfalls. Gravity, doing its relentless work, was pulling some of them in on themselves. Others leaned toward the street, buttressed with four-by-fours anchored to the sidewalk. Nature was also doing its part. Determined scrubby bushes and even small trees sprouted wild—no doubt from seeds shat out by birds—from open windows and rooftops. Tenacious wall-eating vines clung to facades. Beneath the weeds on empty lots lurked rusted junk, trash, litter, garbage, tires, and other urban detritus. From pockets of packed earth along the sidewalks stood obstinate small maple and ginkgo trees, budding green now like some sad memory of spring. In a month the weeds around them would be waist-high. Here and there were clean rebuilt blocks, evidence of fitful attempts at renewal, and some walls were adorned with colorful murals bearing themes of African American pride. These stood out jarringly from the surrounding rot. It was easy to imagine those living here, growing up here, feeling like social discards, which they were.

It was also surprisingly roomy for a ghetto. This was partly because so many houses had been demolished, creating open lots, and partly because the wide streets had been built to accommodate traffic from the western suburbs. Views from intersections were particularly broad. To the southwest, just a dozen or so blocks away, was the Baltimore skyline, a cluster of towers, old and new, that spoke of power and money, the *white* city center—*just over there*—both near and far. Its proximity, if anything, underscored the sense of isolation and neglect.

Such was Pony Head's unlovely turf. Sandtown was all that the larger city did not wish to be. Baltimore had plenty to boast about. Roughly six decades after the city began rebuilding its dilapidated core, transforming its distinctive Inner Harbor into a tourist destination —hotels, museums, new sports stadiums, restaurants, and glitzy entertainment centers that attracted millions annually—Sandtown remained what it had long been: poor, drug-infested, and violent. With a murder rate that ranked it consistently among the deadliest neighborhoods in the world, this was the side of Baltimore made notorious by the revered HBO TV series *The Wire*, the part that had earned the city its nickname "Bodymore, Murderland." One of the city's oldest Black neighborhoods, Sandtown was by almost any measure the worst. It was named for the spillage from horse-drawn wagons hauling loads from a sand quarry at its western edge in the nineteenth century, creating small drifts in the streets and sifting into kitchens, living rooms, and cellars. Now the sand was gone, but the neighborhood was famous for something else: it was exhibit A of intractable urban failure, a negative of the dazzling new image Baltimore strove to project.

For Pony Head, it was just home. He had grown up here, on the same block of Carey where he now sat. We picture cities as monumental gray blots on the landscape, but they are actually mosaics, patchworks of hundreds of distinct neighborhoods, each as blinkered as a small town. Sandtown, for all its dangers and faults, was still a community. For those rooted here, it was comfortably familiar, in the true sense of the word, a place of family and friends, of shared history and experience. Anger and violence, poverty and hopelessness were part of it, but life here was not all grim. The streets, for those who belonged, could be lively and fun. And for many, for those like Pony Head, Sandtown's very infamy was a source of perverse pride.

If you could make it here . . .

And Pony Head wasn't just making it, he was thriving. A thickset, confident, genial man, his light brown skin flecked with tiny moles around his eyes, he was prosperous and content. His birth name was Jan Gray. As boys, he and his buddies made silly chalk drawings of each other on the sidewalk, just up the street. One produced a crude sketch of Jan as a pony, exaggerating his pronounced noggin—he'd always had a high forehead—and he became Pony Head. At thirty-nine, still with a tall cranium and now with a dense black beard that sometimes reached his chest, the name seemed even more apt. More people knew him as Pony Head, or Pony, than by his real name.

Everybody who engaged in the street life of Sandtown had a nickname. It certified that they belonged and might also help shield their legal identity from hazards like bill collectors and the law. Pony sold drugs, mostly heroin and grass, as had his father before him, until he was murdered. Pony joined The Game when he was still in grade school, working as a gofer and a lookout for corner crews. It was both lucrative and fun. There were more benefits as he grew older. Girls swooned for him. The mix of drugs and money and guns was irresistible. After many years of hard and dangerous effort, the neighborhood corners were his.

His domain was two blocks wide, between Calhoun Street on the west and Carrollton Avenue on the east, reaching north to Mosher Street. The southern border was Edmondson Avenue, one block south from where he now sat. His territory bordered two small parks,

Harlem Square and Lafayette Square. This thin rectangle, five blocks long, was prize drug turf. More than once Pony and his crew had had to defend it. He oversaw the cutting, packaging, and distribution—in small glass vials with red plastic caps—of a popular heroin brand he'd named "Sweet Dreams." Fifty vials per pack, a dollar each. It was a hot product. Pony's corners were open seven days a week, from seven in the morning until seven at night. White kids would drive up from South Baltimore and buy fifty packs at once, dropping $2,500. Say what you will about addicts, they make steady customers. On an average workday, Pony Head and his crew, what he called his "little clique," would pull in a predictable $10,000, and on good days, twice that. Not that he was personally pocketing that much. Most of the take went for re-up, to pay his workers—each earned fifty dollars a day—and to cover losses.

Losses were a bitch. There were so many ways to lose product and money that it took formidable management skills to turn a profit. One of the features of any illicit trade is the need for self-protection. When people steal from you—your rivals, your own people, others—you are on your own. If you can't defend your corners, you are out of business. Pony did not regard himself as a violent man, but he did what he had to do.

There were also perils completely outside his control. Some of the worst thieves he contended with were city police. One of the department's busiest, most in-your-face street units during Pony's big years was the SES (Special Enforcement Section), which had a star squad called the Gun Trace Task Force. It was created to do smart, aggressive policing, targeting the city's most violent actors, confiscating their weapons, and using the amazing tools of computer-assisted ballistic analysis to connect them to specific crimes. What it became instead was an organized crime unit, not in the traditional law enforcement sense but in the purely criminal sense. The Gun Trace squad was a gang with badges, whose members preyed upon dealers and convinced themselves—even as they enriched themselves—that they were doing God's work. If you were doing good, the logic went, who would begrudge you a healthy cut? Beyond straight-up theft, they broke into cars and houses, invented charges to justify searches, faked videos to establish alibis, and robbed dealers—or alleged dealers. And this unit was not just tolerated on Baltimore's force, it was *praised*, albeit mostly by itself. Wayne Jenkins, its commanding sergeant, and his men regularly posted photos posing before captured money and guns, boasting of their accomplishments. This was particularly galling to those on the force who knew that few of the unit's cases resulted in convictions. More often they fell apart in court, as judges ruled its reports and testimony unreliable. Well before fellow officers learned of the unit's illicit activities, many city cops were skeptical of its methods and disgusted by its grandstanding. Nevertheless, those who spoke critically of the squad were met with ridicule. "You were just accused of being jealous," said one detective. It amounted eventually to a yearslong departmental charade, with Jenkins leading the cheers for himself. He and other leaders of the outfit were decorated and promoted. If fellow officers were deterred from calling them out, which of their victims dared to report their crimes? And to whom?

So, like every dealer in the city, Pony kept his product hidden. He had a lot of hiding places and shifted them constantly, which, inevitably, led to more losses. An entire shipment once vanished from a rooftop hiding place. Who had taken it? One of his own workers? A random civilian who had stumbled on it? The cops?

Then there were the honest cops, a different brand of trouble, busting him or his crew, keeping their arrest numbers up. One day Pony was nabbed carrying almost $2,000-worth of product. That was immediately lost. Add in attorney fees to defend himself, and the financial hit ended up being more painful than the prison stretch. He could afford a good lawyer, and while he had been to jail seven or eight times for possession with intent to distribute, and once for assault, he had always managed to dodge what he considered a serious charge. All of this, too, was part of The Game.

So, being the corner king in Sandtown was a mixed achievement. Pony had his struggles, but he still made plenty. And it was enjoyable, especially the social aspect. Friends everywhere. Little kids would follow him up the sidewalk, cadging for quarters or dollar bills. He was generous and shared liberally with his very large family—he counted eighty cousins in all. It was *amazing* how they turned up when he was flush. He had a steady woman with expensive tastes, and he liked to show a little flash himself: pristine designer sneakers, necklaces, watches, rings, and chains. He had a long gold chain he suspended from his belt, from which hung one of the fancy wallets from his collection. He projected prosperity and calm authority. His voice, graveled by cigarettes, was usually low. Here, in the hardest of neighborhoods, Pony Head, who had left school after eighth grade, was that most American of success stories, the entirely self-made man.

His friends and family did not consider him a criminal. The Game was just a fact of life. Pony had simply risen to the top, taking advantage of a clear and present opportunity in a place where opportunity was scarce. In time, a successful corner king could even acquire a measure of security. If you stood your ground long enough, and were bold and lucky enough, as Pony had been, you earned a rep sufficient to back off the competition. Even your respectable neighbors tolerated you somewhat, so long as the shooting incidents were kept to a minimum. This was one of the arenas—community relations—in which Pony excelled. He cultivated goodwill, but he could also project quiet menace. He was loath to do it, but various neighborhood improvement efforts over the years had caused him headaches. For instance, an entire block of Carey Street, right across from where he sat that night in May, had been renovated. The rebuilt houses looked fabulous, like new, with warm red-brick facades, bright white trim around new windows, marble stoops scrubbed clean. The block looked like an ad for urban renewal, with spiffy, appealing homes on one side of the street and decayed ruins on the other. Into the fresh, newly refurbished side of the street had moved respectable, middle-class homeowners. Pony was good with that—until they started calling the cops on his crew working across the street. He spread the word that unless this stopped, some of the fine cars his new upscale neighbors parked before their fine homes might start catching fire, which would be a terrible shame. The calls stopped.

This was mild stuff, easily managed. Pony was no one to trifle with, but he was also amiable. People liked him. He had achieved something like tenure. He felt so firmly ensconced that he believed any threat to him would be countered not just by his crew but by the whole community. Sandtown looked after its own.

This is one of the reasons the warning hurled his way that May evening, as he sat literally minding his own business, didn't register.

It came from Tana, walking past jauntily. Pony knew and liked him, a wiry, very dark-skinned teen with a loping stride, a homeboy. He had watched Tana grow up, one of the kids on the block who had sometimes followed him around in years past. Pony had gone to school with his mother, Annette, and had even hung around with her a little before she began, as he put it, "dibbing and dabbing" in the product. He had known Tana's father, a big jovial Jamaican dude, before he got arrested and deported back home. He knew churchgoing Delores, and that Tana had been mocked as a "church kid." Pony had admired how the boy, even when very small, had always held his own out on the block, cheerful and smart, with a quiet dignity that belied his situation. Proud. Surprisingly poised. Always dribbling a basketball. In his school years Tana had often sat with Pony in the mornings before shouldering his backpack and heading off to classes, and then returned in the afternoons. The kid was the same age as some of Pony Head's own. Pony had an avuncular feeling for him.

But now the kid had developed swagger, especially since his older half brother, Rell, had been busted and sent away. Tana had assumed leadership of their little drug operation. They were calling themselves "TTG," for "Trained to Go." Tana wore wide, loose, low-slung jeans and tight T-shirts that showed off his slender torso. He wore gold caps over his front teeth so his smile gleamed like the grillwork of a luxury car. His face had matured, acquiring overlarge features—big, heavy-lidded, bulging eyes and a long, sloping, wide nose, the tip of which fell just short of his full lips. A receding chin exaggerated those jutting features, giving him an exotic face to match his exotic name.

Tana came up the sidewalk with a phone held to one ear, bobbing to some internal beat, and called out, "Pony, you ain't from around here no more. You washed up." He was laughing.

Pony jabbed back in the same spirit: "Yo, this is *my* block. Yeah. How many times I'm gonna tell you that, yo? This seven hundred Carey Street is *me*, dog. All the way down to Edmondson Avenue, yo."

This was "the dozens," good, harmless neighborhood fun. Tana kept at him.

"Cuz, yo, I shouldn't see your name on nothin' else around here," he said, still with the phone to his ear, still smiling. "Flat out. I mean, we ain't gonna have this talk no more. Next time I'll just bang you, like, shabangbang shaboing."

Pony scoffed.

Tana added, "Crack your head."

"I mean, why the fuck you be rubbin' on my arms, yo?" Pony protested, laughing.

Then Tana moved off, still talking into the phone. Pony thought nothing of it. Young 'un strutting his stuff on a Sunday night.

Tana and Rell sold a heroin brand called "Checkmate." This didn't concern Pony. Demand was bottomless. When you put more heroin on the street, more buyers showed up. He had let it be known, however, that he expected a cut from anyone peddling on his corners. This he considered only fair. He had secured the turf. It had not come free, so why should sharing it be free? So while he expected a fee, he did not consider Tana and Rell competition. And even if he were, Rell, whom Pony considered the more menacing of the brothers, was locked up. Tana was just a nice kid.

He didn't give the exchange a second thought until a month later, when, on his way to a corner store, a little homeboy named Tev, Tevin Haygood, one of Tana's TTG crew, stepped out of an alley across the street and fired two shots at him. Both missed. Luckily, the boy hadn't dared come close enough to make them count. Tev was another one Pony had watched grow up—*cute kid*, was how he saw him—but like Tana, he'd grown into a cocky teen. They had exchanged words a few days earlier, Tev acting like a hard case, boasting of being a "shooter," and Pony dissing him, telling him to knock it off. The shots, Pony figured, were just Tev's wounded pride. Unless . . . unless it had something to do with Tana's challenge? Had the kid acted on Tana's orders? Pony wondered about it and dismissed it, which says something about his world, where being shot at was a thing anyone *could* dismiss. As he saw it, the attempt, however outrageous, had been timid and half-assed. Having made his point, Tev would not likely try again or, for that matter, cross his path anytime soon. Pony was a serious player. Nobody had gotten hurt, yet. He chalked it up to teenage bluster.

Many months later he learned otherwise and from an unlikely source. He got a call from a cop named Joe Landsman, who had busted Pony for the first time fifteen years earlier and several times since. Over the years, they had developed something like professional respect, a mutually beneficial relationship. Landsman was straight, honest, and good at his job, too good. He was a serious pain in the ass, but Pony had learned to deal with him. One of the ways he had avoided a heavy charge all those years was by offering information, selectively. Landsman was plugged in extraordinarily well for a cop, but no cop knew Sandtown like Pony did. He could explain things to

Landsman, point him in the right direction, or sometimes even serve up a rival—offering useful hints, like where the target stashed his drugs or gun, who had been present at a shooting, what phone numbers were being used to conduct business, and so forth. If the man wound up in jail, it was a win for both cop and dealer.

When Landsman had started asking about Tana and Rell, Pony demurred. These were his homeboys. He considered them friends, even as their reputation grew more menacing. They had a different, harder attitude toward The Game than he did. They bragged less about the money they were making than about the bodies they dropped. Tana called them his "highlights," posting videos and photos of himself on social media—juvenile, crazy stuff, flaunting guns and money, *asking for trouble*. The two especially angered Pony when they killed one of his friends, Bub, Brandon Littlejohn, a good basketball player and a ladies' man, who wore his hair in intricate, tight, slender braids that flowed behind each ear. And then, to make things worse, Tana and Rell had attended Bub's funeral service. Pony found that chilling. There they were, paying their respects, offering condolences, sharing the grief, looking their victim's stricken loved ones straight in the eye. That was cold. Pony knew that Bub had been tempting fate—he was rumored to have been helping the police—but he was one of them! The killing had bothered him enough to share what he knew about it with homicide detectives. *What were these boys doing killing their own people?*

Pony had even heard that the brothers drew up lists of those they intended to kill, and sometimes did so for hire—rewards were posted online, up to $10,000. They had taken their crew's name from that Waka Flocka Flame rap, "TTG." "I'm all about that fucking bread," the lyrics went, which Pony could understand, but for Tana and Rell, that didn't seem true. They seemed to be less about bread than their rep, like they aimed to become known as the baddest brothers in the baddest blocks in Baltimore.

He had considered this to be mostly Rell's influence, but after Rell went away, it had grown worse. Might he be on their list? He didn't believe it, but he was a careful man and began taking precautions. He stopped hanging around on his corners. He didn't vanish, and his crews continued to work, but he stayed out of sight. He found a spot two stories above the sidewalk, on the small inset balcony of a house at the corner of Carey and Harlem—the woman who lived there let him use it. It afforded a wide view of the surrounding corners but kept him up and out of sight.

Still, whenever Landsman asked him about TTG, he would have nothing to offer. It went against Pony's code. As bad as they were, he had no personal beef with them. Besides, informing on them looked more and more like a way of making yourself a target. That's why they had killed Bub. Despite everything, he still considered Tana a friend, which is what he told Landsman.

"I'm telling you, these guys are not your friends," the cop said. "They don't care anything about you."

"No, we cool," Pony said.

Landsman complained, "They're trying to kill you, and you're protecting them!"

"Nah," said Pony. "You got it wrong."

Landsman said he could prove it. And so, months later, Pony found himself wearing headphones, high up the George H. Fallon Federal Building, a dark gray monolith on Baltimore's modest skyline that housed various federal agencies, including the office of Maryland's US Attorney, listening to a recording.

During his imprisonment, Rell called his brother almost every day. In the spring of 2014, he had been in the Maryland Metropolitan Transition Center, a lockup for inmates nearing the end of their terms. All calls by inmates were recorded and available to police on a restricted database. The inmates knew this, but given the high volume of calls every day, few worried that their conversations were being monitored. Who would have the time? Landsman, it turns out, trying to learn more about the brothers. Listening to one of Rell's calls, he was startled when he heard Pony Head's voice. It was from the night Tana had taunted Pony. Tana had had his phone to his ear as he moved down the street, and during the shouted exchange with Pony, he and Rell had been talking.

This is what Landsman wanted Pony to hear. He told him, "They were talking about killing you."

Pony scoffed.

Those wild shots fired by Tev? Landsman suggested they had been Tana's idea.

"No, no, no," said Pony. He was used to cops getting things wrong. He told Landsman that he'd known Tana forever. He was harmless— at least to him. "No way," he told Landsman. The theory didn't fit.

"Just come in and listen," said the cop.

The prison call began with the standard automated voice asking whether the recipient was willing to accept an inmate call. A young woman accepted, Booda, Rell's little sister.

"What's up, Shawty? What you doin'?" Rell asked, and then gave the slow laugh that punctuated nearly every sentence he spoke. It made him seem dopey.

"Nothin'," said Booda, impatiently. She said she was eating and getting ready to go to work.

"Still working at the same place?"

"Yeah."

"What you doin' other than working?"

"Gettin' high."

Booda was not chatty. She suspected Rell was calling to talk to their brother, which he promptly asked to do.

"That what you call me for? 'Cause that's not what I'm here for," she complained.

"I thought you said you was goin' to work!" Again, the lazy laugh.

She forwarded the call.

Walking up Carey Street, Tana greeted Rell warmly, singing out, "Ter-relly-relly!"

"What's up, Shawty?"

Tana told him that he'd just been beaten on a deal to buy two pounds of marijuana—"jiffies," in their coded slang. He had attempted to buy them by mail, paying up front, but instead of sending him the dope, the seller had shipped him two ordinary red bricks. He'd been had.

"Boy, you know I got *got* fifty-eight hundred doin' that dumb-ass shit."

"For what?" Again the giggle.

"On the jiffies. The jiffies didn't come. Two red bricks came. Got me for fifty-eight hundred."

"You said what came?"

"Two red bricks . . . Yeah, two of 'em came. Got the shit out of me for fifty-eight hundred, but I'm right back at it. Yeah, hell, yeah."

"Damn," Rell said, and giggled.

You could tell that Tana was outdoors, moving, a breeze buffeting the cell.

"That was all you had?" Rell asked.

"Fuck no! *Hell* no!"

Rell laughed.

"But he got me good."

"They say Nellie got shot," said Rell.

Donnell Cawthorne, one of the older dealers in Sandtown, had been shot two nights earlier a few blocks away, hit in the chest and the back. At the scene, police found seventeen shells on the pavement.

"I don't know what happened with Nellie," said Tana. "But yeah, that nigga was opened up like a motherfucker. His guts was coming out. I asked 'em how many times he got hit. They said seven. I think it was more than that!"

They had a good laugh about it. They were close, these two, and bantered in a relaxed, cheerful way. One could sense Tana *performing* for his older brother. He was carefree and happy, taking his imprisoned brother on a stroll through their familiar streets—on the recording, Pony Head could hear other voices, laughter, shouting. Tana called out to people as he passed, carrying on short conversations. "What's up, James!" he shouted, then, to Rell, "James looking at me all crazy." Then, loud enough for James to hear, "I don't know what's up with James, yo."

He handed James the phone.

James said, "Smiles! What's up?"

"Just chillin'." Again the giggle.

"Why, you smilin' right now, ain't you?"

Rell laughed.

"You smilin' motherfo . . . All right, yo. Love, my nigga."

When Tana came back on the line he was singing again: "These bitches come and go / . . . make my love bells sway / motherfucker don't play . . ."

Tana was in a playful mood. He joked with some children, handing over a twenty-dollar bill. He sang some more. Rell laughed. As he strolled, Tana boasted, improvising a rap, "Nigga got balls . . . Motherfucker don't play . . . what it is . . . They call me Buffy, baby. You want to hear my highlights, nigger? . . . Shabangbang shaboing . . ."

Then, as he approached Pony's corner, he said, "Po-ony writin' his name on our rapper list."

Pony looked over to him.

"Pony you ain't from around here no more," Tana told him. "You washed up. Cuz, yo, I shouldn't see your name on nothin' else around here."

This Pony remembered. He heard himself answer, "Yo, this is *my* block," and so on.

Then Tana spoke to his brother, part of the conversation Pony had not heard: "Pony tell me, yeah, that niggers about to start having to pay if they want to motherfucking sell some shit down here. They gotta ask him."

Rell laughed.

"You heard me?"

"Yeah." Again the giggle.

"I told Pony, 'Boy, your ass gonna be opened up like a quarter piece [a hole the size of a quarter].' Matter fact, fuck a quarter piece, like a fire hydrant."

"Uh-huh," Rell concurred.

"Got these old heads down here, yo," Tana complained.

Here was context Pony had not considered. It was more chilling now—*you washed up . . . bang you, like, shabangbang shaboing . . . crack your head . . . like a fire hydrant*. Tana had been serious about coming after him. Tev's shots suddenly appeared in a different light, as Tana following up on his threats. The more Pony thought about it, the more he was convinced that Tev would never have come at him on his own. He wouldn't have dared.

Pony Head was shocked and hurt. These boys had looked up to him. He thought he had their respect. Landsman had been right.

His hard-won turf had become too dangerous for him. There and then, high in the federal building, he resolved to quit The Game. And he followed through. He ceded his corners immediately. TTG took them over. They would own Sandtown. They would even appropriate Pony's brand, relabeling their own product "Sweet Dreams."

Also, there and then, Pony decided that he was going to do whatever he could to help Joe Landsman take them down.

3

The Fulton Avenue Wall

The Fulton Avenue Wall, circa 1885.

*Caste is insidious and therefore powerful because it is not
hatred, it is not necessarily personal. It is the worn grooves of
comforting routines and unthinking expectations, patterns of
social order that have been in place for so long that it looks like
the natural order of things.*
—Isabel Wilkerson, *Caste: The Origins of Our Discontents*

When that Harvard study ranking Baltimore as the hardest
place to escape poverty was released in April 2015, the city
was convulsed by the Freddie Gray fallout. It was the latest of many
periodic outbursts by Baltimore's Black residents protesting racial
subjugation, poor living conditions, police brutality and corruption,
and lack of opportunity. Like the one that followed the murder of Dr.
Martin Luther King Jr., in April 1968, which left six dead and hundreds of homes and businesses burned, this one degenerated into a

wild lashing out. Hundreds of people were arrested, scores of businesses were looted and damaged, and more than two hundred vehicles and buildings were set on fire. Police were the primary target of the community's ire, and twenty cops were injured. It was a very old story.

Things might have been different. A century before slavery ended, Baltimore had the largest population of free Black people of any city in the nation. Just prior to the Civil War, in 1860, only 8 percent of the roughly 18,000 African Americans in the city were enslaved. Black Baltimoreans, despised by many of their white neighbors and considered a threat by enslavers, carved out their own fragile, isolated culture. After slavery was abolished, many of the newly liberated migrated to the city. Capable and hardworking, they might have shaped the city into a model of American integration, a showplace of racial harmony. But race hatred did not end with slavery.

Baltimore was always an amalgam: part Northern in character and part Southern, partly urban and industrial and partly a hub for both agriculture and fishery. Its Northern mercantile character was strong, with ships that plied the oceans, including whalers, and a sturdy industry of watermen who worked the vast hatcheries of the Chesapeake Bay, what H. L. Mencken would one day call "the immense protein factory." Its Inner Harbor port launched the tobacco, corn, and fruit grown on southern Maryland's plantations and in turn received the world's bounty. After 1830, the port was also a railroad terminus, for the Baltimore and Ohio Railroad, which brought iron and grain from the Midwest and fostered heavy industry along the waterfront. So Baltimore evolved a distinctly rowdy, urban flavor, starkly at odds with the placidity of the flat, well-watered farmlands to the immediate south on both sides of the bay. The city's rich racial and ethnic pastiche, infused by waves of immigration, made for such a volatile mix that the city earned the nickname "Mobtown" for its riotous politics and street crime. At the same time the city reflected the distinctly southern character of the state around it. Forcibly imported Africans were off-loaded in chains at Baltimore to provide slave labor for the vast estates stretching west of the Chesapeake all the way to the Potomac River and south from Annapolis seventy miles to St. Mary's City. Farms and plantations also covered Maryland's sizable portion of the Eastern Shore, from the bay's headwaters near Newark, Delaware, to Assateague Island and the Virginia border, 140 miles south. Most of the state was as Southern as Alabama. Wealthy enslavers dominated the state government in Annapolis, so even as the city grew ever more distinctly Northern, it remained under the thumb of those who had more in common with Jefferson Davis than Abraham Lincoln.

Baltimore's booming early nineteenth-century economy formed priorities of its own. Demand for skilled labor opened opportunities for Black residents and its proximity to the slave fields made it a destination for those fleeing bondage or fortunate enough to have purchased their freedom. Among them was Frederick Douglass. Sent to work in Baltimore's shipyards by his "owner" in the 1830s, he found his way into the city's free Black community and then fled north to a lifetime of heroic, passionate advocacy for America's founding principles.

During the antebellum years, Baltimore's free Blacks were not equal citizens. They were barred from voting, organizing, investing, and borrowing. Maryland's government took steps to prevent their numbers and influence from growing. State laws allowed for free Blacks convicted of petty crimes—at trials where only white citizens were allowed to testify—to be sold into slavery. Fearful of violent freedom uprisings, particularly after Nat Turner's ill-fated attempt in southern Virginia in 1831, the authorities decreed that free Blacks entering Maryland could stay legally for only ten days. In an era when the inherent inferiority of Black people was considered a given by most whites, their basic human rights were routinely and flagrantly ignored. Even those few among the privileged caste sympathetic to the race didn't want them around, cherishing the impossible fantasy of shipping millions to faraway continents. Lincoln himself toyed with this idea.

Southern sentiment was so rife in Baltimore that Lincoln, traveling to his inauguration in 1861, had to be spirited through the city under cover of darkness and in disguise to avoid a plotted assassination. During the Civil War, Confederate sympathizers clashed with Union troops in Mobtown's streets.

After the Civil War, Maryland as a whole remained defiantly Southern and racist. The city's story isn't any better. Baltimore's response to growing numbers of Black residents reflected what Du Bois described as "a thing in the South which for two centuries better men had refused to even argue—that life amid free Negroes was simply unthinkable, the maddest of experiments." To avoid such madness, the city shunned and isolated its Black inhabitants. First overtly, by law, and then more subtly, with social barriers and strict covenants, it confined them to the least desirable neighborhoods, crowding them into substandard housing served by inferior schools and health care, and denying them opportunity. Black people were barred from most white-collar careers and restricted to only the least attractive and lowest-paying blue-collar jobs. These ghettos predictably became sinkholes of poverty. And in the classic style of racist subjection, the very effects of these policies, unemployment and destitution, disease, poor academic performance, crime, and appalling living conditions became "proof" that the underlying racist assumptions were true: *Just look what happens to neighborhoods when they move in!*

None of this stopped Black people from coming. At first it was the newly liberated traveling north, looking for work and to escape the persecution of white supremacist vigilantes. Then it was the need for laborers in Baltimore's factories and shipyards, although waves of European immigrants, mostly Irish and German, continually

displaced them. Hemmed in by apartheid dictates, the city's growing Black population found no place to live other than already overcrowded ghettos. Many prospered anyway, building businesses that
catered to their own shunned community. Black people needed bar-
bers, grocers, butchers, lawyers, doctors, and undertakers, too. Those
who thrived did not, however, gain greater social status in the larger
community, or mobility. Racial barriers were popular and explicit.
The city's eminent newspaper, *The Sun*, ran an article in 1909 noting the growth of the Black population under the headline "Negroes
Encroaching," with six columns of photos at the top of the page under
the heading, "Where the Blight of the Negro Is Most Seriously Felt
in the City." In 1910, Mayor J. Barry Mahool, considered a social pro-
gressive, said, "Blacks should be quarantined in isolated slums." A year
later, Mayor James H. Preston began demolishing well-established
middle-class Black neighborhoods downtown to make way for urban
renewal projects, mostly to widen major roads, what author Antero
Pietila termed, "Baltimore's first government-sponsored Negro
removal project." When a few well-to-do Black people tried to buy
homes in adjacent white neighborhoods, the city enacted a law explic-
itly forbidding it—the first such in the nation. It stood for seven years
before being struck down by the Maryland Court of Appeals in 1917,
not because it so clearly discriminated against Black people, but
because it was worded so sloppily that it had inadvertently restricted
some white people from purchasing property. That same year the US
Supreme Court ruled that overt racial zoning was unconstitutional,
but even as the laws fell, the walls held firm.

Conditions aggravated by poverty and overcrowding became a
justification for maintaining strict color lines. Perhaps the starkest
was Fulton Avenue, near the western boundary of Sandtown, a wide
avenue with a green median that had spacious homes on both sides.
As white residents moved out, speculators bought up the big houses
on the east side of the street, stripped out bathrooms and put up

flimsy interior walls, installed crappers in the backyard, and sold them to slumlords at exorbitant, jacked-up prices. So housing on the east side of Fulton Street, the Black side, transformed into crowded tenements even as the west side of the street, the white side, prospered. The grand homes on the west side were still single-family residences in the early 1940s.

Black residents could gaze across the divide at another world, homes with indoor plumbing, porches, and lawns that grew more and more opulent as you traveled northwest.

"It could have been the Moon," said historian Louis S. Diggs, who grew up on the Black side of the street. "I recall many days looking far up, wondering what it was like up there."

There was tenacity in these ostracized people. Through the Jim Crow years, Sandtown blossomed. By the 1930s, it and the adjacent Black neighborhood of Uptown were home to a flourishing Black middle class and a vibrant, creative African American culture. Those who managed to hold on to steady jobs in Baltimore factories bought houses, cars, and other staples of middle-class success and supported within their segregated borders a vivacious and sophisticated nightlife. Pennsylvania Avenue, defining the neighborhood's eastern edge, was lined with restaurants, jazz nightclubs, bars, and theaters, which featured some of the nation's most accomplished entertainers—all Black. By mid-century, such venues had vanished.

The decline began after World War II, as blue-collar factory jobs dried up, victim of industrial migration to the Sunbelt and then overseas, in the larger American shift from a manufacturing to a service economy. Those who could afford to move out of the city did. Housing plunged in value, leaving block after block of deteriorated row homes, converting Sandtown into a showpiece of urban decay.

Two huge trends were at work, the automobile and race hatred. During the decades when Black residents multiplied and spread out in the city, whites fled in all directions except due south into the

Chesapeake Bay. They left on wheels, part of the great automotive transformation—some would say ruination—of American cities. The city dismantled its elaborate and extremely convenient trolley networks, tore up the rails, and widened and smoothed city streets. It built expressways to facilitate the daily commutes of suburbanites, who still reported to office buildings downtown. In the evenings they made the short reverse drive out to Baltimore County, whose pristine green hillsides were sprouting new homes like chickweed. The county, stretching north to the Mason-Dixon Line, wraps like a horse collar around the city (but does not include it), extending along both sides south to the industrial eastern and western banks of the Patapsco River—the entrance to the city's Inner Harbor.

Settlement of the county was a gold rush for homebuilders. (As Garry Wills described it, "Fields were cut up into lots, ribs of wood clothed overnight with brick, and the supple corkscrew of water rose from a thousand lawn sprinklers. . . . Mini-mansions in pockets of shrubbery.") Spanking new ranch houses with plastic shutters sprouted on quarter- to half-acre lots in newly planted neighborhoods with bucolic names like Springlake, Pine Ridge, Pot Spring, and Woodlawn. These new "subdivisions," not neighborhoods, had roads that led nowhere, curved byways, and cul-de-sacs that suggested you had *arrived*. They were planted with saplings no taller than a ten-year-old, but which promised soon enough to become leafy bowers in whose shade you might stroll and mingle with—*wink, wink*—your exclusively white neighbors. Roughly one-third of the floor plan for these new suburban dwellings was garage space. A wide driveway led to the cavernous two berths, one for Dad's car, one for Mom's, with a two-story brick and vinyl-sided box alongside for humans, an appendage often smaller, in fact, than the average Baltimore row house. An alien watching from orbit might have concluded that cars, not people, were the dominant life-form, with a new world designed for them. Shopping centers surrounded by acres of asphalt were built to accommodate parking. Then the county built its own massive expressway, the Baltimore Beltway; although part of the Interstate Highway System, it leads not out of state but wraps from one end of the horse collar to the other—Arbutus to Catonsville to Pikesville to Towson to Rosedale to Dundalk—connecting the (also new) shopping centers and malls and (eventually) office parks with fields of concrete around them for parking. Part of the Beltway's magic was that it enabled white families, other than whisking into and out of downtown on highways and elevated expressways, to avoid the city altogether. White folks could play and shop and eat out and eventually commute to work entirely in suburbia, as edge cities gradually overtook downtown as locations for company headquarters. They could live their lives in near-perfect racial insulation, never encountering a human being with dark skin.

Baltimore's apartheid was impervious to landmark advances in racial equality—federal laws forbidding discrimination in housing, banning discriminatory lending and segregated schools, the civil rights movement, the Voting Rights Act of 1965, and so on. As the county grew, it became whiter and whiter. Its population more than doubled between 1950 and 1970, but its already paltry proportion of Black residents fell by more than a half, from 7 percent to just 3 percent. Segregation was enforced. Racial zoning was policed so strictly that in 1972 the county executive, Dale Anderson, its highest elected official, ordered real estate agents to report to the police any sale of a home to a Black person. There was no law against purchasing a home while Black, but being hauled in for questioning, having word of the transaction broadcast to your sure-to-be-outraged neighbors, effectively discouraged the practice. Such steps were politically popular. Anderson was reelected by a wide margin. Spiro Agnew, who preceded him in the office, had priests and rabbis arrested in 1962 when they led protests at a segregated county amusement park. And even Agnew, who as the county's top zoning officer had helped shape the racial enclave before Anderson's tenure, was not considered to be enough of a racial purist. When he ran for governor in 1966, he was attacked for not battling the Black menace more aggressively. His Democratic opponent, George P. Mahoney, ran with the thinly disguised racist slogan "Your home is your castle: protect it," hoping to attract suburban voters terrified of Black people. The county was a lot less violent than the city, for sure, but every social class has its own flavor of crime. Land was trafficked in the county's boom years as freely as drugs on city corners. Agnew had begun harvesting bribes and kickbacks in his zoning office in the 1950s and continued to collect them on his steady rise to county executive, Maryland governor, and then US vice president.

None of this was seen as criminal by those profiting from it. Just as Tana and Rell embraced the world they found, men like Agnew embraced theirs. Why shouldn't he, as arbiter of valuable zoning permits, effectively in a position to hand out bags of gold, profit by the choices he made? He certainly thought he should. After he was forced to resign the vice presidency in 1973, confronted with a forty-page federal indictment itemizing his payoffs (including one delivered to the White House), Agnew entered a dodgy *nolo contendere* plea and would continue to assert his innocence until the day he died. There was so much money being made, who could begrudge him his share? No doubt Agnew believed it was his due. And he was not alone; Anderson went to prison in 1974 for the same crimes.

All these efforts at exclusion, some corrupt and some in the open, worked. In 1974, the US Commission on Civil Rights described Baltimore County as a "white noose" strangling the city socially and economically. Those who pointed to the success other ethnic groups had in escaping ghetto life—Italians, Germans, Polish, Irish, and Jews—failed to note how Black Americans had been systematically denied paths to wealth and social position. They had been prevented from migrating to more affluent areas, to neighborhoods with better schools and more jobs. During the years of Baltimore County's explosive growth, the new Fulton Avenue wall was the city-county line.

I grew up on the white side of the wall. In my swollen baby-boomer high school class of 1969, there were 570 students, only three Black. This was Dulaney High School in Timonium, a northern suburb only about ten miles as the crow flies from Sandtown. Living in our apartheid community, we did not see ourselves as racist—far from it. I was shocked and offended a few years later, visiting South Africa for the first time, to find "White Race Group Only" signs posted on the beaches and elsewhere, as if I had not grown up in the same world. My suburban white cohort was raised to fully embrace racial equality—in principle. How easy to be color-blind where there is no color to be seen! In the carpeted living rooms of our new cul-de-sac houses, we thrilled to the stirring rhetoric of Dr. King, rooted for civil rights protesters, and were horrified by baton-swinging, bullheaded, racist Southern sheriffs, with their fire hoses and snarling dogs, by the burning crosses, white robes, and blunt hatred of Southern bigots. These were the villains of our childhood. All the while we were cosseted in the warm folds of liberal virtue, secure in our advantages, which, for the most part, few of us recognized. Summer job? No problem. You could caddy for tips, join a landscaping crew (all those lawns!), pack bag lunches for summer campers at the nearby McCormick's factory, lifeguard at the local pool—where you could earn money baking on a golden tan while keeping a watchful eye on the bikini girls and Speedo boys—wash dishes for a strip-mall restaurant or make sandwiches a few doors down, or, when you got out of high school, land a job at the local supermarket for sturdy union wages (even health benefits!), earning enough to pay your way through college. The world as it should be: learning the value of hard work, showing up on time, applying yourself to the task at hand, smiling for customers, nodding to bosses, training for long-term success, which never seemed for any of us to be in the slightest doubt.

Children embrace the world they know. Only once in a great while was there a discordant note. I can remember playing baseball on the diamond behind Dulaney in the spring of 1968, after the assassination of Dr. King, and seeing the smear of black smoke on the blue southern horizon as riots consumed the city. To steal Diggs's metaphor, it might as well have been happening on the Moon. After graduating from the nearly all-white Loyola College in 1973, I started work at the *Baltimore News-American*, then the city's largest-circulation daily newspaper. The city's populace was already more than half African American, and yet the paper employed not a single Black reporter or editor. This was despite a historic tradition of Black journalism—the *Baltimore Afro-American* had been an important national newspaper for over eighty years. The city's preeminent—read *white*—newspapers ignored the Black half of the city's population except to report on crime, sports figures, or occasionally entertainers. The worst of it is that, at the time, I did not even regard it as odd, revealing, unwise, or even . . . perhaps the word I am reaching for is, *wrong.*

The city's Black population continued to grow—from 15 percent in 1920 to 24 percent in 1950—and determined efforts by civil rights lawyers and fair-minded politicians gradually lifted the old barriers. By 1980, Blacks were a solid majority in the city, but only the very old remembered the glory days of Sandtown. Ten years on, Blacks were 60 percent of city voters, and Schmoke, the city's first Black mayor, was presiding in Baltimore City Hall.

The city was changing. Even the city-county racial wall had begun to erode by the time Montana Barronette was born in 1995. The county, pressured by federal efforts and court rulings to pro-vide affordable housing to people of all races, began moving—snail-like—toward integration. Whites were even being lured back into the city, not to live but to play. By the end of the century, Baltimore was basking in the glory of a remarkably successful decades-long effort to rebuild downtown and the Inner Harbor, but it found itself flat-footed when critics pointed out how little this transformation had touched nearby neighborhoods, like Sandtown, with far more urgent problems and needs.

The triumphant Inner Harbor renaissance of the 1980s and '90s, part of a renewal process that had begun a quarter century earlier, was a classic example of Baltimore's persistent Black-white disconnect. You had to have been there to fully appreciate the change. The back end of my old *News-American* building faced the harbor across East Pratt Street. The water smelled bad and was littered with refuse. Every time it rained, gutters and drains delivered more of it. I never saw the Inner Harbor waters actually catch fire, but it was easy to imagine. Around this dark, lapping mess stood the vacant shells of the city's industrial past. It was spooky, certainly not a place for a waterfront stroll. From time to time, one of the old behemoth buildings would burn down—sparked, one always suspected, by hopes of an insurance payoff—and what a spectacle that was! I watched one go up like a torch, with flames jumping from its rows of broken windows. The conflagration was so hot that, standing on the sidewalk across six-lane East Pratt Street, I had to turn around to avoid scorching my face.

All these ruins were then swept away by sheer municipal willpower. The city and state, along with the Greater Baltimore Committee, an association of the town's leading citizens, bought up over a thousand structures surrounding the harbor, relocating seven hundred still-breathing businesses. The empty buildings were leveled, creating acres of open space around the harbor, and the water was cleaned. The Maryland Transportation Authority was persuaded to reroute a long-planned highway project that would have cut through the harbor area, and the USS *Constellation*, an 1854 sloop of war, was towed in, parked at a central pier, and opened as a museum. A wide promenade was built along the water's edge. In 1976, a flotilla of tall ships sailed in to celebrate the event, commemorating Baltimore's maritime heritage, and paddleboats and sailboats blossomed around them. City fairs were held weekly on the newly cleared waterfront. And, lo!, people began showing up—*white people*, drawn out of their leafy county bowers into the heart of the riot-scarred Black city. They came in such shocking numbers that when the city's indefatigable mayor, William Donald Schaefer, announced plans for the project's next phase—Harborplace, a festive, airy mall housing restaurants and novelty shops—he faced a citizens' revolt.

Take away the open space? Build a mini shopping mall that nobody would ever patronize after the novelty wore off? Schaefer had to defeat a referendum to move ahead, and James Rouse, the project's developer, proved the naysayers wrong. He built a stunning festival of a market, modeled after Boston's Faneuil Hall Marketplace (which Rouse had also built), that drew five hundred thousand visitors on its opening day, in 1980, and entertained its seven millionth visitor—the goal for the first year—after only three months. Harborplace turned out to be just the beginning of the renaissance. The Inner Harbor sprouted office towers, four-star hotels, farm-to-table restaurants, the Baltimore (now National) Aquarium (Schaefer famously donned an old-fashioned striped swimsuit and straw hat and clutched a rubber duck for an inaugural plunge in 1981 into its seal pool), the Maryland Science Center, performing arts venues, and then two giant new sports stadiums—Oriole Park at Camden Yards for the baseball team and Ravens Stadium for the football team swiped from Cleveland. Baltimore became a worldwide model for urban revitalization, winning awards and attracting millions of tourists and regular suburban visitors. Orioles and Ravens games alone regularly brought in visitors by the tens of thousands. There were design awards, front-page stories, and glossy spreads in national magazines. It was swell. Schaefer, attaining the status of a living legend, became governor of Maryland.

He and his city basked in the unfamiliar glow of universal approba-
tion . . . until along came Baltimore's own Hieronymus Bosch, David
Simon.

A former *Baltimore Sun* reporter, Simon went about skillfully
torching this shiny new image, detailing the lives of Black Baltimoreans still trapped in the old urban ghettos. All that planning effort,
all that money, all that political clout, all those accomplishments and
awards—and for what? Here were Black Baltimoreans, still mired
in the same old shit. Sandtown was still Sandtown. In 1991, Simon
published *Homicide: A Year on the Killing Streets,* which became the
NBC series *Homicide: Life on the Street,* and then cowrote with former
city homicide detective Edward Burns *The Corner: A Year in the Life
of an Inner City Neighborhood* (Lexington, just over the bridge from
Sandtown), which became the HBO miniseries *The Corner.* Then,
collaborating again with Burns, along with scores of talented writ-
ers, actors, and filmmakers, he created his masterpiece, the gritty,
acclaimed HBO series *The Wire,* which aired from 2002 to 2008.
Cumulatively, Simon painted his version of a Bosch hellscape, a tryp-
tic of his adopted hometown as *Bodymore, Murderland.* The series was
jarringly realistic, right down to the actors speaking in fluent local
Bawlmerese. So authentic was *The Wire* that, even as it painted the
city as drug-infested, murder-ridden, and universally corrupt, Baltimore, dazzled by the Hollywood spotlight, threw open doors to its
production crews, and prominent locals—including former mayor
Schmoke—signed on for cameos.

Simon was not the first to suggest that the renaissance had displaced and ignored the city's poor Black residents. The criticism had
been in the air throughout the decades-long project. It had been conceived by white suburbanites for white suburbanites. The earliest
phases of the project, in the 1950s, had bulldozed old Black neighborhoods to clear space for gleaming new towers and entertainment
centers, what Garry Wills called "tall, sterile buildings . . . products

of reverse 'extraction,' gleaming molars stuck in the rotten maw . . . as much out of place as if they had come from Mars." As these new structures rose—the Charles Center, Morris A. Mechanic Theatre, Baltimore Civic Center, and so on—many of those dislocated wound up in public housing or in slum dwellings in neighborhoods like Sandtown. In the eyes of its critics, the new Baltimore was slick and fake and ultimately cosmetic, displacing what was messy and troubled but real. Black people had always been a huge part of the city's fabric, and their erasure gave the lie to the word "renewal." The truth was that Baltimore's story was largely a failure of whites and Blacks to live together. The renaissance just extended the history of exiling those with darker skin to the margins. Resentment about this was easily drowned out by the ringing of cash registers, the roar of baseball and football fans, and the kudos of white newspapers and magazines. Simon gave it voice. He was a social critic with global reach, a loyal TV audience, and a mantel full of Emmys. His portrait stung.

It stung because those behind the renaissance really were good people who were trying to save the city, who certainly did not consider themselves racist but the opposite. Otherwise, why would rich businessmen who lived mostly elsewhere care about Baltimore at all? The accusation nettled the civic boomers behind the great revival. The reinvention of the Inner Harbor did, in fact, help everyone. City schoolchildren, most of them Black, were a big part of the audiences at the aquarium and the science center, and the gleaming new venues— hotels, bars, restaurants, shops—created jobs and were open to anyone with a credit card. But how, in a city as segregated as Baltimore was and remained, could such a grand civic undertaking be perceived in any but racist terms? If *they*—the moneyed white folks behind the rebuild—could work magic like that at the waterfront, why couldn't *they* lift neighborhoods like Sandtown, too? Why build attractions for tourists and sports fans when Black people needed basic things like affordable housing, better schools, and good jobs? The plaint assumed that millions invested in one way—backed by government loans and guarantees—would work wonders of a different sort if invested in social betterment. It made more sense to many than the old trickle-down logic that the Inner Harbor boom would lift all, eventually. That sounded like more of the same white-people bullshit Black Americans had been hearing forever. Mountains had been moved to build a gleaming playground for the very white people whose mass exodus had left the city in the lurch.

At around the time Simon's work began to appear, and shortly before Montana Barronette was born, the powers behind the renaissance accepted the challenge. If they could transform the trash-choked Inner Harbor into a global tourist destination, they could certainly reverse fortunes in one of the city's historically neglected Black neighborhoods. There was dispute over where to center the project, some pull and tug between West and East Baltimore, an old rivalry, but Mayor Schmoke, true to his West-side roots, prevailed, and the effort settled on Sandtown. More than 40 percent of the families living there met the federal definition of poverty; one in six adults were unemployed. Rouse, the genius behind not just Harborplace but also the much-heralded planned city of Columbia in Baltimore's southwestern suburbs, committed his home-building foundation to turning the Sandtown neighborhood into a model of urban renewal. Backed by Schmoke and the established herd of municipal and business leaders, more than $130 million poured in over the next decade. Charitable organizations both secular and religious joined, and some deeply committed activists literally moved in, investing not just money and expertise but *themselves*. It was a full-on assault, aiming to improve not just dwellings but lives. There were initiatives targeting employment, education, crime, and health care. Everything was thrown into the effort, including the kitchen sinks that arrived with Habitat for Humanity's hundred-home project—Jimmy and Rosalynn Carter showed up to help drive nails. "This will be a drop in the bucket for us to come here," the former president told an audience of over a thousand at the new Inner Harbor Hyatt Regency. "But these drops in the bucket can make a flood tide of change."

That was the plan. Ten years later, by the time *The Wire* was airing on HBO, the flood tide had not washed in. The results of this heroic effort were largely disappointing, enough to call into question the whole approach. Prospects for individuals can be profoundly improved by moving them from a depressed neighborhood to a thriving one, but attempting to remake an entire destitute neighborhood was overreach. While Sandtown's rebuild helped thousands of individuals, it did not alter the lives of most residents, particularly those most in need. It was, after all, during the 2000s that Tana and Rell were mastering the reality of Sandtown's streets. At the end of the decade, drugs were still being sold openly on corners, prostitutes still strolled the sidewalks, schools still ranked at the bottom, and poverty was still the rule. The racist history that had so deliberately created Sandtown was so deeply rooted that it easily withstood even this generous onslaught. In some ways, the neighborhood actually got worse. Those best positioned to take advantage of the various programs and initiatives prospered and moved away, increasing the number of vacant homes. Then came the financial collapse of 2008, which drove many of Sandtown's hopeful new homesteaders into foreclosure.

Crime dipped, but only slightly, and no more than it had citywide during those years, so there was no clear correlation. Those Sandtown residents untouched by the full-court press of improvement, like Delores Burch and her apartment full of grandchildren, were too old or too young or too unskilled or too unmotivated to profit. Instead of becoming a showpiece for urban renewal, Sandtown became a symbol for its futility. The perverse consequences of centuries of racial isolation and poverty were harder to reverse than anyone imagined.

And if that were the whole story, if the intractable failure of Sandtown and the tribulations of his family had pushed Montana Barronette down a greased path into dealing on corners and then into the clean new sneakers of Pony Head, we might argue—as his lawyer later would—that his story was entirely about circumstance. It would be as much an example, perhaps more so, of social failure as personal failure.

Except that isn't the whole story. Somewhere along the way, goofy, genial, smart, poised, ambitious Montana Barronette became a serial killer.

4

Either You Got to Be That, or You Ain't

Tana, front, in a still from YGG Tay's "My City" music video.

Lacking conventional resources for building profitable reputations, they peddled exaggerated stereotypes and parodies that aroused the voyeuristic desires of consumers. They effectively commodified their stigma, converting negative stereotypes—as backward, savage, and provincial people—into a new form of capital that they exchanged for financial success.
—Forrest Stuart, *Ballad of the Bullet*

The day before Tana threatened Pony Head, a young barber had been shot dead a few blocks away. Alfonzo Williams wasn't the first murder victim who would eventually be linked to TTG, but his was the first for which Tana was named as the killer. It is particularly shocking because it arose from something so seemingly trivial.

It happened on a balmy Saturday afternoon. More people than usual were out on the stoops and sidewalks along a long, sloping row-house block of West Lafayette Avenue. Allise Bridges and her half sister Leandra Williams were taking the air outside their home, a three-story brick row house painted rust red with a marble stoop. They were new to Sandtown, as were their mother and their brother Alfonzo, known to his friends as "Twin," who was, at twenty-three, three years older than Allise and a year younger than Leandra. He was a big, burly, jovial, round-faced fellow who liked to dance and sing—"He *thought* he could sing," says Allise. Alfonzo had moved out of state for a while but had returned when a former girlfriend gave birth to his son. He wanted to help raise the boy. That afternoon he had come home from a haircutting shift and, as was his custom, rounded up all the kids on the block and marched them up to the Everything Cheap convenience store on the corner to buy candy. He had lingered there with his friend Gotti, Daniel Purdie, to purchase some Percocet pills from a wiry teenage dealer on the corner, and then walked back down to the house to stretch out on the steps. He lit a cigarette and popped open a beer. Music was playing nearby. There was a buzz in the air about a big pay-per-view TV event that night, a long-anticipated welterweight fight between Floyd Mayweather and Manny Pacquiao. A neighbor one door down was hosting a fight party, and folks were anteing up to help pay the fee. So the mood was festive. The sisters were still getting acquainted with their new neighbors and had dressed to attract attention, Allise in a shirt that showed cleavage and Leandra in a clingy dress.

They caught the eye of the teenage drug peddler, who came loping down the sidewalk, small, lean, athletic, with big sleepy eyes and jutting lips, smiling, showing off gold fronts. Perhaps "leering" would be the right word, because the sisters said he greeted them by saying, "You so fine, I'll take you *and* you."

Like they were supposed to be honored. That's how they would remember it. In another account, the dealer opened with a wise-crack about Leandra's thighs, which were ample and amply exposed beneath the short hem of her dress, saying, "You need to cover them up." Whatever he said, the sisters were insulted. They chirped back at him sharply, Leandra telling him not to sell his pills in front of their house. The sisters remembered what followed like this:

"What do you mean?" the young man said. "I do what I want."

Sharp words were exchanged. Then Alfonzo spoke up.

"Yo, you don't talk to my sisters like that," he said. Williams stood up and towered over the teen. "That's not the way you talk to them. They not hood rats."

The young man backed off immediately.

"My bad. We playin'."

He asked if Leandra was Alfonzo's girl.

"She's my sister, bro," he said.

That's all there was to it. A neighbor stepped up to say that he also didn't appreciate drugs being sold in front of his house. Alfonzo, characteristically, tried to make peace. He talked with the dealer, who said he had grown up just a few blocks away. They shook hands. Alfonzo invited him to come back that night to watch the fight, and said, "We'll save some drinks for you."

They never saw the fight. Just before it was supposed to start—it was now dark outside—Alfonzo went out to the steps to wait with Gotti and Leandra for a pizza delivery, and the slender dude reappeared, emerging from a nearby alley. The hood of his sweatshirt was up, and he was carrying a gun.

Allise, who was inside, had never heard gunshots before. They had moved to Sandtown only recently; they had lived with their mother in the county and in East Baltimore. She thought she was hearing fireworks. A man across the street had been setting off some earlier. Pop after pop after pop. Then she heard Leandra scream, and she thought, *That's just her acting stupid*. When Allise got to the front door, her brother was slumped on the steps, bleeding. The shooter had fled.

Nine bullets had hit Alfonzo, in the chest, arms, and neck. The neck shot is probably what killed him. Alcohol in his system interfered with the trauma team's efforts to stop the bleeding. He died on the hospital table. The shooting was witnessed by many, but when the police came, nobody would talk except the horrified sisters. They told the police who they thought the shooter was and didn't understand why no one else would, not even Gotti, who had been sitting on the steps next to their brother.

They soon learned why. Tana was infamous.

At some point in our lives—most often in youth—who doesn't want to be a star? Perhaps the desire is strongest among those with little hope of distinction. And where the line between fame and infamy blurs, being feared counts.

Forty years before, when it was harder to get noticed, the uncontested star of Baltimore's streets had been a diminutive street tough named Maurice King, known to one and all as "Peanut," a nickname often applied to those of small stature. Whip thin, dark-skinned, with a face like a balled fist, he had been arrested for the first time when he was seven, for stealing candy. He graduated to stealing groceries —he was one of five children raised by a woman whose refrigerator was often empty. Grocery theft led to bicycle theft. Peanut adopted a simple code: *If you want something, take it and run.* By his teens he was a burglar, and after a stint in the reformatory and then another stretch in prison, he emerged full grown and better schooled in his self-help strategy. Soon he was selling heroin and within a few years had his own shop. In short order, he was managing the heroin trade in Baltimore.

At the height of his success, Peanut made crazy money. Prosecutors—likely exaggerating—would later project his earnings at $50 million annually. Even if the real amount was just a fraction, he was a rich man. Perhaps aware that his salad days—likely even his life—would be brief, he spent lavishly and lived with flash. He was risibly ostentatious, wearing diamonds and furs and startling bespoke suits and, in a distinctly personal touch, bedroom slippers—a foot ailment made shoes uncomfortable. He bought himself a stainless-steel DeLorean, even though he didn't have a driver's license. He gambled wildly. Casinos comped him for travel, rooms, and shows, providing private planes to deliver him and his entourage to, say, a Sugar Ray Leonard fight or a Diana Ross concert. He smoked cigarettes from a diamond-studded holder, hired himself a stockbroker at Legg Mason, Baltimore's premier investment firm, to place still bigger bets on the stock market. Gifts for his multiple girlfriends—his status made him catnip for some women—came from luxurious shops in Beverly Hills. At a certain point, lavish spending served his stardom. A legend needs to maintain appearances—hence the giant Afro, wide-brimmed fur hats, colorful suits, rings, that ridiculous car. There is a portrait of him seated in a throne-like wicker chair like some African potentate, with glowering bodyguards at stiff attention on either side. Peanut was over the top. It was about maintaining his rep, which was as important as—perhaps even more important than—the money. As Peanut told me many years later, "Either you got to be that, or you ain't."

Stardom is not a peculiarly American dream, but America perfected it. Whole industries are devoted to it. In Peanut's day, there were movies and TV, newspapers and magazines—but good luck getting noticed if you were Black, much less a Baltimore drug dealer. Even those with legit attainments in the arts and sciences usually toiled in the shadows. Attracting notice if you were Black depended primarily on word of mouth in your own community, and violence got everyone's attention.

A continent away, in Los Angeles, teenager Kody Scott earned the street name "Monster" after he beat an old man so badly that the victim's face was permanently disfigured, prompting police to ascribe that name to the unknown (to them) assailant. This launched Scott's career with the Crips gang, in which his outrageous exploits in and out of prison gave Monster what he most craved, fame. Occasionally his crimes were mentioned in TV and newspaper reports. He would later change his name to Sanyika Shakur and write an autobiography. The whole point, as he explained it, was the reputation, primarily in his old neighborhood, of his "set."

"We're *not* a secret society," Shakur once said, speaking of his crew. "Our whole thing is writing on walls, tattoos on necks, *maintaining visibility*. Getting media coverage is the shit! If the media knows about you, damn, that's the top. We don't recognize *ourselves* unless we're recognized on the news. . . . There's a lot of talk about loyalty and mission and all that with the gang, and that's part of it, but my initial attraction to these guys I saw who were in gang life was that these dudes were Ghetto Stars. And I wanted to be a Ghetto Star."

The graffiti was advertising.

"When you shoot somebody, you say your name, loud," he said. "And I wouldn't hide my face. You leave people alive, knowing that the word will get out on who did it. You go to parties and you shoot in the air and say your name. Or you go to parties and you shout-whisper your name in girls' ears, tell 'em what a badass you are, or tell 'em, 'Tell so-and-so, he can't kill me.' You'd primarily use females, because they had the gossip thing down. They are very important, because if they are impressed, they spread the word."

The very idea of a "ghetto star" makes sense only in a community that values violent criminal behavior. In the ghettos of Los Angeles or Baltimore, the emergence of a characters like Monster and Peanut and Tana was, as Du Bois put it, "a phenomenon to be awaited."

In fairness to Peanut, he was no Monster. His effort to "be that" meant mostly ostentation and generosity. He lived it up in Baltimore like a man with no future, and his run lasted about eight years. It ended abruptly at age twenty-eight, when he was sentenced to spend the next half century in prison. Vilified as the primary demon of drug distribution in Baltimore, Peanut had never seen himself as a bad guy. Unlike Monster, he did not revel in the violence his business required. Like many corrupt men, he at least partly believed the canned piety of his rationale, that he was a champion of the people, gathering riches to better his oppressed community. He hadn't invented the city's lust for heroin; he was just filling a public need. He provided liberally for his family and friends, donated to charity, sponsored youth basketball leagues, and threw block parties, serving hot dogs and steamed crabs. Like Sandtown's corner king Pony Head a generation later, he reveled in his local status, only on much larger scale. Peanut also knew the importance of intimidation, even if he did not see himself as a violent man. He insulated himself from actual bloodshed by employing enforcers, some of them Vietnam vets addicted to his product and willing to put their training and experience to work. So when Peanut went down, he went down on drug charges, not murder, even though everybody knew there was blood in The Game.

When he was finally freed, thirty-seven years later, slightly stooped, chastened, and more than a little gnarled with age, he found Baltimore's Black community pretty much as he'd left it. Another whole generation of kingpins had come and gone—David Simon had named some of the characters in *The Wire* after them.

Except, the violence had gone mad. It had eclipsed the drugs. Peanut was horrified. Handguns were everywhere. Children had them and used them. The city's murder rate, already bad in the 1980s, had more than doubled and would have been much worse if local trauma units weren't so skilled at keeping victims alive. And even though nearly all the victims were Black, mostly young Black men, there was sympathy enough in the community for paeans to pop up for shooters in music and videos. A certain sort of young woman seemed drawn by a reputation for killing. Such women slept with these new fierce local gangstas, had their babies, and measured them mostly by how well they provided. So what if these hood rats were vicious? Their world was vicious. They were the fearless ones, the ones who refused to knuckle under to unfair drug laws or to the corrupt and racist cop enforcers. They were the ones who abandoned school and scorned jobs that paid minimum wage, who refused to play by the rules of a society that had kept their race down for centuries. They would make money however they could and go down fighting. Ghetto stars. They weren't succeeding on a scale equal to Peanut's—their turf was tiny by comparison—but there were more of them. Just about every Black neighborhood in Baltimore had its own armed and deadly local crew, each with its tinpot corner king. But, oddly, even as their domains shrank, their notoriety grew, beyond even Peanut's wildest dreams.

In the twenty-first century there were more ways to get noticed. Forget about word of mouth or occasional horrified reports in local media. The internet had arrived. People had been creating their own myths forever—Monster scrawling his name on walls in LA, Peanut posing like a tribal chief—but with Facebook, Instagram, Twitter, YouTube, and other social media platforms, everyone had a *global* audience. Every person was the star of their own production. It was still hard to stand out in the din of universal self-promotion, but ghetto stars had a way. Blood still drew attention.

So, in addition to all the other things pulling Tana into The Game, add this: the spotlight. By age nineteen, he was notorious not just in Sandtown but also to a select underground media culture that cheered him on. He knew it and cultivated it. By the time he hurled his challenge to Pony Head, Tana's rep was already trending on platforms Peanut had never imagined and even Pony Head knew little or nothing about.

Gunplay on Baltimore's streets had become a spectator sport. Social media was like a dark chorus reacting to each new outrage. There were Instagram accounts detailing every shooting, posts that generated a running commentary, urging people not to snitch and speculating on why the victims had been targeted. Those killings that received mention in legacy media, on TV or in the dwindling newspapers, were dubbed

"Highlights" by TTG, borrowing the term directly from Instagram. Murders were tallied like notches on a gun grip. And for those with no compunctions about killing, there were even cash incentives. Social research on the internet's role in aggravating violent behavior, whether political or social, has been inconclusive, but there is no doubt that various popular platforms have enabled murderous people with money to select targets and advertise rewards for killing them. In Sandtown, people were targeted for revenge, to settle turf rivalries, or for being suspected of talking to the police. In this climate, even the rumor that there was money on your head could get you killed. There was, of course, plenty of shaming and lament on social media platforms about the carnage, too, about the horror of it all. There were pleas to stop the killing, but there was also the dark chorus of approval. In this new digital realm, reputation spread at the speed of light.

The coin of the realm was authenticity, and there was nothing fake about TTG. The crew had been together in Sandtown since early childhood. Some members were related to each other, either directly or loosely. In a community where generations of women had babies by different men, there were stretched and often bewilderingly complex definitions for familial connection—"his brother has a baby boy by my first cousin," or "his sister's the baby mama of his cousin's brother." So within the tight-knit TTG crew were traces of real kinship. Some of them had, in a sense, raised each other. They had attended school together until they quit, had run errands together for the corner boys, hung together, played football and basketball together, sold and used drugs together, shared earnings and guns and girlfriends and eventually murders. Most of them had children by various women in the neighborhood. They strutted the streets of their dilapidated little world, comfortable, proud, and superbly adapted. After Rell was sent to prison for five years in 2012, Tana became their leader.

There was Binkie, John Harrison, who was the same age as Rell and, like him, was notably slow. He was a slight man with a square,

handsome face and a scruffy beard. His family had been living in Sandtown for generations, and it was the only world he knew—he did not
even have a driver's license. His grandmother had bestowed the infan-
tile nickname, and his buddies sometimes called him "Stinkie." He
had been diagnosed with brain damage from exposure to lead paint
and had struggled in school, dropping out without having learned to
read or write. Binkie cultivated the image of a sullen, menacing loner,
but he was a central player in the gang, its primary enforcer. With out-
siders he was polite but opaque.

There was Tash, Taurus Tillman, a short man with big eyes and
an arresting stare and smile, also the same age as Rell. His mother was
addicted to drugs, and his father was mostly absent, so he had spent
an unsupervised childhood on the streets. Like Tana, however, he had
finished high school, and had then attended a trade school, but he had
never left the corners. He had been to the hardening school of prison,
serving a one-year sentence for selling drugs before returning to the
crew with enhanced cred. Arrested for gun possession while on pro-
bation, he was just one police stop from a return trip to prison.

There was Tev (Tevin Haygood), the youngster who had shot at
Pony Head, so slight and unimposing that he was sometimes bullied and robbed on the streets. He seemed determined to prove himself star material. There was Fat Guy, Guy Coffey, a garrulous, clever
street merchant with a weight problem. There was Brandon Wilson,
nicknamed Ali because he was a talented amateur boxer; and Linton
Broughton, known as Party Marty, or just Marty, with a bruiser's face
atop a thin frame. He wanted to be seen as a killer; he boasted in a
letter to a girlfriend that he had put eight people "on shirts," referring
to the practice of bereaved families silk-screening the faces of slain
loved ones on T-shirts. Marty was an enforcer, someone who kept
the crew's workers in line. There was round-faced and -shouldered,
pudgy Thug, Antonio Addison, who had survived a gunshot to the
head years earlier and had uncles and cousins in The Game. There was

burly Man-Man, Brandon Bazemore, roughly the same age as Tana, who had a better shot than most of the crew at escaping the pull of Sandtown's streets. His stepmother and his father bought a house outside the city and offered to take him with them, but he refused to go, opting to stay with his friends. These, with Rell and Tana, formed the core of TTG, and around them circulated dozens of others, siblings, cousins, girlfriends, hangers-on.

There were also two slightly older men, on the periphery of the gang but vital: Milk, Roger Taylor, and Denmo, Dennis Pulley. These were the crew's drug suppliers, with outside contacts and a lot more experience and sophistication. Both acted as sometime mentors to Tana and Rell. Milk was slender-faced with a light complexion and a neatly trimmed mustache and goatee. Denmo, dark and fully bearded, lived in a downtown luxury apartment building and was planning to launch his own fashion line in New York.

The modern Game was all about branding, and TTG worked at it. Postings on social media may not reveal who a person is, but they do show how they wish to be seen. Many of the crew members had Instagram accounts, tagged "TTG," showcasing themselves together at casinos or upscale venues or in LA or Miami, draped in gold, flaunting—sometimes literally rolling in—piles of cash, pointing handguns, and raising defiant middle fingers to the camera. The themes of these pictures were consistent: joyful defiance, enthusiastic violence, ample funds, and above all, authenticity. No selfie-taking poseurs, they were self-labeled "OGs" (original gangstas). Posts were often punctuated with the "100" emoji, meaning 100 percent real. The word "real" appears a lot. Milk posted a picture of himself on an Inner Harbor promenade holding a thick bundle of cash up to his ear like a phone, huge gold watch on his wrist, with two other cash bundles jutting from the pockets of his custom-tattered jeans, with the caption, "Ain't no way I'm going broke." Tana, handle "ttg_tana," also known affectionately as "Mookman," decorated his posts with emojis of guns and cartoon explosions. They called themselves a "sniper gang," and they were clearly having a ball, traveling, drinking, gambling, spending, even swimming with dolphins—Tana was pictured on a Florida trip in a tank flashing a wary gold-toothed smile as one pressed its snout against his cheek. There was a post of him posing gleefully before a Rolls-Royce, arms spread wide like Jack Dawson on the prow of the *Titanic*—*King of the World!* Brazenness was the point. In another of his posts, Tana is balanced on a blue electric hoverboard pointing his index fingers at the camera with his thumbs up, like guns, boasting, "Idnt kn how to lay lo." Drug transactions were worked out in shorthand on the chat feature. Not everyone who saw and responded to these posts applauded them, and for them Tana had a message, a picture of himself seated on a stoop extending one long middle finger, captioned, "Fuck u haters I kill u all if I could ain't scared of none of y'all cause u kn my aim good!!!! #facts*100*" The fact that he and his crew were still alive was proof that they were winning The Game. One post from Milk read, "If you make it to 25, you A OG *100*"

Then there were the videos. The first, "Be with God," would surface on April 3, 2015. It was expertly produced. Shot in black and white, with superb camerawork and direction, it opens in a graveyard, then moves to a clip from an actual Baltimore TV news broadcast.

The reporter says, "This morning's homicide marks number seventeen for Baltimore City on just the seventeenth day of the new year."

Over the clip, a rapper introduced himself, "Y Double-G Tay," the handle of a baby-faced county kid named Davante Harrison, a gangsta wannabe, who styled himself as a "Young Go Getter." Instead of *Davan-Tay*, he became "YGG Tay." He is dancing and singing in a graveyard, two large, glittering self-promotional pendants bouncing on his chest, calling out those who decried Baltimore's mounting murder rate. Harrison is not there to condemn the bloodshed, he's there to praise it. As he puts it, "Niggas hatin', niggas killing, that's my city's racket." Then comes a news clip from days later, "Man, Woman Found Dead in Car," which notes that the total is now up to twenty-four.

I don't give a fuck
I'm still flexin' hard
That nigga try and pull a move
He gon' be with God.

He boasts about the brutal stakes he and his crew embrace. The video develops into a well-crafted short story with Harrison's glittering pendants—one spelling out "YGG" and the other "Young Go Getters"—as the MacGuffin. They are taken from him at gunpoint in the beginning. Harrison is then shown dancing with Tana, Milk, and other members of the TTG crew, round-faced Thug and Binkie, and one of the rapper's county friends, a skinny string bean called Scratch, Darius Singleton, who wore his flat-brimmed baseball cap sideways, like a character in a comic strip. They all gestured and moved threateningly behind Harrison's rap:

He gon' be with God
If he disrespects my squad
Please don't try to call my bluff
'Cause I ain't a fraud
I'm from the Murderland
This is how we live . . .
It's all about The Game
Selling drugs, banging bitches
It'll never change.

The rapper places a phone call to Tana, who is in the back seat of a car, gold fronts gleaming in the half light, wearing a stocking cap and a dark sweatshirt with white long sleeves. Tana passes the phone up to Milk, driving, and as Harrison continues to sing and dance, they spot the thief on the sidewalk in the act of selling the pendants. As they run toward him, Tana draws a handgun from his jeans, then places the barrel against the back of the thief's head.

While the sequence depicted was fictional, Harrison makes it clear that he is not making this stuff up. Indeed, that's the video's point. Those in his immediate target audience, from Sandtown, would recognize Tana and the others, and word spread widely: *These are no actors; these guys are actual shooters.* Real gangbangers playing themselves, doing what they do, thereby boosting their own and baby-faced YGG's desired profile and cred.

The message isn't subtle. Harrison sings:

I give you real in my raps
I ain't ever flackin'
You don't like it
You need to do somethin', nigga,
'Cause where I'm from
We DO somethin', nigga.

Harrison had been considered the class clown of Milford Mill Academy, a county public high school. Growing up outside the beltway was nothing like growing up in Tana's neighborhood, but Harrison, at twenty, had aspirations that were both upward and downward. He wanted to be a ghetto star, which required he become a genuine street thug. He had attended a community college in the county, where he met Scratch, and pairing with a talented young producer named Davontae Eden, from Reisterstown, northwest of the city, they began turning out highly polished videos of YGG's raps. They picked up support from Milk and then from Milk's higher connections, two drug wholesalers with money to invest and connections to music pros in Atlanta. Sometime in late 2014 or early 2015, Harrison more or less adopted Tana and TTG (Rell was still in prison). He was a soft county kid with money, cameras, and some talent. His audience did not yet approach the tens of millions that watched big-time rappers, but tens of thousands were watching his videos on YouTube, and those numbers were growing. He had big plans and was making real money. With the backing of Milk's suppliers, YGG Tay soon had apartments in LA and Atlanta, the real hub of the rap business. He sent girlfriends to live in them and to help rep him. Mostly, though, his raps were hits in Baltimore's own lively hip-hop scene.

Harrison's dream was no wild fantasy. There was real money in what Forrest Stuart called "ghetto bad man tales" in his book *Ballad of the Bullet*, describing young Black men acting out in "morally charged caricatures of themselves as 'black superpredators.'" The genre was dubbed "drill" music, slang for "shooting" music. The prototype drill rapper was Keith Farrelle Cozart, a Chicago teenager who styled himself as Chief Keef and in 2012 made a rap video with his South Side neighborhood friends called "I Don't Like." They performed it in Cozart's grandmother's living room, where he was staying under house arrest for a felony gun charge. Smoking weed, he and his dreadlocked buddies, handsome young Black men flaunting piles of cash and prison tattoos, danced shirtless, grabbing their crotches, pointing their fingers like guns (the pending gun charge may have discouraged the use of actual hardware), and bragging about their street code:

> *A snitch nigga, that's that shit I don't like. . . .*
> *I done got indicted sellin' all white,*
> *But I won't never snitch none in my life. . . .*
> *I'm killin' those niggas shit they don't like.*
> *Bro-ski got the .30, he ain't tryin' to fight.*

Launched on a YouTube channel, this bare-bones, amateurish act went viral. Stuart writes, "It has amassed roughly ninety million views. . . . It's a truly impressive feat, particularly once you consider that it was accomplished by a sixteen-year-old living in one of Chicago's most maligned neighborhoods." The raw quality of the production only added to the video's authenticity, which was the heart of its appeal. Months after its release it made the *Billboard* Hot 100 chart. Cozart became a celebrity, invited to perform with mainstream acts, eventually signing a recording contract worth millions. Several of his friends on that video also cashed in with their own record deals. They may not have been great artists, but they were *real*, and now they were rich.

Even if you never struck gold like Chief Keef, there were rewards for putting yourself out there online as a drill artist. Stuart writes of his conversation with a young man he called "AJ," reflecting on a rap artist he had known in high school.

"Before this, he was just, like, a regular nigga. Just comin' to school like everybody. Ain't no big deal. Then he dropped his videos and started goin' crazy. Everybody was on his dick. He was gettin' with *mad* girls. These girls was, like, the *baddest* in the whole school! And they was just throwin' it at him! I ain't never seen nothin' like that, bro!"

Chief Keef and his buddies continued their drug use, their violent and criminal behavior, and encountered repeated problems with the law, all of which just burnished their image. At some point, Stuart argues, they *had to* continue their thug life. Their renown depended on actually being the bad actors they portrayed—image shaping the man. If anything, drill music made harsher demands on its performers than Peanut's rep had made on him decades earlier. "It's not long after a young man starts posturing on social media that rivals, and sometimes even strangers, start pressing him to prove his authenticity,"

Stuart writes. "[His] public persona is put to the test. Is he really the hardest man on the block? Does he really use the guns in his photos? He faces a choice—either find a way to affirmatively answer these questions or risk being labeled an imposter."

So Harrison's dream was firmly grounded. *It had happened.* The path, if not well worn, was at least well lit. It was not unlike the allure of NBA or NFL stardom, which inspires obsessive pursuit in millions of boys, even though success anoints only an infinitesimal few. Impossible odds mean nothing to teenage boys. Their life is fueled by dreams. They are all potential. Chief Keef and other drill rappers were a beacon for kids like Tana, whose outlaw behavior was otherwise a dead end. Here was a path to stardom that asked them only to be what they already were. For Tana, the former "baby" on his Harlem Avenue block, the prospect had to have been breathtaking. YGG Tay swept Tana and his gang off their feet. He had far better production values than Chief Keef in his grandmother's living room and had moneyed backers. He put the TTG crew on a global stage, looking cool, brazen, tough, righteous, chanting about their authenticity, living fully and proudly by the harsh code of The Game. These were not some anonymous extras dancing like fools behind the singer, waving their arms around, posing, using their hands and fingers to make shooting gestures at the camera and sometimes pointing real guns, *pretending* to be badass—they were the real deal: *I'm from Murderland. This is how we live!* In another rap, entitled "Errday," in which YGG Tay paired with fellow rapper YGG Dre, Damont Brown—again featuring the Sandtown crew—they boast:

> *On the block like errday*
> *Totin' Glocks like errday*
> *Gettin' cash done errday*
> *I risk my life like errday*

Errday we go get it
Errday we go get it
Errday we go get it
All my niggas go get it . . .
We da reason for the yellow tape
We play our part in the murder rate!

YGG Tay had huge plans. He would open his next video shouting, "YGG Tay taking over the whole fuckin' world!"

This turn to murderous violence had been evolving for years. The drug trade that Tana and Rell had eased into in their early teens came with the usual rivalries and turf battles, and like those who had entered The Game before them, they had to be ready to defend their turf, drugs, and money. But now murder was celebrated for itself. Both brothers demonstrated early on not just a willingness to kill but an avidity.

The first murder linked to the corner gang had happened four years before Tana had threatened Pony Head, before the neighborhood crew had named itself TTG, and had not involved Tana. It was a wild caper that ended badly, especially for a drug dealer called Nut, Jamie Hilton-Bey, a slight man with a trim goatee and steeply receding hairline.

Rell, who was then nineteen, along with Fat Guy and Bub (Brandon Littlejohn), had taken up the profitable practice of robbing other drug dealers, grabbing their cash and product and thus discouraging competition with their own shop. A better idea was proposed to them by an established local gangsta, Rarah, or simply Rah, Ronnie Johnson, a tall, older man with long tattooed arms and a history of extremely violent behavior and poor judgment. Rah was on one of his brief hiatuses from prison.

He proposed that there was more money to be had by kidnapping dealers than by robbing them. Dealers were relatively safe targets from a law enforcement standpoint because they were in no position to report the crime. But they rarely carried drugs or serious money themselves. So robbing them, Rah reasoned, was just nibbling at the edges. Why not grab them, hold them, and demand real money to let them go? Their loved ones surely could cough up more than they were carrying in their pockets.

A fat opportunity presented itself on the evening of May 20, 2010. Bub pulled his car up to the curb on Pennsylvania Avenue where Rah and Rell were sitting, and, pointing down the street, said, "Man, the nigger down there in that house got two hundred and fifty thousand. I know he do."

Bub was talking about Nut, who by all appearances was doing well. He drove a nice car and had a house on Lauretta Avenue that he was fixing up.

The crew drove off to get some guns and help at Rah's uncle's place in East Baltimore, returning in three vehicles—Bub had his, and the others were in two vans, one burgundy, the other blue. Bub parked at the corner of Pennsylvania and Lauretta to watch for cops. Fat Guy drove the blue van, a Pontiac Montana, with Rell in the passenger seat and Rah in the back by the sliding door with his uncle, Meatball, Amos Johnson. Two others, friends of Meatball, trailed in the burgundy van, which would follow in case a cop gave chase. It would turn sideways to block the police, allowing the blue van to escape. They arrived early in the evening, still daylight, and found Nut on the stoop with a woman. Rah pulled up the hood of his green sweatshirt and stepped out. He had a 9mm handgun.

"Bitch, back up!" he told the woman, who did so.

He then grabbed Nut by his shirt.

"Get in the van," he said.

Slight Nut was no match physically for Rah, but he had fight in him. Rah tried dragging him. An older white man who had been painting inside the house stepped out the front door. Rah pointed the gun at him.

"Get the fuck back," he said. The man turned and went back inside. Nut struggled at the end of Rah's extended arm.

"I'm going to shoot you in the head," Rah threatened, but the dealer kept scuffling. It eventually took three of them to wrestle him into the blue van, Rell and Meatball stepping out to assist. They pushed him to the floor prone between the two back seats. Rah and Rell sat over him on either side and tied his hands behind his back.

Nut bargained. He said they could take his car. There was money and drugs in it, he said. The title was in the glove compartment.

"Man, fuck the car," said Rah. "We kidnapping you." What good would the title do them? "We go in the MVA with a stolen title and they be, like, 'Lock these guys up, man!'" He told Nut they wanted $250,000.

"Man, what makes you think I got two hundred and fifty thousand dollars?" groaned Nut. "Ain't no way I got that kind of money! You can talk thirty thousand."

Meatball fished a phone out of Nut's pocket, and they took turns guarding him as they punched up his call list and started dialing his girlfriends and associates, demanding the huge ransom. They got nowhere.

"I don't got no money!" one girlfriend protested.

This went on for hours. Night fell. They drove Nut all over Baltimore, making call after call, threatening, getting nowhere, increasingly frustrated.

They would hold the phone down to Nut on the floor and demand that he make the ask. "Yo, please give them the money," he repeatedly pleaded, to no avail. They drove to the house of one of his girlfriends.

She mocked them—or at least that's how they interpreted it—by hurling a gun and a can of food at them out of an upstairs window.

"She gave us a can of beans!" said Rah, astonished. He threatened to clout Nut on the head with it. But hurting him had not been in the plan—they had no personal beef with Nut.

This was beginning to feel like a mistake, and Rah, the architect, started to panic. They had a police scanner and heard a description of their van being broadcast. Then a cop car passed them going the other way. Convinced that it would turn and give chase, Fat Guy made a sharp left turn, and Rah opened the side door and bailed. His plan at that moment, albeit hurried, was to land on his feet and run. Physics intervened. He went flying, cracking his head hard on the pavement and knocking himself out. He came to with his friends from the trailing van peeling him off the pavement, his head split open and bleeding. They had assumed the police had opened fire and he'd been hit, but the damage was entirely self-inflicted.

The fiasco continued. The two vans met at a gas station on Pulaski Highway in northeast Baltimore and spent more time badgering poor Nut and making increasingly threatening phone calls. No dice. It was now past midnight. Rah was woozy and still bleeding, so the men in the burgundy van drove him to Franklin Square Medical Center, where he told the emergency team that he had fallen off a four-wheeler.

He caught up with the crew early in the morning in Sandtown, his head wrapped in a clean bandage. They did not have Nut.

"Where the money?" he asked.

There was no money, and Nut was dead. The effort had derailed completely when Nut made a break for the van's door, and Rell had started shooting. He hit Nut not once or twice but thirteen times. Eight shots in his torso, four in his arms and legs, and one, for good measure, in his penis. One pierced his aorta, another his femoral artery, so he had bled out rapidly. The shooting inside the van had been so wild that one round had clipped Fat Guy in the thigh. The caper had concluded with Nut dead, Fat Guy bleeding, and no more reward than the petty cash and drugs they had taken from their victim's pockets.

This disaster would claim one more victim about a year later. Bub, who had suggested kidnapping Nut, was rumored to have been talking about this event to the police—which prompted his execution by his friends. Bub never saw it coming. After watching a football game in Harlem Square Park with Tana, Rell, Tash, Fat Guy, and others, he drifted with them over to the basketball courts. It started to rain, so they took shelter in the entranceway to the park's rec center, and, like the teenagers most of them were, began behaving foolishly. Fat Guy produced a spray can of air freshener and a lighter and chased after Tana, launching flaming bolts.

The fun ceased when Bub waved down a woman in a passing car. The idea had apparently been to kill him later, but this forced the crew's hand. Bub stepped toward the car. "Come on," he said, "We goin' to a party." Guns came out. Rell pulled one from his pants, but Tash was quicker. He stepped up behind Bub and shot him twice, then stood over him and shot some more. In all, Bub was hit by seven rounds. The woman stopped and managed to pull his bleeding body into her car. She delivered him to the shock trauma center, where hours later he was pronounced dead. He had just turned twenty.

This happened when Tana was sixteen. He and Rell and the rest of the crew were already notorious. Rell went to jail about a year later. Rah also returned to prison that year. So Tana stepped up, dubbed the group TTG, and began building both its turf and its menace.

After Alfonzo Williams's grieving sisters had named Tana to the police, he was picked up for questioning. He arrived at the homicide headquarters downtown, calm, pleasant, polite, smiling, wearing a black vest over a sleeveless T-shirt. In the interview room, questioned by Detective Josh Fuller, he appeared shocked that anyone might accuse him of murder. Sure, he'd been selling "a little Percocet" that day, and there had been "a little altercation" with the victim earlier in the evening, but that was it. He'd been nowhere near West Lafayette Avenue that night. He'd been with a girlfriend in a room at the Shera-ton Hotel downtown. He said he hadn't checked in under his own name, and he couldn't remember the name on the ID he'd used. His girlfriend backed up his story, but neither hotel records nor surveil-lance cameras confirmed it.

The truth is, the whole neighborhood knew who had shot Alfonzo Williams, but apart from his sisters—newcomers who did not know Tana and could not pick him from a photo lineup—no one would name him. Fuller had a list of witnesses who wouldn't talk.

They were terrified.

Gotti was Fuller's best bet. He had been sitting on the stoop with Alfonzo when the shooter walked up. Gotti knew exactly who Tana was. He had spent his whole life in the neighborhood. Tall and thin, he was ten years older and referred to Tana as "the boy." Sitting oppo-site Fuller and Detective Gordon Carew in the interview room, three weeks after the murder, he fell apart.

He immediately choked up when the questioning started. He stammered that he had seen nothing. He had walked away before the shooting happened. The detectives knew this wasn't true.

"I can see that talking about this makes you upset," said Fuller. "People said you were right there when the shooting happened."

Gotti's head fell to the desk, and he wrapped it in both of his big hands. He was shaking.

"We know you know the guy who did it, who [Alfonzo] was having the argument with. You need to tell the truth about what happened."

"If you don't," said Carew, "you put yourself in the middle, become part of protecting [the shooter]."

There was a long silence. Gotti's head stayed in his hands.

"I'm not trying to get myself or my family involved in this," he said. "I know for sure that he will come for me next."

Another long silence. An internal struggle was taking place. Eventually, just five words emerged.

"His street name is Tana."

"What's his real name?"

"Don't know his name for sure."

"You know his name," said Fuller.

Long pause.

"I wish I did so I could give it to you."

"What we have to determine is if you were part of it or not," said Carew, turning the screw.

"Twin was my friend!"

He described the murderer as "dark-skinned."

"How many times did he shoot him?"

"Seemed like the whole clip to me. The boy kept shooting and shooting, and I was, like, *damn!* And I was stuck, sitting right there next to him."

He said they had all seen Tana coming down the street with a gun.

"How long has he been coming around?"

"Damn near all his life."

Gotti said his friend was shot because the boy felt "disrespected."

"Twin got killed for standing up for his sister."

The detectives arranged for Gotti to review a sequence of photos with Detective Dawnyell Taylor.

"Am I going to have to take the stand?" he asked when she came in. She told him he'd have to take that up with the other detectives. Gotti balked at signing the papers to begin the photo array.

"This says I'm a witness," he complained.

"We use some witnesses, others no," said Taylor. Then she tried to ease his mind, telling him, in effect, that reviewing the photos did not commit him to testify openly. She said, "Look, I know it's hard to do the right thing. What you do down the line, when it comes to trial, your conscience has to be your guide."

Gotti then, sighing with heavy reluctance, opened each file folder she gave him, one by one, and stared at the pictures, saying nothing. When he'd finished, Taylor asked, "Did you recognize any of them?"

"Five," said Gotti, referring to the fifth photo, the one labeled Montana Barronette.

Taylor pulled open file number five again and placed it before him.

"What connection did that individual have to the shooting?"

"That nigga shot Twin," said Gotti. Then he bowed again, taking his head in his hands. "God damn!" He spent a long time with his head down on the table. Then he pleaded, "If I go any farther, I might be the next one!" Then, to himself, "What the fuck am I doing?"

Another long silence, head on the table, hands draped over it.

"God put me here," he said, finally.

"You gotta do whatever God wants you to do," said Taylor.

Taylor got him to write out "He shot Twin" on the form under the photo of Tana.

"I can't believe I'm doing this," he said, mostly to himself.

"We need your signature at the bottom."

"I've got to sign my name?" Gotti hammered the pen down on the table several times, furious with himself. Then he signed. As Taylor left, he protested, "I can't testify. I can't. I need to know if they are going to need me to testify! I can't go on. My own life! My family's life!"

He was left sitting alone in the room.

It was a potentially winnable case, but the homicide squad had an unspoken agreement with the office of the State's Attorney for Baltimore City to file charges only for cases that were slam dunks, and this was not a slam dunk. Sure, Tana's alibi didn't hold up, and they *might* be able to force Gotti's testimony, but the prosecutors felt it wasn't enough. Fuller disagreed.

He knew he had the shooter. He was even more convinced after he saw Tana's homemade rap video. After the interview with Tana, the police had seized his phone and on it found a video he had shot of himself performing a little rap song about the murder, laughing, moving, singing, celebrating. It made perfect sense. Tana and the crew were all involved with YGG Tay's video effort at the time, and who, after all, was Davante Harrison? He was pathetically inauthentic. The money he was making, the attention he received, all of it was reflected glory. TTG was real. Tana was real. And he liked to rap. He was always bobbing and moving to some internal beat, reciting rhymes, celebrating his street life. Why not step out himself? Like Chief Keef, he was *100!* OG! He wasn't rapping fiction. The day after Williams was shot, Tana had started working up a number out on Carey Street, one block away from the bloody stoop, dancing and singing for the camera. Behind him was an ice cream truck broadcasting its own ditty. "Lil bootsie, nigga," he began, announcing he was a little nasty, a little crazy.

> *We out here on Carey Street*
> *Nigga selling them raws, man*
> *Nigga got the grind yeah and we hittin' out back*
> *Coke comin' through niggas,*
> *We drop Ts on the smack, Nigga.*

Behind the row houses around him they were selling "raw," or uncut heroin. These were "Ts," or "testers," free samples of the stuff, trying to establish their brand as purer than competing products.

> *We got the gift right,*
> *We tryin' get it fuckin' back, Nigga.*

They were talented and smart, they had "the gift," defiantly taking back what they had been deprived because of their Blackness and their poverty.

I'm out here droppin' bodies

He pointed to his left, toward Lafayette Avenue, where he'd emerged from the alley to shoot Williams.

Catch a nigga up in the alley
Nigga, catching the news—

Williams's murder had been reported on the news.

Nigga, I'm making mothafuckin' bodies
Nigga, I'm in the trap, Nigga—

He was "in the trap," meaning fully at home, the word "trap" being a double-edged slang term for one's ghetto neighborhood, a place that is both home and a trap.

I handle forty out back, Nigga—

He'd shot Williams with a .40 caliber handgun, which he had ditched afterward.

It came up missin'
I hit a nigga same night with the same jack [gun].

Had he shot someone else the same night? How much of this was fiction, and how much fact? To Fuller it seemed more than coincidental, his pointing toward the scene of the murder, describing himself emerging from the alley with .40 caliber gun. This wouldn't work as a confession, but it was telling, to see him dancing and singing about things the detective knew had occurred. It had to amount to something. It spoke to state of mind, if nothing else. But the State's Attorney wasn't willing. The sisters couldn't or wouldn't say it was Tana for sure, and Gotti was a roll of the dice. So the case languished.

Fuller, who would have plenty more work to do in the Western District in the coming years, would watch horrified as TTG's death count grew, knowing that he had missed a chance to lock Tana away. Getting away with shooting Alfonzo Williams before a slew of witnesses had more than emboldened Tana—it had made him a legend. He was now seen—and likely saw himself—as untouchable. On the street, Tana would saunter up, teasing, "Detective Fuller, when you gonna give my phone back?" Fuller felt like he was being goaded for failing to bring the charge.

But the strangest thing about Tana was that he was always likable. For Fuller it was hard to reconcile the playful, polite, friendly Tana with Tana the cold-blooded killer.

Sandtown certainly had made the connection. By early 2015 Tana had chased Pony Head up to his hideaway balcony, and by the time he starred in YGG Tay's next production, "My City," a cheerful celebration of TTG, he was basking in his rep as the most celebrated shooter in Baltimore.

The video opens with a drone shot on a dreary day of dilapidated row-house blocks, over which YGG Tay proclaims his promise of "takin' over the whole fuckin' world!" It then cuts to him singing and dancing with the local crew—Tana, Thug (Antonio Addison), Milk (Roger Taylor), Man-Man (Brandon Bazemore), and a dozen others—milling and gesticulating before a grand graffiti mural of the word "Sandtown."

Understand that they don't fuck around
If you ain't fuckin', bitch, don't come around
I keep that magic stick [gun/penis] just for you, clown
Hey, Baltimore, that's my fuckin' town.

Expertly recorded and directed, the video jumps from the dancing gang to random rainy-day glimpses of the neighborhood, street intersections, corner stores, the nearby Inner Harbor skyline, Gilmor Elementary School, Lexington Market, a Ravens poster, and then back to the crew, swaying to the rap, waving fistfuls of money, making shooting gestures with their hands.

We 'bout our money but we lay shit down . . .
and if you see it, bitch, don't make a sound

Cut to a passing police cruiser.

I got some shooters that will lay you down
Shout out to my niggas, this is our town.
Got a chopper [automatic rifle] hold a hundred rounds

Cut to Tana mugging next to a boy wearing a backward cap pretending to aim a rifle at the camera.

I keep some shooters, they'll lay you down

Cut to a closeup of Tana, staring smugly down at the camera, arms folded, wearing the same dark knit cap and two-toned sweatshirt he wore as the killer in "Be with God."

It would snag tens of thousands of views on YouTube. Tana was clearly pleased with it. When Rell called him from prison on March 17, 2015, he caught his younger brother in mid-song:

I got some shooters that will lay you down.
Shout out to my niggas, this is our town.

Tana said that the song was getting a lot of play.
"Niggas be running with that. You heard me, Rell?"
"Huh?"
"Niggas be out here runnin' with that."
He sang again:

I got some shooters that will lay you down
Shout out to my niggas, this is our town.

"Niggas be runnin' with that," he said.
Rell laughed.
"Niggas be runnin' with that," said Tana. "Niggas know who he be talkin' about!"
Rell was still laughing.
"You heard me. These niggas funny as shit. Broke ass. Always talking about money and shit. They don't talk that shit to me."
"Mmm-hmm," said Rell, a verbal nod of approval.
"This only the beginning," said Tana.
"Huh?"
"I said, and this is only the beginning with me. Gonna get me a nice little run. A nice run. Get me where I need to be at."

The murder of Alfonzo Williams had seemed senseless. Shoot a man nine times over a brief exchange of words? How do you make sense of that? The shooter and victim hadn't known each other. Other than the momentary confrontation, the big barber staring down the skinny corner kid, Williams posed no significant threat, and he'd even ended the matter by offering his hand and an invitation. Tana, clearly intimidated by Williams's bulk, had walked off. Hours had passed. Tana had had time to reflect. And somehow, quiet reflection had led him to murder. Why?

What conceivable chain of logic might have argued in favor of taking Alfonzo Williams's life?

The decision to kill someone, to take, literally, *everything* from them, is a response so extreme that for most people it is beyond sober contemplation. Where in life's journey does this become an acceptable option? And for something so trivial as Williams's scolding? It takes a great deal of prior conditioning to even consider doing something so drastic.

The year before Tana was born, sociologist Elijah Anderson dissected the forces at work on young urban Black men in a famous essay, "The Code of the Streets."

> At the heart of the code is the issue of respect—loosely defined as being treated "right," or granted the deference one deserves. . . . In the street culture, especially among young people, respect is viewed as almost an external entity that is hard-won but easily lost, and so must constantly be guarded. The rules of the code in fact provide a framework for negotiating respect. The person whose very appearance—including his clothing, demeanor, and way of moving—deters transgressions, feels that he possesses, and may be considered by others to possess, a measure of respect. With the right amount of respect, for instance, he can avoid "being bothered" in public. If he is bothered, not only may he be in physical danger but he has been disgraced or "dissed" (disrespected). Many of the forms that dissing can take might seem petty to middle-class people (maintaining eye contact for too long, for example), but to those invested in the street code, these actions become serious indications of the other person's intentions. Consequently,

such people become very sensitive to advances and slights, which could well serve as warnings of imminent physical confrontation.

Tana's reaction to Williams's chastisement is an old story in this context, but to kill? Yes, because in Sandtown, in 2014, killing, not fighting, was the norm. The "physical confrontation" noted by Anderson had become an understatement. Brawling makes no sense in the world of the handgun—*Bro-ski got the .30, he ain't tryin' to fight.* Even if he dared, Tana wasn't going to take a swing at Williams. He went to get his gun. Williams had scolded him publicly. He knew there were people on the sidewalk and stoops watching and listening, people like Gotti, who knew he was being dressed down and had watched him back down. And this was no longer just a neighborhood matter. Tana was playing on a much bigger stage. His rep was his ticket to fame and possibly fortune. He was Montana Barronette. *The* Montana Barronette. The shooter. *Trained to Go.*

Either you got to be that, or you ain't.

5

Shit Be Catching Up with Them

Protests in Baltimore on April 28, 2015, after Freddie Gray was killed.

I couldn't believe my eyes . . . I stood there on the sidewalk and watched civilization coming apart. Drug dealers on the street, drug runners, old guys guarding the stashes. People with thirty-year-long heroin addictions wandering around, serious crack addicts, with that manic look. And I had this strongly visceral response: This is not O.K. This has got to stop. And it was immediately obvious that nothing the police were doing was going to work.

—David Kennedy

Four floors up in the Fallon Federal Building, which shines like tourmaline over Hopkins Plaza in downtown Baltimore, are the offices of the state's top federal prosecutor, the US Attorney for the District of Maryland. From its windows, you can peer straight down Lombard Street to a century-old American architectural novelty, the slender, fifteen-story Bromo Tower, an exotic structure that marries Italian Renaissance revival—it duplicates the Palazzo Vecchio in Florence—with undiluted Yankee hucksterism. It was built early in 1911 by drug magnate Isaac Emerson, who had hit the jackpot with his effervescent hangover remedy, Bromo-Seltzer. Beneath its square, crenellated peak, the tower has an enormous four-faced clock with letters in place of the usual numerals, spelling out B-R-O-M-O-S-E-L-T-Z-E-R. A man who understood marketing, Emerson incongruously topped the structure with the most American adornment imaginable, a fifty-one-foot-tall, rotating, glowing blue Bromo-Seltzer bottle. For many years this was Baltimore's tallest building, visible for miles in every direction. The tower today houses art studios, and the giant blue bottle is long gone, a manifest aesthetic improvement but a setback for historical accuracy.

The Bromo Tower still commands the view from the Fallon building. As the newcomer to the office, First Assistant US Attorney Jonathan Lenzner was gazing at it one day when he noticed helicopters circling and hovering behind it.

"What are those choppers doing there?" he asked.

"They're stacked up waiting to land at shock trauma," he was told. Behind and beneath the tower sprawls the University of Maryland's world-class trauma center.

Over time, Lenzner couldn't help but notice how the choppers seemed always to be there. Below, on the street, were the regular comings and goings of ambulances. The trauma center was like a MASH (Mobile Army Surgical Hospital) unit on a battlefield. Accidents and illness and violent crime are enough to keep all big city hospitals busy, but in Baltimore, there was war in the streets. In 2015, on average, three people were gunned down every day. *On average.* Some days less, some days more—a lot more. In May, more than a hundred people were shot, only forty of whom died—60 percent was the center's impressive rescue rate. Many of those saved would leave with their bodies shattered, in need of lifelong care. Such carnage had been an ugly feature of the city for some time, but in the second decade of the twenty-first century it spiked dramatically—up 72 percent from the previous decade. Baltimore's body count now rivaled that of New York City, which had fourteen times more people. The Maryland city had become, per capita, one of the most dangerous cities, not just in America but the world.

This was troubling, to say the least, for Robert K. Hur, who served as first assistant under US Attorney Rod Rosenstein, and who would step up to the top job in 2017 when Rosenstein moved to Washington to become deputy attorney general (where he would famously tangle with President Donald Trump). Hur named Lenzner to his old position, tasking him with thinking big, and there was no bigger problem in Baltimore than what they both could see out of their windows. The parade of casualties was like a daily poke in the eye. Victims and killers were often—though not always—torn from the same cloth. The overwhelming majority were young Black men and boys caught up in a violent drug-dealing subculture. But the forces at work seemed implacable. Hur was a Harvard-educated lawyer with a star-studded resume—he had begun his career as a clerk of the US Supreme Court, to Chief Justice William H. Rehnquist. And he realized that if his tenure as Maryland's top federal law enforcement official was ever to be considered a success, or more important, if he would ever be able to consider himself as such, he had to stem the bloodletting.

But how? The issue was a Gordian knot with diverse contributing strands—poverty, poor education, drugs, guns, broken families, a violence-promoting pop culture, inadequate policing. Where might one begin to undo the consequences of more than a century of subjugation, neglect, and enforced isolation, to address the defiant subculture that had taken root? It's not that no one had tried. Baltimore's gun violence had withstood decades of well-meaning but poorly funded social outreach, some of which had inadvertently made things worse, like replacing slums with modern high-rise apartment buildings in the 1950s or enabling residents to find jobs and better housing, only to see them flee and leave their old neighborhoods further depressed. Police crackdowns, periodically in vogue, and mass incarceration had fed deep-seated community hostility without making a dent. Drug sweeps actually *increased* shootings. Children of those arrested were often left parentless, like Tana and his siblings, making them more likely to fall into The Game. It was an infernal cycle. The most recent horrifying surge in Baltimore shootings, much of it centered in Sandtown, had happened over the very years of that enormous public-private effort to turn the neighborhood around.

Sweeping change and social outreach were beyond Hur's powers, but his office was very good at fighting crime. He had nearly one hundred seasoned prosecutors and a support staff nearly as large. He supervised an alphabet stew of federal law enforcement agencies—FBI (Federal Bureau of Investigation), ATF (Bureau of Alcohol, Tobacco, Firearms and Explosives), DEA (Drug Enforcement Administration), HSI (Homeland Security Investigations), and others. Using sophisticated data analysis, The Alphabet Stew could pinpoint the most dangerous places and people in Baltimore and concentrate efforts accordingly. That much was doable. But for the feds it meant a shift in focus, which is not always easy to accomplish in a bureaucracy. Traditionally, the US Attorney stepped in only for crimes that reached across state lines and national borders, to stop banking schemes and criminals who ran huge multimillion-dollar syndicates like the Mafia, ethnic gangs, drug traffickers, terrorists, and the like. Baltimore's plague of shootings was *hyper*local.

As such, it should have been the concern of city police. Even without resources like those the feds enjoyed, the Baltimore Police Department was better positioned. It knew the city intimately. It had officers in every neighborhood, cops who knew Baltimore block by block, who were acquainted with community leaders as well as corner kings and their crews. Good beat cops knew who was feuding with whom. The department's detectives were the ones chalking outlines and peeling bodies off pavement. They were the ones interviewing (or trying to interview) victims and witnesses. Local police were the obvious remedy for local violence—except in Baltimore, the cops were a big part of the problem.

In 2015, all of the department's long-standing faults surfaced at once after the death of Freddie Gray. Racism, corruption, brutality— you name it. The protests that erupted in Black neighborhoods stretched over days. Some turned violent. Citizens battled cops in the streets. When the Baltimore State's Attorney, in sympathy with protesters, indicted six police for causing Gray's death, many cops quietly stopped policing the most dangerous neighborhoods. If city hall no longer had their backs, why take risks? If something went wrong— and in making arrests things often did—you might end up in the dock yourself, the world turned upside-down. The issues and emotions that exploded after Gray's death went well beyond the specifics of his case. Baltimore's Black citizens had grievances against cops too old and too numerous for anyone to count. A subsequent Department of Justice investigation, concluded in 2016, found that corruption, racism, and abuse were endemic. Black residents were arrested many times more frequently than whites, often for insufficient reason or no reason at all.

"The relationship between the Baltimore Police Department and many of the communities it serves is broken," the report concluded. "Officers seem to view themselves as controlling the city rather than as part of the city. Many others, including high-ranking officers in the department, view themselves as enforcing the will of the 'silent majority.'"

Force was more likely to be used against Black people, even during arrests on picayune charges. Whether or not these arrests resulted in prosecution—eleven thousand charges were rejected by the district attorney and central booking during the four-year period studied—the trauma and stigma of a rough collar endured. It was little wonder so many Black Baltimoreans refused to help the police. Yet even this hostility might have been surmountable if the police were good at their job. There was, in fact, a silent majority of citizens in neighborhoods like Sandtown who wanted their streets cleared of drug peddlers, who craved justice for crippled or dead sons, brothers, husbands, fathers, friends. But the department's incompetence alone made it arguably smarter to stay silent. Instead, victims sought their own justice, further feeding the flow to the trauma center.

The DOJ probe ended in a consent decree. The city police acquiesced to sweeping reforms under federal guidance. As all this was going on, Hur's investigators were also assembling a case against the department's Gun Trace Task Force. Led by a fast-talking, bull-necked, boyish-looking, aggressively criminal sergeant named Wayne Jenkins, the task force was supposed to be a "smart policing" effort to link weapons to crimes. Instead, Jenkins molded it into a full-blown thuggish enterprise. An anti-police propagandist could not have invented a more damaging story. An independent investigation would find "a shifting constellation of corrupt officers," Black and white, "who discovered each other over the course of their careers and committed crimes individually, in small groups, and then in larger groups." Carrying out robberies during street stops and searches of homes, submitting false reports to hide its crimes, and committing "massive overtime fraud," the squad made a mockery of police work, stealing from both the department and the citizens it was hired to protect. The Gun Trace unit was, of course, best known in the city's Black neighborhoods, which bore the brunt of its misconduct.

"Over the course of many years, [the unit's officers] victimized vulnerable Baltimore residents who they trusted would either not complain, or would not be believed if they did," the report found. "Until the federal investigation developed evidence of their criminal activity, the corrupt officers were correct: most of their carefully selected victims did not complain, and those who did were virtually never deemed credible when the allegations were denied by the officers."

Charges would come in two years: Jenkins and eventually seven members of his Gun Trace squad would be sentenced to prison. But the rogue unit was still hard at work as Hur faced the challenge of curbing gun violence in 2015. What he heard from his investigators about Jenkins's squad underlined the hopeless inadequacy of the Baltimore Police Department. It was not just incapable of policing the city; it couldn't police itself.

All of this put Hur on the spot. Part of the feds' mission had long been to take the most violent repeat offenders off the city's hands and off the streets, with a program called Project Exile. The feds didn't have the numbers and reach of the city police, but within The Stew they had resources and tools that even well-run local law enforcement could only dream about: sophisticated surveillance methods, data analytics, and experienced investigators and prosecutors. They could work a single case for months or even years, provide protection and even relocation money for witnesses, and then bring accused criminals to trial in federal courtrooms before juries drawn from a statewide pool, not just from local citizens with deep distrust of cops and courts. Unlike state judges, federal judges didn't have to run for election every few years, and they had sterner sentencing guidelines.

The feds also had a prosecutorial weapon ideally suited for cracking down on gangs, the 1970 RICO (Racketeer Influenced and Corrupt Organizations) Act. Originally drawn to go after the Mafia and other national crime syndicates, whose bosses often escaped punishment by relegating their dirty work, RICO had proved useful against any kind of criminal enterprise. A paltry teenage neighborhood crew like TTG may not have been what its drafters had in mind, but TTG shared the same traits as the big syndicates. The crimes committed were group crimes with group responsibility. Dirty work was distributed, and weapons were shared, making it much harder to tie a gun to a specific individual, even with a ballistic match. Except in rare cases, state courts required each defendant to be tried separately. With RICO, prosecutors had only to prove that a criminal organization existed, that the accused belonged, and that the crime served its interests. Prosecutors could put an entire gang on trial. Using this tool against TTG might have seemed like using a sledgehammer to crush an ant, but by 2015 it was no longer just a drug gang—it was, in effect, a serial killer. Extreme problems call for extreme solutions.

So in the summer of that year, the long arm of Uncle Sam began reaching for nineteen-year-old Tana and his Sandtown homeboys, bumptious comers in their own rap-video universe.

Here was a degree of jeopardy the crew could not yet imagine. To TTG, cops and courts were a joke—at worst, a nuisance. Being arrested as a juvenile, even being jailed, was like after-school detention—you hung out with your buds and fought off boredom until the bell rang. As an adult, getting busted and locked up was both a cost of doing business and a badge of honor. It certified you as *100*. Most of the time, when crew members were picked up and questioned, as Tana had been after the killing of Alfonzo Williams, no charges came. They knew Sandtown witnesses were afraid to speak up, a reluctance they interpreted as respect. They were firmly astride their little world, and, as Tana told his brother, this was "only the beginning."

Whether locking up an entire gang would reduce the city's raging gun violence was dubious, at best. Baltimore had made two half-hearted— some might say half-assed—efforts to mount a coordinated response. Both had been called Operation Ceasefire, patterned after the ideas of innovative Boston criminologist David Kennedy, who had arrived, decades earlier, at the key insight in Hur's data: most urban blood-shed was the work of a few violent men. By Kennedy's figuring, three-quarters of city shootings were committed by *one-half of one percent* of the population. For the criminologist, identifying these instigators was just the first step. Locking them up did not make a dent in the larger problem; others just stepped up to take their place. Kennedy was less interested in arresting and punishing offenders than in breaking the pattern, which meant changing the culture. This made sense. Most representatives of that one-half of one percent were very young, potentially malleable. Part of what Kennedy proposed was to reintroduce social disapproval, the very thing Du Bois had noted was lacking in many poor Black communities. In theory, even the most dangerous character wanted to live and stay free. What if he were offered a way off the greased path? Instead of arresting and prosecuting a self-destructive, dangerous teen like Tana, why not intervene *before* he embarked on his killing career, bring him to meetings—often confrontations—with family, community leaders, shooting victims and their loved ones, anyone who might reach him or whom he might respect? Why not try to guide and educate him into safer and ultimately more rewarding pursuits? This approach asked police to step back from their well-defined role of enforcer and to act instead as a facilitator. Kennedy achieved such success in Boston in the 1990s that it was dubbed a miracle. Homicides fell 80 percent from 1990 to 1999. Dozens of cities adopted the program, including Baltimore.

But it was a hard program to sustain. It was expensive, and it required the buy-in of a wide assortment of federal, state, and local agencies—departments of housing and health, social services, schools, prosecutors, community, and police. It was politically challenging because it left local politicians vulnerable to charges of mollycoddling criminals. The police hated it. Identify the worst of the worst and then invite them to community meetings? Offer them counseling and aid? What kind of appeasing, cheek-turning nonsense was that? It didn't help that Kennedy, with wild hair that reached halfway down his back and a thick beard, looked like a hippie or, as some cops put it, "like Jesus." This feeling had played a role in the launch of Martin

O'Malley, a former prosecutor, to Baltimore's mayoralty in 1999, succeeding Kurt Schmoke. Young and white, O'Malley had stunned the
experts by winning against a field of Black candidates, pledging a
crackdown on crime. He immediately disbanded the first Ceasefire
program. The police department adopted its strategy of identifying
the city's most dangerous players—with an eye not to reforming them
but to locking them away.

And O'Malley had some success. A year into his first term, the
number of murder victims dropped below three hundred for the
first time in a decade and stayed down. This may have been mostly
luck, as crime rates fell at the same time in many parts of the country.
O'Malley's push for more aggressive policing, at least in the beginning,
earned some buy-in from the Black community, but the stern tactics
wore thin. At the same time, something odd happened with the murder numbers. They no longer moved in tandem with broader crime
statistics. Even as violent crime overall declined, Baltimore's homicide
rate, the number of those killed per one hundred thousand residents,
held steady at more than seven times the national average. Aggressive
tactics did not slow deadly shootings, and they aggravated the old friction between cops and Black citizens. Despite significantly increasing the numbers of Black police officers, the department remained
majority white and was perceived as such. O'Malley could not undo
the image—buried deep in Baltimore's past—of police as enforcers
of the racist status quo. Still, he had been doing something right. He
increased efforts for drug treatment and kept a lid on what had been
yearly jumps in crime. When he left to become Maryland's governor
in 2007, the violent crime numbers jumped up again. His tenure in
city hall was succeeded by a series of disastrous mayoralties—two of
his three elected successors were indicted, forced to resign, and convicted of crimes.

Operation Ceasefire was resurrected by the one of the three who
managed to honorably complete their term, Stephanie Rawlings-Blake.

She reintroduced the program with much fanfare in 2014. It didn't last. In short order, its director resigned, complaining that neither city hall nor the city police had offered adequate support. Then came the Freddie Gray episode, which upset the table. Any semblance of police-community cooperation went up in clouds of smoke and tear gas. Ceasefire was a casualty once more. Rawlings-Blake, bruised by the fallout, declined to seek another term.

Still, the one part of the program the police liked had legs. Ignoring the truly innovative parts of Kennedy's approach, Ceasefire morphed into a targeting vehicle. It culled details from thousands of criminal files and found links that the overworked department overlooked. Unless a suspect was charged, his name in a file didn't merit much attention. Often the most dangerous characters were precisely those smart enough to avoid arrest. But when their name surfaced in three, five, seven, or more files, even just as prospective witnesses, they stood out. These were characters who tended to be present when shootings occurred. The method unearthed bad actors who might otherwise have escaped notice. And the first big target on the list was none other than Montana Barronette, who by early 2015 was linked directly or indirectly to nine violent crimes. He had been charged in none.

This came as a surprise to West Baltimore detectives. They knew who Tana was—he was Rell's affable little brother, the kid with the basketball who was always so cheerful and polite. The cops considered Rell the dangerous one, and he was in jail. Other than a few minor scrapes as a juvenile, Tana had a clean record. But the stats didn't lie. In the years Rell was locked up, his younger brother had done more than take over their drug operation. On the street, which was always way ahead of the cops, he was well on his way to becoming a legend. Even if the city had intended a David Kennedy–esque intervention, it would come too late for Tana.

*   *   *

On June 29, 2014, eight weeks after the Williams murder, Terrell Jarrett was killed on Carey Street, a five-minute drive south of Sandtown in South Baltimore. Once a close friend of YGG Tay, Jarrett, known as Hell Rell, had made the mistake of misplacing a substantial amount of the rapper's money and drugs. Confronted about it by YGG, Hell Rell had slapped him, another mistake, this one fatal. Thousands were offered for his killing, which was captured by a surveillance camera, one of many mounted on poles or over storefronts in the area. Hell Rell, a sidewalk dice enthusiast, was interrupted by a shooter who strode up to the game, pulled a handgun, and drilled him in the chest and stomach. Word was that the reward money had gone to Binkie (John Harrison) and Tana. Tana would be heard cryptically alluding to the shooting a day later in another of his prison phone chats with Rell, who was still months away from release.

"I had to make channel," said Tana, referring to the TV news. "I had to make the internet."

Rell knew exactly what his brother was talking about.

"Where at?"

"Over on the other part of town on Carey."

Rell gave one of his lazy laughs.

"It'll be all right," said Tana.

"Yeah."

Tana sang:

It'll be all right.
It's gonna be all right
It's gonna be OK.

Four months later, two other local gangbangers, James Blake and Ronald Langley, were killed. Their mistake had been trying to kidnap Milk (Roger Taylor), who, working closely with a major drug importer named Shongo Owens, was financing YGG Tay's career.

The kidnappers grabbed the wrong person, not in a figurative sense, because Milk was certainly a dangerous fellow, but literally *the wrong person*. They took Scratch (Darius Singleton), the rapper's gangly buddy with the askew baseball cap, who had borrowed Milk's car. After realizing they had the wrong guy, Blake and Langley stripped Scratch, took his money, and let him go. When word reached Milk and YGG Tay, a bounty was offered. Both Blake and Langley were shot dead, and once more Tana and Binkie were named by witnesses and on social media as the likely triggermen, celebrated, and rewarded. Langley was set on fire, which would become an occasional TTG motif. His blackened remains were discovered in November behind a West Baltimore elementary school.

Next came Beezy, Brian Chase, another Sandtown homeboy and something of a dandy, with big soulful eyes, a neatly trimmed mustache, a tuft of hair beneath his chin, and long dreads he wore dangling down the back of his neck. He was known as something of a motormouth. His body was found in a small fenced-in backyard, his face planted in dog shit, to the enduring amusement of his killers. Beezy's mistake had been telling people that there was a price on Binkie's head, that he'd been "green-lit." This may or may not have been true, but rumor alone was dangerous—it might make Binkie a target. Given Beezy's talkative nature, he may not have had a purpose in saying it. He liked Binkie. The rumor had surfaced in a conversation with Donte Pauling, a mutual friend. Beezy told Pauling that he thought Binkie was "crazy for keep coming around here like he ain't got all that money on his head." This had to be taken seriously. Beezy was in a position to know. He was a member in good standing of a prison organization called BGF (Black Guerilla Family) that had loose designs on expanding its reach outside lockup and muscling in on drug corners. The gang was potentially threatening. Behind bars it had a well-defined structure, with "ministers" of defense, information, and so forth. On the outside it was less formidable but dangerous enough to threaten a local crew like TTG. When Pauling repeated what he'd heard to Binkie, Binkie was alarmed. He said, perhaps speaking euphemistically, he would have to "holler" at Beezy the next time he saw him and "get him out of there."

That happened on January 4, 2015, when he and Tana spotted Beezy on a Mosher Street sidewalk. It was early evening. They were cruising the neighborhood in a Mercedes, Tana behind the wheel, Binkie in the passenger seat. Pauling was in the back seat, and he tapped Binkie on the shoulder to point out their mutual friend. They stopped the car, and Tana and Binkie got out, Binkie pulling up the hood of his sweatshirt and putting on gloves. Pauling waited outside the car. The two caught up to Beezy on foot. They walked with him a short distance, and then Tana returned.

"Yo, what's up? What the fuck?" Pauling asked, knowing of Binkie's beef with Beezy.

"I don't know," Tana told him. Binkie "be geekin'," he said. "I ain't going to be the last one being seen with that nigga."

Tana then drove off, leaving Pauling on the sidewalk. Minutes later, Pauling heard gunshots, and then saw Tana cruise past again. Some minutes passed, and then more gunshots.

Pauling later learned the reason for the delay between shots. Left for dead by Binkie in an alley, Beezy had managed to crawl off to a fenced yard, where both Tana and Binkie caught up with him and finished him off. There were fourteen holes in his body, one directly through his throat, which might have been a coincidence but could also have been a message that Beezy had talked too much.

Weeks after the shooting, Binkie was questioned by Dawnyell Taylor. Binkie came to the precinct station with his mom. He was polite—"Yes, ma'am," "No, ma'am"—unruffled, and unhelpful, perfectly willing to chat about himself but astonished that anyone would want to question him about a murder. Taylor thought he looked like a little kid. He presented himself as such.

"Lately, I been in the house, mostly," he said. "Havin' to watch the kids. Lately, I ain't been hangin' around like I used to."

He told Taylor that Sandtown was like his family. "It's just a big family, for real, for real." He'd had nothing to do with the murder. Beezy had been "like a cousin," in the local sense. Binkie's cousin Shaneya was Beezy's brother's "baby mother." He admitted that he had seen Beezy on the night he was murdered. They had talked about "round the way stuff." He thought Beezy was a "cool guy, funny, outspoken."

"Really?" asked Taylor. She said she had interviewed a lot of people about Beezy, and no one else had described him as "a cool guy."

"To everybody else, he was kind of a mess," she said.

Binkie chuckled. "I did say he was outspoken."

Binkie was more candid with Pauling. Days after the shooting, when Pauling asked how he'd gotten Beezy to walk off with him, Binkie said that he'd made up a story. He'd said that he was on his way to rob someone who had just sold a car and had thousands of dollars on him. Beezy took the bait.

"Basically, it was his own greed," Binkie explained.

The excuses for plugging people kept multiplying. It had started with the disastrous kidnapping caper, then suspicion about snitching—Bub (Brandon Littlejohn)—to disrespecting Tana personally (Alfonzo Williams) to preying upon or endangering the crew's drug supplier (Blake and Langley) to merely repeating a potentially dangerous rumor. Then there were those killed for a payoff. Death had become TTG's business.

It became the penalty for any interference with the gang, such as bullying the crew's pimply thirteen-year-old corner kid Tevin Haygood, the one who took those wild shots at Pony Head (Jan Gray). Waiflike, with his cap on backwards, Tev was working to harden his image. Acne had left scars on the edges of his prominent cheekbones, and he'd begun promoting himself on Instagram as bad news. He'd posted, "I'm TTG," with symbols of a gun blast and a pistol. "You can ask Niggas they'll vouch for me *100* *100* . . . STAMPED ✔." Nevertheless, out peddling weed, Tev still looked enough like a child to be regularly shaken down by a tall man with a stylish goatee and a gun named Marquez Jones. He had a distinctive look, long and lean from tip to toe, the length of his head accentuated by a goatee that he tapered to a point. Jones showed Tev no respect whatsoever. Whenever he saw him, he stooped down and patted the teen's pockets, taking whatever he found. This was enough of a problem for TTG that Tana told his old friend Davon Robinson that he was going to have to kill the skinny dude. Then he reconsidered. *Tev* needed to shoot him. It was time, he told Robinson, for the kid "to look after hisself."

Tev was chilling on the sidewalk with Tana and other members of the crew on Monday afternoon, March 2, 2015, when they saw Jones emerge from the Harlem Park Elementary Middle School, a low, modern red-brick building on West Lafayette Avenue with a broad expanse of open space around it. The group was on a corner across the street, standing before a sepia-toned wall mural depicting a sphinx, Thurgood Marshall, Duke Ellington, George Washington Carver, and others. They watched Jones saunter off toward Calhoun Street in the distance.

Tev eyed his persecutor sullenly, and boasted, "He ain't goin' keep walkin' around here like he ain't done nothing."

"You keep lettin' him," said Tana.

"I ain't have no gun," said Tev.

Tana remedied that. He walked Tev over to his red Honda Accord and gave him a 9mm handgun.

When Jones got to the Calhoun Street corner, his good friend Donte Pauling pulled up to the curb and waved to him. The two talked for a few minutes, and then Pauling said, "Let's get the fuck off the corner." They walked halfway up the next block to a friend's row house, where Pauling knew he could tap into the Wi-Fi from the front porch. It was six doors up, a house with its brick front painted gray, tall narrow windows, and an ornate oak front door. Pauling sat on the top marble step to tap at his phone. Jones stood alongside him, leaning on the stoop railing.

They both spotted a boy striding purposefully toward them, angling across the street from the next corner. The kid had a ski mask over his face and had pulled his hood up.

"Who the fuck is this?" asked Pauling.

"I don't know," said Jones, in what would be his last words.

Then Pauling recognized Tev, even with the hood and mask. He relaxed. Tev was just one of the neighborhood kids, no threat. Kids sometimes walked around masked and hooded like that, playacting. Not this time. Tev strode straight up to Jones and raised his arm— Pauling thought they were going to slap five—and then he heard the familiar *pop!* of a gunshot. The first round hit Jones in the face. He flinched and lurched toward the boy, who fired again. Pauling ran, dropping his phone in his panic. He didn't stop running until he rounded the Calhoun Street corner, hearing more pops behind him. When he looked back, Jones was facedown on the sidewalk, and Tev was gone. He had been picked up by Tana in the red Honda. The whole thing had happened in seconds. Pauling tried to calm himself. He found a bullet hole in his pants. He was shaking. He walked tentatively back up Lafayette to retrieve his phone. Blood was pooling under Jones's head. His front teeth were gone. His eyes were open wide and fixed in a lifeless stare.

The round that ended him had entered behind his right ear and passed through the base of his brain, killing him instantly. His front teeth had been knocked out on the concrete during what the medical examiner called "terminal collapse," meaning the absence of an instinctive effort to break the fall. He was already dead when his face had hit the pavement.

Tana was apologetic when Pauling ran into him a few days later, still angry about his own close call. Tana explained that he had cautioned Tev to shoot only Jones. He wanted Pauling to meet with Tev to smooth things over, to avoid any bad blood. As for Jones's death, he commiserated about the loss of a friend but said Jones had it coming. "When people be growin' up they be doin' certain shit, and shit be catching up with them," he said.

By early 2015, Tana's name appeared in the homicide files for each of these murders, and people in Sandtown would whisper his name to police, but none would agree to testify. So even as TTG broadcast its guilt on social media, the murder cops couldn't build a case strong enough for the city's new young State's Attorney, Marilyn Mosby.

But a street rep like Tana's could last for only so long before *shit be catching up.*

Somebody took a shot at Tana in June. He was riding a dirt bike in the streets, a favorite pastime, and the rounds sent him flying. He wasn't hurt, and he thought he knew who was behind it. He told Tyree Paige, one of his young hitters, that the shooter was a friend of Dirty, Lamont Randall, a heavily tattooed, high-ranking member of the BGF who had recently been released from prison. Dirty had designs on TTG's turf. Tana had tried to negotiate. He approached Davon Robinson, himself a BGF member, and Robinson had agreed to meet with Dirty and try to smooth things over, but then Robinson had been busted. The meeting never happened. Then the shots. Game on.

On the night of July 7, Paige, on the corner selling, saw Tana, Binkie, Man-Man, and Thug preparing for action outside a local convenience store. Man-Man went inside to purchase masks and gloves. They had two vans and at least one automatic weapon that Paige would later describe as "big." They told Paige they were going to get Dirty, who was at that moment sitting on a stoop with some friends a few blocks away on West Fayette Street.

"Y'all ready?" asked Tana before they entered the vans and took off.

A surveillance camera on an apartment building down the street caught the action: Vans pull up alongside cars parked in front of the row house, and masked men with guns jump out. Flashes of gunfire light up the darkness. Then the shooters dash back to the vans and race away.

Dirty was left flat on his back on the sidewalk in his sleeveless white T-shirt, pale blue jean shorts, and new Adidas sneakers. He was riddled with holes. He'd been hit seventeen times, one round leaving a gaping aperture in the middle of his forehead. Blood drained from his head down to the curb. Three others with him were also shot. Jacqueline Parker, a broad-framed middle-aged woman, was lifted from a pool of blood, leaving a large maroon stain on the sidewalk beside her empty black sandals. She had been shot eleven times. Burly Gerald Thompson was also dead, shot nineteen times. A fourth victim, Ashley Johnson, would survive. These three had just been sharing a stoop with the wrong person. Police found fifty-three shell casings scattered on the bloody sidewalk and in the street.

Even with the constant gun violence, a triple murder still attracted attention in Baltimore. The killings made the TV news channels and the newspapers. The reports listed the names of the victims but revealed nothing about who the killers were. There was no mystery whatsoever in Sandtown or even on the city homicide squad, which listed four "persons of interest" in the index of the case file: "Antonio Addison (alias: Thug), Brandon Bazemore (alias: Man-Man), John Harrison (alias: Binkie), and Montana Barronette (alias: Tana)." No one was arrested.

When Paige had heard the crescendo of shooting in the distance, he figured it was Tana and his boys. He caught up with them the next day. They were basking in their success. One of them told Paige excitedly, "We *wore* him out!"

Paige was also with Tana a week later when he collected a reward from Milk. Returning to his Honda Accord, Tana removed a bundle of cash from a brown paper bag and carefully counted out $10,000. He told Paige that it was "for Dirty." Milk later approached the families of the innocent victims and offered them cash to make amends.

The triple murder alone—three of the forty-five murders so far in Baltimore that month—caught the attention of Cliff Swindell, the new Maryland supervisor of the Operations Intelligence Division, FBI Safe Streets Task Force. A day after the shootings, city chiefs summoned all the heads of The Stew for an emergency strategy session. The local brass noted that this incident was part of a madly accelerating trend and asked for help. As it happened, Swindell already had two local cops on his team, Dan DeLorenzo, from Anne Arundel, Baltimore's southern suburban county, and a gung-ho city detective named Mark Neptune. In their citywide ranking of murderous gangs, TTG now topped the list.

Removing the gang would not be easy. TTG was an especially small target for the feds. It had few dealings outside Sandtown, much less across state lines. It was a close-knit group inside Baltimore's most alienated neighborhood, a weed with deep, stubborn roots. Members lived and worked in the same blocks where they had grown up. Many in the community were either connected to them and hostile or terrified of them and silent. Witnesses and informants would be scarce.

Neptune told Swindell that for any hope of success, they would need one cop in particular.

6
Here Come Landsman

Joe Landsman

When Mr. Bucket has a matter of . . . pressing interest under his consideration, the fat forefinger seems to rise. . . . He puts it to his ears, and it whispers information; he puts it to his lips, and it enjoins him to secrecy; he rubs it over his nose, and it sharpens his scent; he shakes it before a guilty man, and it charms him to destruction. Otherwise mildly studious in his observation of human nature, on the whole a benignant philosopher not disposed to be severe upon the follies of mankind, Mr. Bucket pervades a vast number of houses, and strolls about an infinity of streets. . . . He is in the friendliest condition toward his species and will drink with most of them . . . but through the placid stream of his life, there glides an undercurrent of forefinger.

—Charles Dickens, *Bleak House*

Sandtown knew Joe Landsman, and Joe Landsman knew Sandtown.

For years he had haunted its vacant houses, its alleys, its hiding places, and its corner drug markets, first as a uniformed cop patrolling housing projects back in the early 2000s; then in plainclothes making drug buys and busts for Western District operations; next, beginning in late 2007, as a homicide cop—this being Baltimore's murder central; and then as a young sergeant, back in uniform, supervising a squad of other officers. Landsman was the neighborhood's scourge. He had busted just about everybody who was anybody in its bustling drug industry. In honor of his talent for popping up unexpectedly, corner boys and their lookouts had dubbed him "Mario," after the runty Nintendo character with the round nose and bushy black mustache. They had lots of euphemisms for the police: "Po" and "Knockers" and "Twelve" and "Five-Oh" and "Four-Five." The call "Timeout!" was an all-purpose alarm. But when Landsman appeared the alarm was particular: "Landsman! Here come Landsman!"

He didn't really resemble Mario, much. He was short, had thick black hair, and was often unshaven, with a dark beard that crept far up his cheeks. And he was usually scruffy, dressed in jeans and a T-shirt. He moved in a slight hunch and had a sidling, boyish manner and a quiet intensity that made you think his mind might be napping or elsewhere, begging you to underestimate him. He was nobody's model for a cop, much less a supercop. For that his older brother Jay Landsman Jr., a captain in the Baltimore County Police Department, looked the part, square-jawed and clean-cut. Beside Jay, Joe came off as the brother you'd expect to find in the basement playing video games, dark, slight, rumpled. Comfortable on his own. Absorbed completely in his own thing. He avidly collected sports memorabilia, football and baseball cards, which were displayed on custom shelves in his downstairs den, but apart from that and whatever time he logged now as a husband and father of four, Joe Landsman was all police. He had skills that one colleague termed, simply, "ridiculous."

In a sense, he'd been at it his whole life. He had grown up immersed in police work. It was the Landsman family trade. His grandfather had been a cop, the city's first Jewish lieutenant. His father, Jay Sr., was one of the squad supervisors featured in David Simon's book *Homicide,* and when Simon made *The Wire,* he named the sergeant commanding the series' fictional homicide squad after him. Lean and dark, with a thick mustache, the real Jay Landsman Sr. looked nothing like the rotund, pugnacious actor, Delaney Williams, who played him on-screen. Jay Sr. himself also appeared in the series in a recurring role, as Lieutenant Dennis Mello, and managed to make his screen time memorable, with his thickly authentic Bawlmerese and mordant wit—dismissing officers after a routine pre-shift briefing with, "Don't get captured." Jay Sr.'s brother was also a city cop with the homicide unit. When Joe was old enough, out of high school, he went right into police work, as had his brother and as would his two sisters.

This bewildered Christina, Joe's wife, who had a thriving real estate business in the western suburbs. A college grad with a somewhat wider scope, she wondered aloud to Joe why all of the Landsmans had dutifully donned the badge. Couldn't they see other options? Hadn't school or life or wonder exposed them to anything else?

"You guys think that police work is *everything,*" she said.

Her statement struck Landsman momentarily speechless, before he could stammer, "Well . . . *isn't it?*"

The thrill of the chase, the mental challenge, the *human* challenge, the risks, the sense of doing good, even the ugly side—all of it. What else could be as satisfying or interesting? As children the Landsmans had played hide-and-seek in the body bags their father stored in the garage for his body-removal business, which requires a brief explanation. Body removal was something Jay Sr. started on the side. With a wife and growing family at home, he was then working, as he put it, "a million hours a week for the police and getting paid for shit," so he was always looking to supplement his pay. He already had a construction business that kept him busy on weekends, but then he spied a market niche that maybe only a murder cop might recognize. It seemed that funeral homes were reluctant to transport bodies from crime scenes to the morgue and then from the morgue to their establishments. Murder scenes were tragic and messy, and the city didn't exactly pay top dollar for the work, but there was plenty of it. Years of working horrid death scenes had inured Jay to squeamishness. He saw dollars in those chalk marks on the pavement. Securing the necessary permits and approvals, he bought stretchers, three vans, a hearse, and the body bags, and enlisted some of his homicide squad buddies as drivers. They also offered crime-scene cleanup services. In time, he was servicing the city morgue, the state anatomy board, medical examiners in several counties, and thirty funeral homes. Hence, there were body bags in the garage.

Joe learned to drive behind the wheel of a hearse. He was already a veteran of murder scenes. He'd started going out on calls with his dad when he was still in grade school. He thinks he was ten when he saw his first dead body, and it wasn't in the fastidious perfumed hush of a funeral parlor. He'd jumped in the van with his father on an early morning call, playing a video game in the passenger seat, when they rolled up on a young man sprawled on the pavement who wouldn't get any older. He had been shot several times in the head. It was ugly, jarring, bloody, and indelible. Perhaps a normal ten-year-old boy would have been scarred. Landsman wasn't. Maybe it was his pedigree. The scene excited him, motivated him. Here was something visceral, not something on a screen or pictured in a schoolbook. It was real, and it was happening in his world every day. It was his father's work. It would become his.

When Joe was a cadet the department enrolled him in some classes at Baltimore City Community College, encouraging him to pursue a degree, but he had no patience for it. Books didn't hold his interest, nor did competition for rank and status, which the college degree would have helped. He just loved the work. The streets. He started on patrol in the Eastern Division, and then moved over to the public housing gig, which started his long run in the Western. He was just twenty-seven when he achieved his goal, the homicide squad, the youngest murder cop in the department's modern history. Even when he was promoted and became a supervisor, he still kept one foot in homicide, as part of a department task force. Along the way he acquired an encyclopedic recall of arcane, invaluable local knowledge—who was killed when and where and allegedly by whom, who had witnessed what, who was working what corner and for whom, who was related to whom and how—so to him the names Tana and Rell were more than familiar. He had known them both for years.

He had watched them grow up, from a distance. During those years, he must have done a thousand surveillance ops, starting when he was still in uniform. Multiply that thousand by five or even ten, and you'll have an estimate of the number of hours he'd spent hiding out in vacants (unoccupied buildings), watching and waiting, peeking through an empty window, or cramped in the back of an undercover van staring through peepholes. It was a challenge to stay hidden. Sandtown had eyes everywhere and a sixth sense for surveillance. If Landsman was ever spotted in an unmarked car, its make and model were remembered, and from then on whenever one rolled into the neighborhood the nearby corners would shut down until it drove away. Any strange man, especially a white one, seated in a parked car for longer than a few minutes was assumed to be a cop. Landsman tried arriving very early in the morning in a car with tinted windows and climbing into the back seat to watch. Soon enough, any car with tinted windows was suspect. He tried everything. The department had a white van with signs on the sides that could be flipped; one side said "Baltimore Gas & Electric," and on the other was the universal yellow-and-black symbol for radioactive material—presumably to discourage anyone from coming close. Landsman was in it one night, parked, when the idling engine gave out. He didn't want to sacrifice the spot, so he sat in the back for hours, sweltering. This was an especially unglamorous side of undercover police work. He had two jugs at his feet, one filled with water and the other—because he couldn't get out of the van to relieve himself without giving himself away—filled with urine. Hour after hour he sat. Sometimes it took all night to catch one brief glimpse of action. Often nothing at all happened. It was boring as hell, and on this night he was melting. In the darkness he reached down and took a big swig from . . . the wrong jug. On another night, radioactivity warning or no, a group of young men surrounded the van and started rocking it violently back and forth, giving Mario a good shaking before they departed, laughing. Landsman waited for a few minutes, then crept out, looked both ways, and hustled up the street to his unmarked car and drove off.

Vacants were better. When he picked out a likely one, he would creep in hours before dawn, sometimes climbing a fire escape, and pick his way up a dark staircase to an upper-floor window or the roof. He had one favorite spot on Biddle Street occupied by a homeless man who seemed to welcome the company, and they got along well, until one morning Landsman stumbled on him and another man going at it with a naked prostitute. That convinced him to find another spot. Once in position, he had nothing to do but wait for daylight. The houses would talk to him in creaks and moans. There were sometimes gaping holes in the floors and ceilings, from which pieces of the past snowed down whenever a truck or bus passed below. Landsman saw rats and mice and wildlife he didn't expect to see in the inner city, like racoons, opossums, enormous spiders, and snakes. Some of the long-abandoned dwellings were eerily grand, even beautiful, with big high-ceilinged rooms that had large fireplaces and doors that swung open to spacious courtyards and the desiccated remains of what might once have been lovely gardens. All was in ruins. Landsman wondered about who had lived there. One of his favorite spots was in what he assumed to have been a railroad shed or workshop, a cavernous space with rails that ran straight through, probably from Baltimore's long-lost trolley era. Nearly all of these hideaways were littered with needles and empty drug vials that crunched underfoot. Wherever he set up, though, no matter how well concealed and careful he was, the neighborhood found him. Once, a favorite hiding place, an old row house, was set on fire. He doubted it was a coincidence. Staying completely concealed was impossible because, in order to watch, he had to lift his head over a window or ledge. Invariably, before long, down on the street a boy would catch him at it, point, and shout "Mario!" or "Landsman!" and that was that.

The nickname, at first, was insulting. Did he really resemble a squat mustachioed cartoon character? Then a kid he busted explained. Like the Nintendo character, Landsman was always jumping out of unexpected places. The nickname was playful. Once discovered, he would be greeted with scornful laughter and cheerful insults. Most of those lookouts were, after all, just kids. Mario was part of the fun.

The kids had it about right: the consequences of getting caught were usually laughable. Baltimore judges were not inclined to come down too hard on street sellers anymore, especially the young ones. Even for the older dealers, getting nabbed was mostly just a nuisance. The tougher ones would laugh and shrug it off as a price of doing business. They were so inured to occasional trips to juvie or the city jail that it hardly fazed them. How could they take Landsman seriously when the whole system he represented was a joke? Most of the people they knew used drugs. They were bought and sold everywhere. Selling drugs on the corner might have been a crime, but there were the customers, lining up every day, whatever happened. In that larger context, Landsman's untiring effort *was* comical, if not pathetic, like trying to empty the ocean with a spoon. It felt that way sometimes to him, too. Once, in one of his better busts, he'd set up on a rooftop and watched Pony Head, the bearded corner king, hand out product to his workers. He'd busted Pony and seized the drugs. This bust was no joke; it had the potential for serious jail time. But Pony hired an expensive lawyer who managed to get Landsman's evidence suppressed. The charges were dropped. After that, whenever Pony Head saw Landsman he didn't just laugh—he complained to him about his attorney's fee: "You cost me five grand!"

Still, Landsman kept doggedly at it, doing his job day after day, month after month, year after year. He was playing a longer, deeper game. Not all of those he busted were cavalier, and not all were in a position to skate like Pony Head. A good many didn't spurn him when, having arrested them, he offered to listen. Young and scared, surrounded by cops who were hostile or indifferent, they had Landsman. Mario. His was a face they knew. A *friendly* face. Someone they could talk to.

Landsman had a gift. People liked him. Many of those he busted even ended up liking him. For one thing, like Charles Dickens's Inspector Bucket, he didn't bring a ton of moral outrage to the work. He was just a cop, doing his job, and they were just dope sellers, doing theirs. Life had assigned them adverse roles, and Landsman, in his own way, respected them. He knew the work was demanding and often dangerous, and he knew a lot of the young men doing it were smart, ambitious, and in many cases decent at heart. They fascinated him. His job had thrust him into their world, and for reasons both professional and personal, he was driven to understand it. Enough so that he saw every bust not as a victory but as an opportunity. Seated in an interview room across the table from a suspect, he wasn't Mario anymore. In those rooms, information was a commodity, something that could be bartered for a reduction in charges or maybe just for an innocuous favor, like a phone call or a Coke and a sandwich. And Landsman kept his word. Over the years, a good many of those on the wrong side of the law came to trust him, even seek him out. Even a veteran like Pony Head, a trusted source when it suited him, became in time something like a friend, so that when his homeboy Bub (Brandon Littlejohn) was gunned down, he had somewhere to take his outrage, someone to tell about the brazen young killers who'd had the gall to show up at Bub's wake. Little by little, Landsman learned a lot. So when the FBI's Cliff Swindell came calling, Landsman could tell him a quite a bit about Tana and Rell.

Landsman was the one who had busted Rell in February 2012, sending him to prison. Having heard Rell's name in connection to the murders of both Nut (Jamie Hilton-Bey) and Bub, he'd resolved to get him off the streets, even if only for a few years.

He'd known right where to find Rell, too, on his usual corner, just across the street from Harlem Square Park on North Calhoun Street. Catching him in the act wasn't easy. Rell had grown up doing this, and he had skills. But Landsman was a supervising sergeant now, and he could deploy a number of officers to keep watch. He knew that the drugs Rell sold were kept somewhere nearby, and he could guess the likely places. Just one row house down, past a narrow vacant lot, was a vacant covered in faded gray Formstone with the front door and first-floor windows sealed with cinder blocks. Nobody was going to just wander in there off the sidewalk. So while keeping eyes on Rell on the corner, Landsman positioned an officer in a nearby vacant on the other side of the block to watch the rear of the house he suspected. Over days, they observed Rell or his partner Tash (Taurus Tillman), wander back, climb a fire escape, and crawl through an empty second-floor window, then emerge a few minutes later to pass product to the hitter who delivered to customers. After documenting the pattern, Landsman and one of his officers pulled up in a marked car and, after a brief chase, arrested the two. Rell had $900 in cash, Tash $600. Inside the vacant they found a small drug shop, a plate with cocaine residue, small orange-capped vials used to package the drug, and hidden in the ceiling, a quantity of cocaine and more empty vials.

Even with all that, Rell was out of jail a little more than a year later. Landsman persisted. When Rell went right back to work, the observant sergeant scooped him up again for violating the terms of his parole. Rell returned to serve his full term. This was the period when Rell was making daily jail calls to Tana.

As troubled as the Baltimore Police Department was, it had its share of exceptional cops trying to do the job right, fighting a Sisyphean battle against the city's mounting violence. That triple murder in July 2015, the one that left bodies on the sidewalk and fifty-three shells scattered on the pavement, would contribute to a monthly total that matched an all-time record of forty-five, set in 1972, when there had been a quarter million more people living in Baltimore. More than ever, shooters got away. The meeting the triple killing prompted with The Stew amounted to a cry for help from Kevin Davis, who had been appointed interim police commissioner after the Freddie Gray unrest. He threw open the doors of his department, creating something he dubbed BFED (Baltimore-Federal).

It lasted only a few months. No matter how deep the feds' pockets, and no matter how impressive their tools, they were peering at city neighborhoods through a telescope. They could surveil the hell out of a community or a suspect. They could place tiny cameras in key places that recorded in high definition day and night. They could tap phones and track calls and texts over a period of time, so that they could draw detailed maps of organizations. They could geo-locate phones in order to pinpoint a suspect's whereabouts at any moment to within twenty feet, placing them, say, at the scene of a shooting. When they seized guns they could perform ballistic tests *on the spot* that could link them to shootings going back years. They could analyze blood droplets for

DNA to tie killers to victims. But all this crime-busting wizardry was useless if they did not know exactly where to point it, and Baltimore's cops couldn't give them enough to keep them busy. Even when The Stew was given a target, it had little chance of *penetrating* such small local networks without someone to point the way in. For that they needed cops who not only knew the turf but knew the people. And there were too few Landsmans to go around.

In fact, Swindell was lucky to get the one Landsman there was. Joe's career had very nearly crashed during the 2015 street protests, which had forced an all-hands-on-deck response. Landsman cleaned up—haircut and shave—and donned his blues to join the ranks facing down passionate crowds. That is why he looked like a boy scout in the image that made him briefly notorious. On a night when he was on riot duty, a young Black man with long dreadlocks wearing a black T-shirt that read "Fuck the Police" strode out of the mob and up to the line of cops, screaming repeatedly, "Arrest me!" He stared at them bug-eyed, either very angry or very high, possibly both, screaming, "I dare you! I'm right here!" One of the cops stepped out of the line and sprayed mace directly into his face. The man froze, then staggered back a step or two. Grabbing a fistful of his copious hair, another cop pulled the man roughly down backwards to the street. The crowd was even more riled up now. Bottles flew and crashed to the pavement. Landsman and two others, an officer and a man in civilian clothes, stepped forward to help the protester up. The downed man, hands now cuffed behind his back, wouldn't or couldn't stand, so the officers counted to three, then lifted and dragged him to the relative safety of the sidewalk, as best they could. There Landsman and the others poured water over his face to clear the spray from his eyes.

All in a night's work, as far as Landsman was concerned. But there had been cameras everywhere, and video of the episode was taken from several angles. Clips of it were posted online. The blasting of mace and violent pull-down by the hair were seen as shocking examples of police brutality. Someone snapped a photo—or froze one of the videos—just as Landsman and the others lifted the man to drag him off the street. In that moment, Landsman was looking off to the left, keeping an eye out for flying bottles, mouth open—with all the tear gas it was best not to breathe through your nose—and in the frozen frame he looked for all the world like he was grinning glee-fully. There was certainly nothing amusing about what was happen-ing. But a picture is worth a thousand words, even if the story it tells is false. This one shot around the world on the internet, and suddenly Landsman, the "smiling cop," was poster boy for the sadistic, heart-less Baltimore police. With his left hand gripping the downed man's loose pants, pulling them away to show his underwear, his right arm threaded under his manacled hands, and the apparent grin—it really does look like he is laughing—the shot perfectly encapsulated what the protests were about, a downed, handcuffed Black man being bru-talized by police, and worse, the cop clearly enjoying himself. Many of Landsman's own colleagues were outraged. Copies of the picture were posted around headquarters the next day, and he was summoned to the commissioner's office.

Landsman swore the image did not convey the truth. The com-missioner, then Anthony Batts, opened his own laptop and found three videos of the incident, each showing the full sequence of events from a different vantage. All showed the protestor—Larry Lomax—taunting and daring the police before being sprayed, roughly pulled down, and cuffed. It was clear that Landsman and the other officers had acted to move him out of the street at some risk to themselves. Out of harm's way, the videos captured Landsman helping to rinse Lomax's eyes. An internal affairs probe cleared him of wrongdoing. Lomax later won a civil lawsuit against the cop who administered the blast of mace and the one who yanked him down by the hair.

Fallout from the freeze-frame would dog Landsman for years. For a time, it remained easily searchable online—"smiling cop"—and would even cause some friction with friends and acquaintances. Some of his colleagues continued to hold it against him, although his reputation in the department was secure.

Landsman reported for work with the FBI Safe Streets Task Force on October 15, 2015, bearded and scruffy once more, driving out to the agency's Windsor Mill field office, just outside the beltway northwest of the city near the sprawling Social Security complex in Woodlawn. For Landsman, it was like dying and going to heaven. The task force had license to bear down on one case for the long term, and had a fabulous surveillance and detection toolkit. It also had money to pay and protect informants—assets largely unavailable to city police. Then there were subpoenas. In a federal case, the task force could compel reluctant witnesses to testify, and they could better protect them. The identities of grand jury witnesses were hidden. If the target pleaded guilty, witness names would never be revealed. If it became necessary for witnesses to take the stand in court, there was plenty of time and money to relocate them and give them a new identity. It often took a year or more for a case to move from the grand jury to a courtroom, so there was time to get all that done. None of these things were true in state court.

Landsman joined the task force's two local detectives, Neptune, a prematurely bald, bearded, fit city cop, whom he knew, and DeLorenzo, who was also bearded and wore his hair so close-cropped he might as well have been bald. Both had the kind of arms young men work at, richly tattooed, wore their tattered caps backwards, and like Landsman were, despite their very casual appearance, dedicated cops. One of the elaborate scenes inked on DeLorenzo's arm showed his son laying a wreath before one of the lion sculptures at the National Law Enforcement Officers Memorial in Washington, DC; another tattoo was a line from Thomas Paine's *American Crisis* pamphlet series, "If there must be trouble, let it be in my day, that my child may have peace." Both men were Landsman's age and shared his cheerful passion for the work. Beside them, with his tousled crop of black hair, Joe looked much younger, but he outranked them, and to Neptune and DeLorenzo he was "Sarge."

Tana had come to the attention of Neptune and DeLorenzo that summer in an investigation called Operation Pedestal Gardens, after the West Baltimore apartment complex out of which it operated. Its target, Deandre Smith, known as Blue Black, was one of two major wholesale drug suppliers under investigation. The other was Shongo Owens, whose probe was dubbed Flat Rate, after the Priority Mail shipping boxes he used to import his product. These two were supplying much of Baltimore with large amounts of heavy, addictive drugs—heroin, cocaine, fentanyl, ecstasy, PCP. They had both grown rich. Owens also promoted rap artists, like YGG Tay, and was affiliated with Future, the popular Atlanta rapper and producer. Keeping watch on one of Blue Black's stash houses in Baltimore County, the task force watched one buyer take delivery of a drug shipment and then drive off toward the city. They lost the car but traced it to one Montana Barronette.

By the fall of 2015, the Pedestal Gardens and Flat Rate investigations were winding down—both Smith and Owens would eventually plead guilty and depart for prison, the former for ten years, the latter for twenty-five. Neptune saw an opportunity. Why not point the task force next at Tana and TTG? Instead of going after the Sandtown crew piecemeal on drug charges and sending them to prison one by one for relatively short terms, like Rell's, why not pull out the sledgehammer, the RICO Act, and scoop up all of them at once? The quantity of drugs they were selling wasn't that consequential, from the feds' perspective, but the rising number of murders was. In state court, prosecutors would have to link each homicide to a specific shooter, a near-impossible task, but with RICO, the US Attorney's office need only establish that the gang was a criminal enterprise and that all the blood trails led back to it.

As a killing machine, TTG was revving up. One of the first things Neptune and Landsman did was draw up a list, beginning with Nut in 2010, who they suspected had been shot by Rell. Then there was Bub, shot down by his supposed friends; the seemingly inexplicable shooting of barber Alfonzo Williams on his front stoop; Hell Rell (Terrell Jarrett), who had unadvisedly slapped the rapper YGG Tay; James Blake and Ronald Langley, who had targeted Milk (Roger Taylor) but taken his buddy Scratch (Darius Singleton) by mistake—Langley's body set on fire; and tall, thin Marquez Jones, shot in the face while visiting with his friend Donte Pauling. With the triple murder that summer, there were ten victims on the list so far, eight of them in the previous year and a half. Here was an urgent public menace.

But official reception to the proposal was tepid. The FBI was more interested in high-yield cases like Pedestal Gardens and Flat Rate. It was easier to make a drug case than a murder case, and the impact of taking down a major drug pipeline, posing with mounds of seized contraband, was arguably greater. That kind of bust often pulled in some of the city's most active triggermen, because rich dealers were the ones paying for contract murders, and the killers were part of their organization. Swindell saw Pedestal Gardens and Flat Rate as models. The FBI had latched on to Owens's supply scheme and had seized large shipments from Los Angeles on commercial carriers—FedEx, UPS, and others. Both syndicates were so profitable that even big intercepts of their product hardly fazed them. Such losses were just written off. In this context, TTG was distinctly small potatoes. While working the Owens case, it became clear to the detectives that Milk had been the primary conduit for the Sandtown crew. To Swindell, Milk was a better target than young Montana Barronette.

In fact, Swindell was puzzled about why the city had not taken Tana off the streets already. All they needed was a felony drug charge.

Wouldn't that be enough to lock him away for years? He called Landsman and Neptune to his Windsor Mill office to talk about it.

"You know the reason that the Blue Black case is successful and this one isn't is that they put drugs on the table," Swindell said.

To Neptune, this was patronizing. He and Landsman and DeLorenzo had years of experience combating gang murder and drug dealing on the streets. It was hard for the task force supervisor, sitting with all his federal advantages, to imagine the difficulty of building such big cases at the local level, particularly in Baltimore. Witnesses ran away and hid, and even if you found them, it was hell getting them before a grand jury, much less a courtroom. City cops had few of the feds' options for protecting or coercing them. And, besides, the case they envisioned was not just about drugs, it was about violence, about serial murder. Swindell's comparison to Pedestal Gardens missed the point. Infiltrating and taking down TTG would require a lot more than putting big drug seizures on the table. It was going to mean cultivating sources, finding and developing informants and witnesses, DNA and ballistic analysis—everything The Stew had to offer. The comment set Neptune off, and he didn't hold back.

"Are you fucking kidding me?" he said to Swindell. "You have no clue how to make a case like this!"

The two men ended up screaming at each other.

Landsman was with Neptune on this. They argued: *Barronette is a serial killer. He is out there murdering people. We're getting this from our sources. We know this through homicide files.*

Swindell: *If you want Barronette so bad, why don't you grab him with some coke and put him away for five years?*

Detectives: *Because he's killed a dozen people, and he needs to go away for life! What are you talking about, five years?* By their reckoning, if they hung a drug charge on Tana—who had no adult priors—even if they caught him with a gun, the best they could hope for in Baltimore's courts was maybe a year in prison. *This task force is called Safe*

Streets, they argued. *Our job is to be a violent gang task force, not a drug task force. We're not serving our purpose out here if we're just putting this guy away for drugs. He runs an entire West Baltimore neighborhood by fear!*

They would eventually see that Swindell's challenges owed less to resistance than to an aggressive management style unfamiliar in their own department. He was an active, hands-on supervisor, and he pushed upward on their behalf as aggressively as he pushed down. When weeks went by without action after he had requested another detective, Jeff Lilly, on Landsman's Western District squad, Swindell invited city commanders to a briefing in Windsor Mill and outlined what the task force had done and was doing, which was met with warm approval. Then he laced into them. Why hadn't they delivered Lilly? Swindell, who was Black, pointed out that his entire task force team was white. He was trying to diversify it, not just because the FBI wanted it, but because having a Black detective, like Lilly, would be very useful working in Sandtown. He got Lilly the next day.

Neptune, Landsman, and DeLorenzo set about bending the task force to their will. They had worked RICO cases before but had never run one. Even the FBI agents they worked with had little experience doing so or in compiling a wiretap authorization. They regarded the detectives' ambition as laughable. Still, a good manager doesn't quash initiative. Swindell didn't order the detectives to desist; he just didn't offer to help. How likely was it that three Baltimore cops could score a federal wiretap and manage a sprawling RICO case on their own?

That's what they set out to do. How hard could it be? Their FBI colleagues' attitude seemed to be, *OK, dude, whatever. Call us back in six months.*

What they needed was a way *inside* TTG. If they could get a wiretap on, say, Tana's phone, they could monitor it over time and eventually infiltrate the whole crew. But getting court approval for that first federal tap was a high hurdle. The paperwork was byzantine, a bureaucratic nightmare to the uninitiated. Some of the applications ran to a hundred pages. You had to know which phone number to target and show that it was being used for criminal purposes.

There was even pushback from the two federal prosecutors assigned to work with Safe Streets, Matt Sullivan and Laura Gwinn. Sullivan was relatively new to the job, and, at least as the detectives saw it, seemed reluctant to undertake such a major federal murder case. Gwinn seemed to share his reticence. She was smart, tough, experienced, and savvy. When Wayne Jenkins, of the soon-to-be notorious Gun Trace Task Force, approached her about partnering with the task force, she sniffed trouble immediately. "He's like a used car salesman," she complained. "I don't like him. I'm not using him." Swindell agreed, and Jenkins and his rogue crew were kept at arm's length. Gwinn was good, but she was nearing retirement. What Neptune, DeLorenzo, and Landsman were pushing was a big deal. It would take months to gather the evidence just to prove that Barronette, Sivells, Tillman, Taylor, and Harrison et al. ran a business that was criminal, much less tag them with all the unsolved murders. The trial alone, if they got that far, would take months. It would attract a ton of attention. Somehow the Sandtown crew, most of its members at that point still in their teens, didn't seem to warrant it. So the prosecutors sided with Swindell.

They needed that first phone number. The gang was smart about phones. Each member had several and changed them often. Rell had been picked up once carrying six. The ones used for business were held close, so knowing which to tap first called for inside knowledge. In other words, sources.

This was, of course, Landsman's forte. Soon after he joined the task force, he delivered a gift. A priceless one. Over the years, it seems, he had become something like friends with Guy Coffey (Fat Guy), the driver Rell had accidentally shot during the Nut kidnapping and murder. Landsman and Fat Guy went way back, and Fat Guy knew TTG well.

And, as it happened, he was willing to help. Not just willing, *eager.*

Cop and street dealer had met for the first time more than nine years earlier, on the evening of April 5, 2006. Guy, just fifteen, had been with his buddy Steven Woolford on Wheeler Avenue just up from the bridge over Route 40. Woolford was seen passing heroin to someone parked in a blue SUV. Guy was nearby.

As the subsequent arrest report explained, "The actions of Guy Coffey, standing in the street looking in all directions while Steven Woolford was involved in a suspected illegal narcotics sale were consistent with the actions of an individual looking out to alert police," apparently meaning that he seemed to have been looking out *for* police. Landsman was the arresting officer.

Guy looked younger than fifteen, with baby fat that rounded out his face and frame. He had short hair, buck teeth, and a slightly turned-up nose. The most memorable thing about him in this first bust was his defiant silence. He would not give even his name. When you manacled most kids that age and hauled them into lockup, they were terrified. Guy seemed unfazed, almost like he had been trained to resist. It was so peculiar it was comical, and Landsman never forgot him, the little fat kid trying to look so fierce. Landsman was nice to him.

Guy slipped through the juvenile system like an oiled seed and was back on the street in days. Landsman busted him again about three weeks later. Same deal. A drug buy on the basketball court in Harlem Square Park, with Guy at a distance. But this time Landsman noticed that the fat kid was not just looking out, he was *overseeing.* It seemed, despite his youth and soft appearance, that Guy was actually in charge. He commanded a surprising amount of respect. Everybody knew Fat Guy. He styled himself hard-core. His father, who had the same name and nickname, had been a prominent dealer in the neighborhood years earlier, before being sent to federal prison, where he died. The son had stepped out like the new king of the block, an heir. Landsman, again, treated him kindly.

If he aspired to follow in his father's footsteps, Guy succeeded. More busts, more jail time. He eventually aged out of the more forgiving juvenile system and would spend the next ten years in and out of real prison.

When he bounced back out to the streets in 2015, after serving a four-year stretch, he went right back to doing his thing. In July of that year, just months before joining the task force, Landsman was investigating a murder. A police informant had been killed, shot in the back of the head in broad daylight, near the corner of Edmondson and Warwick Avenues. A member of that neighborhood's gang had posted on social media, "Remember bitches . . . Snitches end up in ditches!!!"

Without much to go on, Landsman watched that corner closely. Much of the surveillance work he had formerly done in person, peeking out of upstairs windows or disguised vans, was now much easier. The city had mounted cameras high on poles all over Sandtown, providing a live high-definition feed. Combined with security cameras inside and outside the neighborhood's few commercial establishments, Landsman could watch almost everywhere from the comfort of his desk at police headquarters.

He watched for hour after hour, trying to get a feel for the corner players, who associated with whom, where they congregated, where their stash houses were. He was at this when he spotted a rotund figure he recognized immediately. Well over three hundred pounds, with a hairline that had started to recede, his old buddy Fat Guy was unmistakable.

He wore sweatpants that were stretched so tight over his wide legs that they resembled, the detectives joked, jeggings (stretch-fit tights that looked like denim). He was selling. He kept his stash between his buttocks. From time to time, clearly unaware that there were cameras above, he would place a young lookout on the sidewalk, retreat around the side of a building, and then squat and reach back into his pants to extract the product. Landsman sent a few of his men out to arrest him, and when Guy arrived at the station, he was no longer the risible hard case Landsman remembered. He grinned when he saw the familiar cop and greeted him like an old friend. Ordered to hand over his stash, he squatted and withdrew a package of heroin from his butt. Everyone laughed. And right away he said he wanted to make a deal.

Jovial, relaxed, and talkative, Guy chuckled with Landsman over the severity of his teenage pose. He said he had wised up. He complained that there seemed no way off his treadmill of arrest and prison. He was sick of it. He had just become a father. Selling drugs was the only way he knew to provide. Landsman had some money to pay informants and offered Fat Guy an alternative.

He would become a dream CI (confidential informant). When he found he could earn money talking, it was hard to shut him up. He started by laying out the whole story of the informant's murder at Edmondson and Warwick Avenues, explaining who had done it and why, leading detectives to the killers and to the guns they had used. His information was golden. He was paid $1,000 for that assistance, and immediately asked, *What's next?* Fat Guy shot to the top of the local informant scale. He was a hard worker. The respect he had on the street and his history of moving freely between gangs gave him unprecedented access and knowledge. It also, perilously, made him feel immune to suspicion. Most CIs were acutely sensitive to danger. The penalty for snitching was death. So they often hedged on specifics, taking care to avoid giving information that might be traced to them, and they wanted to be far away when arrests were made. Not Fat Guy. He held back nothing, and when it was time for busts, he wanted to be there.

Once he called Landsman and said, "The guy you're looking for is in the bar," giving the address.

"Where are you?" Landsman asked.

"I'm in his car outside."

Another time he texted a tip about a suspect, describing the car he was driving and its location. When Landsman's men pulled up behind it, the car fled. They declined to chase it because they'd seen their CI in the front seat. Fat Guy came back pissed. Why had the cops backed off? He would have been paid more if they caught the man.

So when Landsman moved to the FBI task force, he brought this gift. The feds paid CIs even better, and he could keep rewarding Fat Guy indefinitely. First off, Guy told them all about the Nut kidnapping fiasco, directly linking Rell to the murder. He didn't just know Tana and the rest of the TTG crew; they considered him one of them. They had grown up together. They trusted him. He was also a living, breathing Sandtown search engine. If he didn't know the answer right away, he'd go find it. He was the key to Neptune and DeLorenzo's wiretap effort. He knew all the gang's phone numbers and which ones were used for business.

To get the court order, Swindell insisted that they document at least thirty "dirty" calls from Tana to someone else in his drug crew. They first had to photograph Tana using the targeted phone as he placed at least one of those calls, proof that it was employed for criminal enterprise.

With a camera trained on him inside a car with the detectives in late November, Guy placed a phone order with Tana. He punched in the number and then put the phone on speaker.

"Hey, man, I need to get up," he said, using their coded language.

On November 24, the exchange took place, Guy collecting ten grams of heroin from Tana at a gas station, paying with money provided by the task force. It was their first controlled buy—a foothold.

With the number Tana had used for this deal, they could subpoena Verizon, his service provider, for records of all the calls made from that phone over the previous eighteen months. The top ten most-dialed numbers would point to his closest partners. Between Fat Guy and their own records, they linked those numbers with names—Rell,

Binkie, Tash, and so on—mapping TTG's structure. Next, they needed to show that each of these target phones were also dirty and engaged in drug selling. This would enable "tolls," permission to monitor them for a limited time, usually for ten days to two weeks. If there were no calls from Tana in that time, they had to start over, find a new dirty number. And these guys ditched phones regularly.

Absent a tip from an informant, finding the new numbers was labor intensive. Insurance databases were helpful, because someone involved in an accident or making a claim had an incentive to be reachable, so gave their readiest number. Arrest records were good, too, because they often contained contact numbers for phones seized from suspects and those of witnesses. Jail calls were also useful. The task force could listen to these on their in-house database. Inmates making these calls, talking to their friends or family, often revealed useful information. Nowadays few people memorized the phone numbers of even those closest to them. Locked up, their cell phones confiscated, they were often looking for those numbers, which those on the outside gave freely. It was one reason Landsman began listening to all of Rell's prison calls. Once the detectives had new number, they had to establish that it was dirty, which meant showing their target using it. They would park near a drug corner and record themselves placing a call to the phone and then video the target answering. They would speak gibberish until he hung up, but they had him.

The write-up had to be exhaustive. Judges wouldn't authorize a wiretap until every other investigative avenue had been explored. For this they had Landsman's long experience investigating and arresting members of the crew. The application stretched from thirty pages to fifty to a hundred.

Meanwhile, TTG was doing its part to support the detectives' argument for urgency. On November 8, they killed a burly, bearded young man named David Moore, also known as Day-Day. Moore had been caught on video shooting and killing someone else, a friend of Tana's. When Tana was shown the clip, he assured his friends, "I got him." Get him he did. Moore was walking ahead of two friends on Gilmor Street when a car pulled up alongside him, and two young men wearing face masks and hoodies stepped out and shot him nineteen times, killing him.

Tyree Paige, who had witnessed the gang gearing up for the triple murder in July, was sufficiently disturbed by this killing to tell police that he recognized Tana as a shooter, despite the mask and hoodie. He had seen him wearing the same outfit, minus the mask, the day before. The shooter had been wearing pricey black and white Air Jordan sneakers, and Paige had been with Tana at the Mondawmin Mall when he'd bought ones exactly like them. A week or so later he heard Tana take credit for killing Day-Day. At a restaurant with Tana, Milk, and YGG Tay, the subject came up.

The rapper asked Tana, "Did you take care of that for me?"

"Yeah," said Tana. "I got it."

One more murder was added to the list just before the end of the year. On December 28, Erika MacKenzie stopped at a bodega on Baker Street and sent in her ten-year-old son to see if they sold toothpaste. Baker is a wide street that passes on the south side of Matthew A. Henson Elementary School. It has the same low, wide-open feel of all of Sandtown. MacKenzie parked just outside the store looking west toward the broad intersection and the school. When her son returned to say that the store did sell toothpaste, she sent him back in to buy a tube, and as she waited, she heard a loud pop from behind her, and then saw a woman run past with her hands covering her ears. Seconds later she heard more pops, louder than firecrackers, very close. In her side mirror she saw three men chasing another, running and shooting. The fleeing man fell just behind her car.

The shooters then ran back to a red car parked nearby. One of them returned, stood over the fallen man, and fired down at him, these shots much louder. This shooter then ran back to the car, which drove away.

MacKenzie went to the fallen man. He was still alive but horribly wounded. He had eleven holes in his torso. One of the rounds had passed through his heart and lungs. He was dying fast, trying to crawl toward the curb. MacKenzie called 911. She recognized him, an athletic young man with a thick neck, sparse beard, and sleepy eyes. It was Dominique Harris. He had played baseball with her children in the street. She got down and held him until the police arrived.

Harris was twenty-two. He had many friends in the neighborhood and was known in his family as a quiet young man who liked to draw and make music videos. But away from home, he was also known as Shotgun and was in The Game. Earlier that day he had been robbed at gunpoint by Binkie and had pursued him with a gun. TTG had found him first.

So as 2015 closed, the effort to target the Sandtown gang congealed. The detectives gained an important ally in the US Attorney's office, Robert R. Harding, a senior prosecutor who was chief of the office's narcotics division. Harding, who had been working in Baltimore for a quarter century, was known for handling big racketeering cases, and, like so many, was friends with Landsman. The detective sent Harding the growing TTG murder timeline with some background information, and the chief prosecutor showed up at the task force's next meeting in the Fallon Federal Building with Sullivan and Gwinn. He listened as the prosecutors once more explained their preferred strategy and then came down preemptively, in favor of the detectives' argument to target the gang as a criminal organization.

"This is how we move forward," he said, ending the discussion, and then assigned Sullivan to start writing the RICO memo.

Then Landsman's hard-won street connections yielded another valuable informant. While reviewing Rell's prison calls, he had heard the one in which Tana threatened Pony Head—*Next time I'll just bang you!* He had recognized Pony Head's voice right away and had invited him to the Fallon center to hear the full phone conversation, to show him that the taunt was more than just talk, and the brothers actually viewed him as a threat to their business. It was enough to bring the old corner king into the investigation. He offered convincing neighborhood context and vivid testimony about TTG's growing menace. With Fat Guy setting up buys and providing current phone numbers, and Pony Head filling in backstory, the task force was no longer looking at TTG through a telescope; it was on the inside. And Landsman was just getting started.

Approval for use of the RICO Act came as the year was ending, and with it, to everyone's surprise, the exhaustive wiretap application bore fruit. The first wiretap would go up on Tana's phone on Wednesday, January 20, 2016.

7

The Ballad of Ronnie Jackass

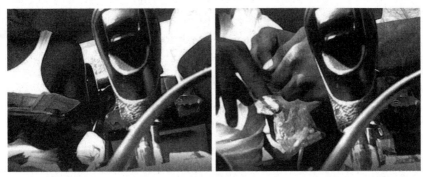

Ronnie Johnson making an undercover drug buy on August 11, 2016.

McWatt was the craziest combat man of them all probably,
because he was perfectly sane and still did not mind the war.
                              —Joseph Heller, *Catch-22*

Ronnie Johnson had his father's name, so as a child he was "Junior," or "Ronnie J." But once he embarked on his career as a monumental screwup, his father told him the "J" stood for "Jackass."

"Rarah" or "Rah," as Ronnie was known out and about, had been the brains—one hesitates to apply the term "mastermind"—behind the horribly botched kidnapping of Nut (Jamie Hilton-Bey), which had ended in Nut's murder, a stray bullet hole in Fat Guy (Guy Coffey), and Rah's own busted head. Ronnie Sr. would have found all of this completely in character, just the latest in a long string of extremely poor decisions.

Rah was born in 1983, the only child of his father, who worked on an asphalt crew, and his mother, who was sickly and nearly always at home. Statistically speaking, the intact family—they had a place on Pennsylvania Avenue, the eastern boundary of Sandtown—had given Rah a certain edge over Tana and Rell, who had been exiled to the streets as teens. No advantage, however, was enough to defeat Rah's delinquent fate. He was no stranger to Sandtown's drugs and violence. When he was thirteen, his cousin Dante Willis, standing beside him on the sidewalk, was shot in the head and killed by members of a rival drug crew firing from a passing car. It was at about that time that Rah stole a handgun from his father. He found a hiding place for it in the neighborhood in case he or his friends needed it, there being a good chance they would. Rah was not and never would be one to question the violence around him; he was fine with it. He adapted. In his world, having a weapon was simply prudent.

When he started at Frederick Douglass High School a few years later, Rah was big for his age and cultivated an intimidating mien. He carried the gun to school and made sure his classmates knew it. Tall and athletic, he played shortstop for the baseball team, liked to talk, and had a cheerful, outgoing manner—but also a bad temper. He wasn't afraid to fight and did so often enough—coupled with his frequent absences—to get kicked out. He was sent to Francis M. Wood High School for a new start. The gun went with him.

There is a certain inevitability about an armed teenager. Rah had come close to using his gun several times. When another eleventh grader exchanged words with him and came at him, Rah warned, "Walk up on me, and I'm gonna shoot you." The boy took a few steps toward him and then thought better of it. Sixteen-year-old Rah felt relief. He would have shot him. Not long afterward, he did shoot someone. It was at a family cookout held by his aunt on June 24, 1999, in O'Donnell Heights, a public housing project in southeast Baltimore. The party erupted into a brawl. An argument between Rah's

cousin and the father of her baby fired up family and friends on both
sides, and in the melee, fists were supplemented by sticks and clubs.
A boy named Tavon Kintchen fatefully homed in on Rah and took a
swing at him. Rah showed the gun and warned him off, Kintchen kept
coming, and Rah shot him, one round to his left chest.

Kintchen went down, and Rah, his blood up now, stood over him
planning to finish him off. But the gun jammed. This was a miraculous break for both teenagers. It meant that Kintchen would live, even
though his life would never be the same, and that Rah would get out of
prison before he was an old man. The shooting had happened before
many horrified witnesses, including Kintchen himself, of course. The
bullet clipped his spinal cord and left him paralyzed from the chest
down. He would spend the rest of his life in a wheelchair, struggling
with a long series of maladies until his death two decades later. Rah
didn't think to run away or hide. He walked back into his aunt's house,
which was where he was arrested that night. He was charged with
attempted murder, first degree, which is exactly what it had been. Tall
and ornery, he was considered old and mean enough for adult prison,
and that is where he went, sentenced to twenty-five years. The judge
suspended sixteen of them, which was about as generous an outcome
as Rah could have wished for. So began his real education.

Prison was a shock at first. Rah had been a formidable figure in
high school, with his gun, his size, his athleticism, and his willingness to fight, but he was no match for the full-grown inmates around
him now. He was sent to Eastern Correctional Institution, the state's
largest prison, holding well over three thousand inmates. It was set
in the tidewater flatlands of Maryland's Eastern Shore, and while its
security classification was medium, there was nothing medium about
its menace. It was overcrowded, run by corrupt guards and gangs, and
only borderline manageable. Rah had to fight almost every day. He
saw people stabbed and killed, in one instance right in front of him.
He saw another man held down and raped. He had an uncle and a

cousin in the same prison, both BGF leaders, but they took no notice of him for the first eight months or so. Rah would later say they were "seasoning" him, giving him a long and frightening taste of going it alone in his dangerous new world. Perhaps they wanted to see how the kid carried himself. Rah fended for himself as best he could and grew up fast. One day his uncle slipped a folder under the door of his cell with confidential papers introducing him to the gang, what it stood for, what it offered, what it demanded. The introduction began, "This is a way of life."

Rah, of course, knew about BGF, even if he didn't know its origins, rules, or methods. It had grown out of the Black Panther Party movement in California prisons during the 1960s, a time of Black Nationalist fervor and occasionally violent acts of defiance. Vestiges of its revolutionary origins remained—gang members still called each other "comrade" and held organizational titles like "minister of justice" or "minister of defense"—but BGF was no longer a political movement. It was a criminal protection racket for select Black prisoners. It existed both in and out of prison but was far better organized and more powerful inside. Members were strictly regimented, held to exacting standards, and punished if they fell short. Rah's uncle, George Curry, was the gang leader at Eastern. He and his comrades were feared and respected. In that world, it was a luxury simply not to be bothered, which BGF membership offered. Just to be introduced to the gang felt like an honor to Rah. It was a brotherhood. The papers named every gang member in the prison. It was a long list. Rah knew many of them and had observed their special status. If he was asked to join and chose to take its dark and florid oath—*If I should ever break my stride, and falter at my comrade's side, this oath will kill me / Should I ever be untrue or forsake the chosen few, this oath shall kill me / If I ever sought to do harm or allow harm to come on a brother, this oath shall kill me*, and so on—the gang offered him important things he did not have. First and foremost, safety. If he was sitting at a cafeteria table

and someone took a swing at him—this had happened—every comrade in earshot would rally to his aid. And it offered community. In
prison, the safest way to live—and this is how Rah had lived—was to
stick to yourself, avoiding contacts that could lead to trouble, which
nearly all could. BGF offered something like family and, for Rah, with
his uncle and cousin in key roles, real kinship. Comrades were, the literature promised, like fathers to sons, brothers to brothers. The papers
also outlined how he would be expected to carry himself, and they set
guidelines for righteous conduct, which, as far as he was concerned,
was how he had been trying to act since he'd gotten there. For Rah, it
was irresistible.

There was, of course, a downside. That opening line, "This is a way
of life," was more accurate than perhaps intended, in that joining the
gang and enlisting in the violence that sustained it was quite likely an
invitation to a lifetime behind bars. Mutual support meant he would be
protected, but it also meant that he would have to protect his comrades,
follow orders, fight, and even kill. Gang membership wouldn't just jeop-
ardize his hope for an early release, it would likely lead him into new,
serious crimes. BGF smuggled contraband into the prison, everything
from tobacco to weed to harder drugs. The other road would have been
to tough it out by himself. With good behavior, Rah's relatively merciful
nine-year stretch might be shortened, and even if he served it all, he'd
still be a young man on his release. So it was a big decision.

Rah, Ronnie Jackass, didn't hesitate. After an introductory period,
he took the full oath in 2001. He was eighteen.

And right away prison got better. He no longer looked over his
shoulder. He was surrounded by comrades. Membership and his
family ties to the leadership gave him immediate status, and a path
to more. Whatever BGF asked, he gave, enthusiastically. And as his
prison years passed, he matured. He got smart about the uses of violence. As long as the victim of a beating or a stabbing didn't die, and
as long as no guard was attacked, penalties for such behavior were

acceptable. Inmates guilty of such acts were most often disciplined by losing "good time" or privileges. Efforts were made to spread the dirty work around so that no one gang member would be sanctioned too often. Rah earned a reputation for boldness and intelligence, and managed to avoid trouble with prison authorities. He began climbing BGF's well-defined ranks, becoming a minister of justice, which made him responsible for policing the gang and further insulated him from actual violence. When a gang member broke the rules, he meted out the punishment and tried to make it appropriate. He did not administer the penalties himself. In minor cases it might be nothing more than twenty push-ups, or running laps around the exercise yard, but for more serious offenses he might order that the offender be beaten or even killed. He realized that a reputation for fairness earned respect, and he took the responsibility very seriously. He saw himself someday running the whole organization.

And he somehow managed all this without extending his term. He was paroled on June 24, 2005, at age twenty-two. The only thing he was really good at was jail.

Full of good intentions, Rah set out to earn his GED (general equivalency diploma) and find a real job. He soon discovered that his prison record made him all but unemployable. Falsifying an application sometimes got him briefly employed, only to be fired when his past was discovered. Soon enough he turned to Sandtown's more attainable way to earn. He started selling drugs. Tall and rangy, with tattoos up and down his lean muscled arms and a wild spray of braids, he looked like an athlete, but now the games he played were for much harsher stakes. By then he was a BGF commander, an important rank in jail but one with significantly less influence on the streets. As one former member put it, asked if BGF had a hierarchy and written rules, "Don't nobody follow 'em, but, yeah, I would say so." Most of the time Rah couldn't even find the people who were supposed to report to him. He was back to fending for himself.

Still, the title alone had its benefits. Women were excited to meet him, to have sex with him, to bear his children. Eventually he would father five by four different women. To a young man who had just spent eight years locked up, this was no minor perk.

The fun didn't last long. Rah was busted in March 2007 for selling drugs in Sandtown by an undercover team run by Joe Landsman, who was then a Western District supervisor. Rah was exasperated. He'd been caught red-handed, selling ten vials of drugs for forty dollars to one of Landsman's CIs. "Man, I served a CI, didn't I?" he lamented, sitting in a police cruiser, clearly disappointed in himself. Rah had avoided the drug trade as a teen, but after failing repeatedly at legitimate employment, he'd taken it up in desperation. All those years in lockup had left him without street smarts. Now he faced another prison term, for what? Forty bucks? He was ready to accept his father's verdict, *J for Jackass*. He vowed to never sell drugs again. This time, awaiting trial, he was sent to the Jessup Correctional Institution, a maximum-security prison beyond the runways of Baltimore/Washington International Airport in Anne Arundel County, southeast of Baltimore.

Once more, BGF came calling. He was tapped to "take a hit," an expression that worked two ways: performing a hit, attacking someone, and thereby *taking* a hit, a likely severe penalty. The target was his cellmate, Adam Herbert, who stood accused of betraying the gang. It was not an invitation Rah could refuse. He stabbed Herbert, who survived.

He was, of course, caught. Stripped naked and left alone in a basement cell, he was then cast to the lowest rung of Maryland's prison system, the North Branch Correctional Institution. Set in the mountains at the far end of the state's long westward arm, it is Maryland's "supermax," housing its most dangerous inmates. Rah was now housed with the criminally insane and with violent men with little or no hope of release and nothing to lose. His cellmate was serving a murder sentence of ninety years plus life. Inmates were killed in their cells. Some were so terrified they never left their cells. He would hear men howling like animals at night. His gang affiliation was no help— BGF meant little at North Branch. Nobody was safe. Rah figured he'd never get out of the place alive.

So he sat down and wrote a letter to the one cop who had treated him decently.

Joe Landsman went to see Rah when he was returned to Baltimore in the summer of 2007 for trial. The police sergeant drove with one of his colleagues out to Jessup to fetch him. Rah's lawyer had agreed to a proffer session, at which his client promised to trade information in return for consideration on the drug charge.

So Rah, garbed in his bright orange jumpsuit, was driven to city police headquarters, a weathered gray stone building with rows of aqua-paneled windows on a long, curved front that faced South President Street. It was just a few blocks north of the Inner Harbor. In the homicide squad's fifth-floor conference room, the lawyer listened with some amazement as Rah started talking. In his brief sojourn of freedom, he had been fully embraced by the street thugs in Sandtown— these were years when Rell was just a young teen and Tana still a boy. The very things that had screwed up Rah's life—shooting Kintchen, joining BGF, stabbing his cellmate—had made him a legend. He knew or got to know all the local players. He had become friends with Blue Black (Deandre Smith) and Shongo Owens, Milk (Roger Taylor), Denmo (Dennis Pulley), and Pony Head (Jan Gray). To the homicide cops, Rah was a magic key to any number of criminal puzzles. His lawyer leaned back, smiled, and shook his head. The details were amazing. His stories resolved old cases and gave new leads on current ones.

To cite one example, Rah at once cleared up three outstanding murders and a mysterious home invasion. The body of Kevin Sewell had been found on a street in East Baltimore on June 14, 2006. Sewell had been shot dead. It was no robbery. He had forty-seven grams of cocaine in his pockets and bits of what looked like packing material from a mail shipment. Earlier that same day another young man, Donald Lewis, had also been found dead in the same neighborhood, gunned down. This, too, had been no robbery; he had $901 in his pocket. There was nothing initially to connect the two cases, and no leads for either.

Rah linked them, tied both to a third murder, one that was even more confounding, and incidentally exculpated a suspect who had been wrongly charged with it. An elderly woman, Cynthia Riley, had been found dead in her red-brick home on a leafy street in suburban northwest Baltimore the day before Lewis and Sewell were killed. The victim of an apparent home invasion, Riley had been shot several times with a powerful handgun. One shot had been fired at close range into her knee. The bullet had gone clean through. Above her the ceiling tiles had been torn out, and the room was littered with packing material. Investigators speculated that her killer had been looking for something and had tortured Riley to reveal where it was hidden before killing her. Three different homicide cops had been assigned the cases. Riley's murder had been charged to one Raymond Davis, who was found with a .44 Magnum that ballistic tests linked to her killing.

Rah explained the whole thing, connecting all the dots.

"It wasn't supposed to happen like that," he began. "They weren't supposed to do it."

It seemed victim Donald Lewis had been beefing with a local drug dealer named Blake Harris, who had assaulted Lewis's sister. When confronted, Harris had threatened Lewis with a knife. Lewis reported this to the heads of his neighborhood BGF gang, Rah among them. To settle the matter, Lewis and his friend Sewell had been given permission to retaliate. Cynthia Riley was Harris's grandmother. It was common for drug dealers to stash money and drugs with relatives in quiet neighborhoods outside Sandtown. Lewis and Sewell planned to wait for Harris to show up there, steal his money and drugs, and perhaps kill him—Rah was judiciously shy about his own part in this. He admitted that he had been fully on board for the revenge robbery, drug dealers being considered fair game and easy, since they'd never go to the police. He'd even loaned Lewis and Sewell the .44 Magnum. He said a hit had also been authorized for Harris. Rah explained that while he was present when the kill order was given, he himself had not ordered it.

The mission had not gone as planned. As Rah told it, when the two gunmen broke into the house, expecting Harris, they found only Riley. Making the best of it, they'd tormented her into pointing out her grandson's hiding place in the ceiling, pilfered the stash, and killed her.

This, Rah said, had gone too far. Riley's torture and murder crossed a line. They had killed a civilian—a *grandma* no less! No such authorization had been given. Rah also wanted his gun back. Another meeting was held, and it was decided that Lewis and Sewell must pay with their lives. Two acquaintances of the culprits, Raymond Davis and a youth known to Rah only as "Scrappy," had been dispatched to administer justice—again, Rah finessed his part in this. In the aftermath, because Davis took the .44 from either Lewis or Sewell after killing them, he had been wrongly charged with Riley's murder.

It seemed likely to the detectives, Landsman included, that Rah had ordered the hit. He hadn't just happened to be there. But apart from this predictable evasion, his story completely checked out.

And this was just one of the cases he sorted for them that day, holding forth in his orange jumpsuit. Gary Niedermeier, the detective assigned to investigate the Sewell murder, avidly noted the details for that case and then drew up large charts to organize all the other intelligence Rah had unloaded, mapping the very fluid, elusive Sandtown underworld in a way that would prove useful long after this session.

When it ended, Landsman and his partner took Rah to lunch. It wasn't fancy. They bought him a sub at Quiznos in nearby Canton, a Patapsco River neighborhood, then parked overlooking the water. The windows of their car weren't tinted, and many passersby stared in at the man in the orange outfit, but Rah didn't care. He was, however briefly, out of jail. After his nightmarish stint at North Branch, fearing he'd never get out alive, this felt like heaven, eating real food and gazing out over the water. He never forgot it.

As helpful as he had been, Rah got nothing out of the proffer session. His lawyer left worried that he had implicated himself in several more crimes, the Riley break-in and murder and the homicides of Lewis and Sewell. He had been, perhaps, overly helpful. The cops kept their word about the proffer session—no further charges were lodged against him—but city prosecutors were loath to cut a deal. He got four years on the narcotics charge.

Rah was twenty-seven years old when he got out of prison again, in the spring of 2010. And again, his freedom didn't last long. It was during this period, having vowed to no longer sell drugs himself, that he directed his efforts to robbing drug dealers, not unlike the character Omar Little in *The Wire*. Known as an amiable thief, he would stroll up to a dealer on the corner all smiles and easy banter, asking how business was, and then, abruptly, show his gun. Rah recruited a little crew that included Rell and Fat Guy and got to know, to a lesser extent, Tana. He instructed his teammates how to hold their handgun low and close to the belt when confronting a target. Most robbers tended to reach and point with it, so it was obvious from a distance what they were doing. And an extended gun could be slapped aside. Rah's method both protected the weapon and made the robbery less conspicuous.

But these holdups yielded paltry gains. They got away with whatever cash was in their victims' pockets and whatever they could raise selling the pilfered drugs, but that was it. So it was Rah who came up with the idea of kidnapping higher-level dealers and demanding a big ransom. The Nut caper had ended badly, but others worked well enough through the summer of 2010. But the strategy had a drawback. The men they were kidnapping were dangerous and unforgiving. Rah had grabbed one dealer and released him after taking his watch and collecting a sizable ransom. But in October, the victim and another gunman caught Rah driving past and blasted away at his car, hitting it with twenty-one rounds. Miraculously, none of the bullets hit Rah, but in his rush to escape he floored the accelerator, lost control, and plowed into a wall hard enough to fracture both of his hips. Recovering from this mishap in the hospital, he fell in love with Percocet.

Prior to this, Rah's addictions had been primarily to money and excitement, both of which were denied him during his long convalescence. He could scarcely move. The Percocet gave him a nice buzz and took the edge off his boredom. When he did get back on his feet, after much physical therapy, he used a walker, then a cane, and by the time he was moving again, working to overcome a limp, he was hooked on the pills. They impaired his judgment, which was substandard to begin with. Now when he went back to robbing and kidnapping dealers, he always helped himself to a little of their product. More and more, the money he stole went to support his habit. So now Rah was not just armed and dangerous, he was nearly always high.

This may help explain why he was in the frame of mind to publicly attack his young girlfriend, the mother of his infant child. They got into an argument during a routine hospital visit. Guards intervened, and then the police. The reports said Rah had knocked her down, kicked her, and tried to choke her. This landed him back in jail, coming down hard off his painkillers. Things got worse. Investigators discovered that his girlfriend had been only fifteen when she conceived their child, so statutory rape was added to the assault charge. He then managed to make things still worse for himself. Facing another long prison stretch unless he could convince his girlfriend not to testify, he started leaning on her in calls from prison. He wanted her to deny the attack and swear the baby had a different father. These calls were, of course, recorded. Obstruction of justice was added to his sheet.

He was thirty-two years old when Maryland released him next, on November 20, 2015. Most of his previous sixteen years had been spent in prison. He was personally acquainted with every lockup in the state. Like many men in his position—indeed, like himself five years prior—he firmly resolved that he would never return.

But, once again, he began badly. Rah did what anybody does after a three-year stretch in prison; he went to see his friends. One of them was Blue Black, still at large but headed for a hard fall. Rah was amazed to find that Blue Black and his associates had gotten rich. His old running buddies were driving new foreign cars and power trucks, flashing jewelry, buying homes out of state, taking glamorous vacations. Years earlier, or as they now said, being old-timers in their thirties, "back in the day," they had robbed dealers to get spending money; now they were like corporate executives, presiding over regular wholesale deliveries of heroin, pills, cocaine—which the feds were quietly monitoring and occasionally seizing—and supplying emergent local street gangs like TTG. Sheltered from the hazards of street dealing, they were raking in more money than they'd ever dreamed of.

"Look what we got, man," Blue Black boasted to Rah. "We got mostly everything we need."

Rah was welcomed back warmly. His working days were over. All he had to do was hang and "be cool." Blue Black handed him $500 and twenty grams of heroin. Rah sold the heroin for $2,000 and brought the money back.

"No, man," Blue Black told him, "I gave that to you for yourself."

Rah started taking drugs again, Percocet and Xanax mostly, a dangerous mix because the latter can intensify the opioid high. They left him stupefied. When Blue Black lent Rah his new Ford F-150 King Ranch truck, Rah was so high he immediately smashed it into four different cars. First he hit the car in front of it as he tried to pull it away from the curb.

"Just leave, man," Blue Black said.

So Rah backed up rapidly and collided with the car parked behind. Panicking, he turned the wheel and tried to gun out—and ran into the side of a passing car. When he tried to speed away he hit one more, sending the truck sideways and bouncing it over a curb.

He found himself the center of attention. The drivers of the cars he had hit and curious passersby gathered to confer. No one wanted to confront Rah, who had deposited himself on the curb and assumed what he called his "gorilla face." He was too high and rattled to flee. When police arrived, he stared up at them blankly.

"Don't worry, man," said Blue Black. "It was just an accident."

The police, of course, noticed Rah's condition immediately.

"You really look high," one said.

"I'm not high, man," Rah lied. "They all lyin' on me."

"You just stay here and chill," the cop told him.

Rah ended up in drug treatment, prescribed Suboxone to curb his Percocet cravings. He supplemented the palliative with Xanax, just to take the edge off, another particularly dangerous mix of chemicals. He continued in a steady state of mild stupefaction, a condition obvious to everyone but himself. Heretofore quick-witted and articulate, his speech became slow and slurred and his thoughts scrambled. His friends pointed this out to him, but he didn't see it in himself.

This was dangerous, of course, and particularly so in his world— Rah had made a lot of enemies over the years. Already, just a month after his release from prison, with his vow to never return, his trajectory was trending hard in the wrong direction. Yet, when his old buddy Blue Black asked him to kill a man, Rah had the rare good sense to decline. He arranged for someone else to do it. He knew when and where the victim would fall, so he went to a pizza shop that he knew had a surveillance camera inside and sat under it. He ordered a pizza and ate until the letters "RIP" popped up in a text message in his phone. Then he left, alibi secure.

Things took a turn for the worse when he started hanging around with Larelle Wallace, an old prison buddy known as "Slow Down." The nickname, often shortened to "Slow," stemmed from the fact that Larelle, like many Sandtown natives, had been dosed with enough lead as a child—from old paint or old pipes or both—to suffer brain damage. His family had received compensatory payments from the settlement of a class action suit years earlier. Rah and Slow were a maladroit pair, the one drug-addled, the other drug-addled *and* brain damaged. Together they resumed robbing corner dealers to help feed their habits.

It was disastrous, for the obvious reasons and because Slow was a sworn enemy of another of Rah's old friends, a dealer named Cedric Catchings. Ced was a notoriously violent character who cultivated a demonic image. His hair was shaved on the sides of his head and trimmed flat a good two inches above his forehead, as if he were wearing a fez. His face was decorated with crude prison tattoos, a row of *X*s at his hairline, a teardrop beneath his right eye, a heart on his left cheek, and more elaborate markings on his neck emerging from a scruffy beard. Rah owed Ced big-time because years earlier the dealer had tipped him off that he'd been "green-lit." The would-be assassin was then himself murdered (Rah claimed to know nothing about how this had happened). So Rah and Ced felt like they owed each other. When Rah started hanging with Slow Down, complications arose, because Slow was a close associate of Blue Black, with whom Ced was feuding. This placed Rah precariously in the middle. He had it good with Blue Black and enjoyed his partnership with Slow Down, so Rah resisted when Ced tried to lure him back into his own circle. Ced felt betrayed. He then let it be known that Rah was on his list.

Then Slow was killed. Rah had warned his friend to lie low, but Slow, fatally mellow on Xanax, hadn't listened. Witnesses saw Ced shoot him in the head in broad daylight on Pennsylvania Avenue on April 11, 2016. Rah was shocked and angry, and also frightened because word was out that he was next. So Rah, with Blue Black, decided to kill him first. The dealer put up a $10,000 reward, but Rah needed no financial incentive. He was motivated primarily by revenge and self-preservation. He was high, desperate, and not thinking clearly. He and Blue Black drove by the house of one of Ced's girlfriends, and when they saw his two little daughters playing out front, Rah wanted to shoot them. He hesitated, not out of moral compunction but because he was too powerfully armed—he was carrying an AK-47 and worried that its high-powered rounds might leave the girls' bodies dismembered. This prospect seemed to trouble him more than killing them, because he told Blue Black that he wanted to go back and get his handgun. Shooting two little girls was apparently too much for Blue Black, who told Rah he was crazy and took the assault rifle away.

Rah's bearings, which had steered him so calamitously for so long, were clearly failing him. In retrospect, his desire to shoot the girls made him feel ashamed. He had never considered himself a killer, certainly not of children. It was moral rock bottom for him, a line he had never dreamed he would cross, and it scared him. Yet he knew Ced was gunning for him. If he went around armed, he would surely end up going back to jail—for a convicted felon, possession of a firearm would be enough. If he shot Ced, even in self-defense, he'd also most likely be back behind bars again, and with his record, the sentence would not be short. Rah felt trapped, cornered at last by a lifetime of bad decisions. There was doom every way he looked.

It forced a moment of clarity. How could he hope to escape what BGF had correctly termed *a way of life*?

He remembered the cop who had treated him with respect, who had come to get him from Jessup and had bought him a Quiznos sub and parked before the water with him on a sunny Baltimore afternoon. It was a small thing, but the memory always made him smile.

On April 28, 2016, Rah placed a call to the Baltimore Police Department's Central Division headquarters and asked to speak to Sergeant Joe Landsman.

The detective was driving home from Windsor Mill when the message reached him: "Some guy named Ronnie Johnson left you a phone number and wants you to call him."

Landsman remembered Rah immediately: the walking encyclopedia in an orange jumpsuit who six years earlier had laid bare so much of Sandtown's violent underworld. As it happened, this was the day the FBI task force had finally arrested Blue Black. Landsman knew Rah was friends with him. He called the number immediately from his car.

A woman answered. She handed Rah the phone.

"I'm really tired, man," he told Landsman. "I just want a change."

"For real, man?" asked Landsman.

"Yeah. These guys are either going to kill me, or I'm going back to prison. Things are not going great for me. When can we meet?"

8

We Hunting

YGG Tay in a Baltimore recording studio in 2017. © The Baltimore Sun

I lived for the power surge of playing God, having the power of life and death in my hands. Nothing I knew of could compare with riding in a car with three other homeboys with guns, knowing that they were as deadly and courageous as I was.
—Sanyika Shakur, *Monster*

Three days after nineteen-year-old Markee Brown testified before a federal grand jury, his charred body was found in a North Baltimore cellar. It was April 19, 2016. He had a bullet hole in his throat, the mark of the snitch, and he had been set on fire, which had become something of a TTG signature.

There it was in a new video by the gang's troubadour, YGG Tay (Davante Harrison), this one called "War." Over the chanted chorus, "We want war wit' 'em," a black Chevy Tahoe pulls up in front of a country house. As Harrison struts and raps, a man is carried out the front door, bound hand and foot with a bloody sack over his head. "Nigga disrespect the gang / Now I want him now," he sings, as the victim is tied to a chair in a field and then doused with gasoline. Harrison casually lights a cigarette. His glam female companion delicately takes the match in her manicured fingers and drops it into the gasoline. Immolation as a fashion statement.

Brown's killing made the video seem more than a stylized fantasy. By now, Tana and Rell and the rest were killing routinely, without reflection. It could no longer be rationalized as self-defense. It was simply who they had become—a matter of, as Peanut King had put it, *be that, or you ain't.*

It's not that they thought they would get away with it. They knew by the spring of 2016 that the law was circling them, and for each body dropped, the list of their dangerous local enemies grew. But apparently the risk was exhilarating. They turned up their drill anthems loud, a soundtrack for their adventures. In the words of the rapper Blac Youngsta, one of Tana's favorites:

> *I'll forever be a gunna nigga*
> *I'll forever be a killer gunna.*
> *I'll forever carry blammers*
> *I'll forever, I'll forever, I'll forever*

Forever, of course, was unlikely, which may have been the song's ironic point—forever "youngsta" in the sense that he would not likely grow older. For Tana this was no nihilistic teenage fantasy; it was a life choice. He expected no future. The Game was it, all of it, the hustling, the hunting, the guns, the money, the girls, the drugs. He and his crew expected their run to end badly, and they were good with that. It was a familiar path in Sandtown, one taken by grandfathers, fathers, uncles, brothers, cousins, all either dead or in jail or, in the case of Tana's father, deported. In a larger sense it was a path open and groomed for them by the entire history of Baltimore and America and fore-ordained by the color of their skin, a logical consequence of social and economic isolation, hostility, and neglect. It was an inheritance. They certainly did not see themselves as victims. It is doubtful that Tana and Rell or the rest would have willingly traded places with anyone. They were the opposite of victims; they were slayers. They were winners. The stakes were thrillingly high, the rewards palpable. They were, as their Instagram signatures declared, _100_!!

The unfortunate Markee Brown had appeared willingly before a grand jury on the eighth floor of the gray slab Garmatz US District Courthouse on Lombard Street. He was young and perhaps did not fully grasp the danger. As had Erika MacKenzie, waiting in her car for her son to return with toothpaste, Brown had witnessed the killing of his friend Shotgun (Dominique Harris) on Baker Street the previous December. He knew Binkie (John Harrison) had done it and was angry about it. He wanted Binkie punished.

Brown told the grand jury that he had lived in West Baltimore his whole life, that he had grown up with Shotgun, that he had no job other than "hustling" with him—selling heroin, cocaine, and marijuana out of a vacant on Monroe Street. It was demanding work; they were at it from eight in the morning until eight at night every day. Brown walked the sidewalk attracting customers, whom he would send into the empty house to complete the transaction with Shotgun. Trade was brisk. They had been doing this for two years, a small independent retail shop on a block now controlled by Tana.

They were asking for trouble, which came three days before the new year. Brown, out in the cold, got an urgent call from Shotgun telling him to hurry inside and to "bring some money."

"And what did you see when you entered the house?" he was asked by Assistant US Attorney John Hanley.

"A dude flashing a gun."

". . . Now you said 'flashing' it. What do you mean by he was flashing it? Was he pointing it?"

"Waving it around. Yes, pointing it."

". . . And the guy that was waving the gun, had you seen him before that day?"

"Yes."

"Did you know him well enough to recognize him?"

"Yes."

"And who was the person with the gun?"

"That dude Binkie."

"Binkie?"

"Yeah."

"How long had you known or recognized Binkie?"

"Like four months."

Brown said Binkie was wearing a mask on his head, which he had not pulled down over his face.

"Empty your pockets," Binkie told Brown, who turned over thirty dollars. Shotgun also gave up their complete stash, two fist-size packets of heroin and coke. Binkie then told Brown to leave through the back door. As he departed, he said, he saw Binkie leave through the front door, and Shotgun bolt up the stairs, where he kept a gun hidden in the ceiling.

"So, after you left, did you see anything?" Hanley asked.

Brown said he saw Shotgun run back downstairs, chasing Binkie.

". . . What did you see next?"

"I didn't see nothing; I heard gunfire."

". . . What do you do next?"

"I run up and meet with Shotgun. We run to the block we be on, Payson and Presstman. We run to that block."

They met up with Brown's brother, Andre, and the three huddled.

"The conversation was, who was going to walk back down the street and confront the person we think has something to do with it," he said. "That was the conversation."

So the three set off together back up toward Baker Street. When they reached the intersection, they were ambushed.

"The car pull up, two people jump out with guns in their hands, start shooting and chased us," he said. "I ran. I was away from Dominique. Dominique ran towards them. When I came back to the scene, he was shot up, and that's what happened."

Erika MacKenzie would testify that the shooter, who Brown said was Binkie, retrieved a heavier weapon from the car and returned to finish off his victim. She would tell how she found Harris dying, trying to crawl off the street.

Hanley asked Brown, "How do you know that one of them was Binkie?"

"From the same clothes," he said. Like many teenage boys, Brown was attentive to fashion. Stressful as the situation may have been, he had fully appraised Binkie's ensemble, which he detailed: gray Abercrombie & Fitch winter coat, dark jeans, and "butters," tan Timberland boots. "This time his face was covered up," he said. "When he jumped out of the car shooting, his face was covered up, but he had the exact same clothes on that he had on when we was in the house, the same body frame. You can just tell. If you know him, you can tell it was him again."

Such eyewitness testimony was exceedingly rare—MacKenzie had seen the shooting but could not identify the shooter. Brown could. His testimony was enough for Binkie to be arrested and charged. But the indictment sealed Brown's fate. It referenced an eyewitness who had been robbed earlier. With Shotgun dead, it could only have been Brown. The task force saw the danger. Brown was given money to fly to Georgia, where he said he had family, and he had phoned Neptune to assure the detective he was in Atlanta. He thanked Neptune for getting him out of Baltimore so quickly.

But he wasn't in Georgia. He had pocketed the relocation money and moved less than a mile away, to North Baltimore. Perhaps he felt this was far enough. But the day after Brown's thank-you call, Neptune was informed by Fat Guy (Guy Coffey) that his star witness was dead. Brown had not only stayed in Baltimore, he had continued to hang with his circle of friends, one of whom, it turned out, was the brother of Tana's girlfriend, Jasmine Baldwin. The task force would later find several calls between brother and sister, the first in months, on the day Brown was executed and burned, and another afterward.

On the day of the killing, the task force overheard TTG member Timrod, Timothy Floyd, calling Tana, looking for a gun. More chilling was a call from Rell, now out of prison.

He said: "I'm looking for the gas can."

Brown's death was a severe setback. With the escalating pace of TTG's killings, the task force had begun looking for ways to take the crew's most prolific shooters off the streets immediately. Charges in the RICO case were still months away. Arresting Binkie on a state charge had been a start, but it hinged on Brown telling his story in court—his testimony to the federal grand jury would not be admissible in state court. The gang knew this, too. After Brown was murdered, Tana informed the crew, confidently and correctly, that Binkie was "coming home."

For the task force, nothing was going smoothly. The hard-won wiretap on Tana's phone that had gone live on January 20 plunged the investigators immediately into his violent world. YGG Tay's lyrics were no fantasy. What the detectives overheard in those first months was not just the normal chatter of drug dealing and street crime;

they were listening to soldiers at war. As Tana told one of his associates that April, "We hunting. We ain't doing no hustling, we hunting right now."

Just days after the wiretap began, on January 22, the biggest blizzard ever recorded in Baltimore hit, depositing more than twenty-nine inches of snow. Busy streets were buried in tall white drifts, streetlamps reflecting brightly off silent avenues. An eerie calm descended with the flakes, as if the city were suspended in time. Parked cars became great, rounded white mounds, like crude merlons. National Guard Humvees transporting essential National Weather Service workers foundered in wet, frigid dunes along the Baltimore–Washington Parkway. The storm continued through Saturday, as city residents bundled up and strolled down the empty avenues, marveling at the transformation. Shovels and plows worked ceaselessly, throwing up mountain ranges of dirty snow around parking lots. The steep marble staircase before the Walters Art Museum became a sled ramp. By nightfall Saturday, with snow still gently falling, the city was mostly paralyzed.

And yet the drug trade in Sandtown barely slowed. Early that night, the wire caught a call to Tana from Marty (Linton Broughton), who had responsibility for several corners. One of their workers, a boy called Mike, had been robbed. This was Marty's responsibility, and when he placed the call, he and Mike were tracking the two robbers on foot through the cold, whitened streets. This was just after seven. Tana was in a black Honda he had borrowed from Milk (Roger Taylor), parked a few streets away.

Marty gasped, "Hey, yo, Mike just got robbed by the niggas right here, yo. On Mount and Lanvale."

"Where the joint at?" asked Tana, referring to the handgun that was supposed to protect Mike's corner.

"I got it right here."

"All right. Where the fuck y'all at?"

"You want me to walk? We're on Lanvale walking up. They about to hit Fulton."

"They walking?" Tana asked. "All right, all right. I'm about [to] hit the corner and then pass it to me, baby."

The wire caught Marty questioning his worker: "Those two niggas right there, Mike?"

Mike confirmed it. One was wearing a white coat.

"What kind of joint they have?" asked Tana. What kind of firepower were they up against? Marty said both robbers had guns.

"That's why y'all should have got the one with the ladder [a clip holding multiple rounds]," said Tana. "Y'all heard me?"

"I knew I should have grabbed that," said Marty.

The phone tap caught their continuing, confused efforts at pursuit, Tana in the car moving slowly, Marty and Mike slogging through the drifts on foot. They lost sight of the robbers, then spotted them again emerging from a store.

"They went straight down Mosher . . . going toward Appleton," said Marty.

"All right," said Tana. "You know I know how to handle this. . . . You keep following them, yo. About to grab that other jimmie mack [pistol]."

Tana stopped to fetch the larger weapon from his brother Rell, who was close by. The detectives listening at the FBI office in Windsor Mill were alarmed.

Rell, agitated, asked his brother, "Why the fuck Marty let them go past him, though? He froze? That's when it's his time to shine."

There was more muddled back-and-forth as Tana urged his workers to guide him.

From the FBI's Windsor Mill listening post, an agent called the city police dispatcher.

"You need to find these guys now," he said. "They're going to kill someone."

Meanwhile, the slow chase proceeded westward, toward an industrial property and across railroad tracks.

"Where they went at?" asked Marty. "They went straight down?"

"I don't know," said the exasperated Tana. "Y'all just told me they walked down Mosher!"

"They went straight down Mosher . . . going toward Appleton."

"Where the fuck y'all at? . . . Stay with 'em. Stay with their ass."

"Yeah, they . . . come on, they right there. Come on," said Marty.

"Y'all see them?" Tana asked. "They probably go, they probably go over the bridge."

"Nah, they not going over the bridge. They still walking."

"I'm saying, which way they walking?"

Marty and Mike were having a hard time keeping them in sight. Beyond the railroad tracks was more open space. There was the Calverton Middle School and, across the street from it, the National Guard armory, a fenced-in low red-brick building with a very large parking lot in front. It was dark, and the snow was still falling.

"Man, we far as a bitch talking about following them."

Eventually the two men went into a house.

"Hey, yo, what did they get from him?" Tana asked. "What did they get from his dumb ass?"

"I don't know. He right here."

Marty handed Mike the phone.

"Yo, what'd they get?"

"They took all of it, my phone . . ."

"Aw, no, the phone. What else?"

"The money."

"The money."

"That's it?" asked Rell.

Tana asked Mike, "They had two joints, for real?"

"Yeah."

"You a dumb mothafucka. How much money?"

"I only sold about four bags, so it was probably like forty dollars."

Rell and Tana were not happy with their corner boy.

Marty finally linked up with Tana, and they set off together in his car toward the house the robbers had entered. There were few cars moving on the snow-covered streets, so after Neptune's call, the black Honda was spotted quickly, as it happens, by men on Wayne Jenkins's Gun Trace unit. They rolled their undercover four-wheel-drive truck up behind the Honda and flashed its colored lights.

Tana stepped on the gas. He raced for a few blocks down Lafayette and then lost control at Whitmore Avenue, skidding and slamming headfirst into a snowbank, hard enough to total the car. Airbags deployed, leaving both Tana and Marty momentarily stunned. They both stumbled out and ran in different directions. Marty tossed the smaller of the two handguns he had in the snow as soon as he got out. No one saw where he had thrown the larger one. Somewhere into the snow-covered darkness.

Both were caught. Tana went only a short distance in the deep snow before giving up. He sat down and called for a friend to pick him up. The cops found him first. He had neither drugs nor a weapon on him, so he would be booked and released. Marty did have drugs on him. The first weapon he tossed was found, and he had been seen throwing the second, so he was held and would end up spending months in prison.

The wiretap caught Tana describing the incident to Rell the next day.

"Where the fuckin' car at?" asked Rell.

"Whitmore. Right near Lafayette and, what, Whitmore."

"You parked it?"

"Fuck no."

"Oh, they got it?"

"Banged up. I banged it."

"You say you crashed it?"

"Yeah."

"You got the other what's its name?" asked Rell, referring to the weapon he had given him.

"Nah, he had both of 'em."

"How the fuck?"

"See, I been gave it to him. You feel me? When we first started."

"Who y'all chased by?"

"I don't know. DEA, FBI, and all those lil, um, what is it? Fed squad? . . . Task force."

"Damn."

"You heard me?"

"They was wantin' y'all like that?"

This surprised the agents monitoring the call. Tana seemed to know about the task force targeting them. But he also seemed unconcerned. He said he was about to elude his pursuers when he lost control of the car.

"The bitch wouldn't stop. I tried to slow down and hit the corner, like, whop! The bitch wouldn't stop. So, bam!"

"You told Milk?"

"It fishtailed, it fishtailed. Hit the car, boom! Went straight into the front of the car, boom!"

"So how the fuck they catch Marty?"

"In the school lot. . . . in Calverton lot. . . . His dumb ass throw the bitch [gun] on the corner."

Tana said the cops had found it.

"Which one they find, though?"

"I don't know, probably the black one."

"Fuck."

"I don't know which one. It was little."

Tana said he had come close to catching and shooting one of the men who had robbed Mike.

"I had him. I had that nigga on the feet. I bust him up. But the car [police truck] come straight down, next thing I know the guy running down the middle of the street, like man, man, it's nowhere to go. Snow as high as a mothafuck! Snow as high as shit. . . . Shit up over the top of my boot. . . . I got away but I end up giving myself up. Like, fuck that. You feel me?"

"What they say?"

"We ain't say shit. They booked us, but they ain't found [the gun]. They saw him throw it . . . but they ain't know where. They end up backtracking like finding shit."

The first gun Marty tossed had been found.

"Well, he better hope they don't come back."

"Come back?"

"Yeah."

"And get another? And find the other one?"

The task force would have been determined to find the other gun anyway, but hearing Rell's concern redoubled their interest. It was buried out there somewhere under the snow, where it likely would remain until a melt. Someone would then scoop it up, and they would never recover it.

But they caught a break. Marty made a call from prison two days later, in which he effectively drew a map to the hidden treasure. He dialed Milk, but Tana picked up the phone.

"Who this? Tanner?" Marty asked.

"Yeah, you know who the fuck it is."

Marty explained that when he was caught, he'd had two large packets of marijuana on him. Seated in the back of the police truck with Tana, he had slipped them under the seat.

"I was in the back of the Nissan and kept movin' a lot, and I tried. Yeah, I was slidin' them bitches under the seat."

". . . Man, you should have passed them bitches to me, man," said Tana.

"Hmph, I should have."

"I told you they was about to let me go. Yo, they sucked, yo."

". . . You know where the small jiffy at?" Marty asked.

"Where at?"

Marty described where he had thrown the gun, by the corner where they crashed. This was the one the police had found. He said he had tossed the other, along with his phone, "by the gate . . . over there by the little building."

Looking at a map and knowing the direction Marty had fled, the task force saw that he was probably describing the armory. On Thursday, six days after the incident, Neptune and DeLorenzo showed up there with a group of agents, armed with shovels and a metal detector, only to find that all the snow had been plowed into tall mounds around the armory parking lot. Soldiers brought out a front-end loader and smashed the piles flat, and the agents combed over the hardened snow with the metal detector, finding nothing. It was then decided to scoop the snow into trucks and leave it to melt in the sun. If the gun turned up, the armory would call them. The agents were only a few blocks away when the soldiers called. The first load scooped by the front-end loader had uncovered a black 9mm handgun with a magazine holding seven rounds—the "jimmie mack." They also found the cell phone. Both would prove significant.

Marty's cell phone had a wealth of contacts, call records, texts, and even photos clearly linking him to the gang. Even better, ballistics tests would show that the weapon had been used in the July 2015 triple murder.

Beyond these particulars, the incident, overheard at the outset of eavesdropping by the agents in Windsor Mill—the robbery, the chase, the anticipated shootout—proved typical. This was what Tana and his crew were doing all the time, day after day, night after night. They hunted. They shared weapons and masks and coordinated with each other by phone and text. They also had their own network of informants throughout Sandtown who helped them spot and pursue targets—anyone who stole from them, infringed on their turf, or beefed with them, for any reason. When not busy with their own targets, they pursued those with a price on their heads, collecting sizable rewards. It became clear that TTG was no longer primarily drug dealing, it was hunting. It was a killing machine.

When Tana was released that January night, he returned immediately to stalking the men who had robbed Mike. Just hours after Marty's gun and phone were recovered, he placed a series of calls to a member of his crew whose voice the agents didn't recognize. Tana was looking for a gun and a mask. Neptune relayed the information to police dispatch, describing Tana's vehicle—he made the correct assumption that he'd gone back to his own red Honda Accord—and warned that he was likely armed and dangerous. Neptune and DeLorenzo then drove to Sandtown. Arriving, they found Tana and Rell standing outside the red Honda, surrounded by patrol cars with lights flashing. Worried about tipping the existence of the wiretap, the two detectives parked their car a few blocks away and walked over, pretending they had just happened on the scene.

They needn't have bothered. When Tana had asked why he had been pulled over, one of the patrolmen had said, "The FBI wanted you stopped."

Twice he had been intercepted on a hunt. Clearly someone was listening to his calls. Tana already knew there was a task force looking at him, but until now, he would not have known his carefully guarded phone number was tapped.

Neptune and DeLorenzo searched the Honda carefully, certain that they would find a weapon. They had heard Tana calling for one. They found nothing. Much later they would learn that the car, a gift from Tana's supplier Denmo (Dennis Pulley), had a hidden compartment for contraband. It was so well hidden, it was never found.

For the task force, the cop tipping off Tana to their investigation was unfortunate but the situation was unavoidable. The agents were in a bind. Overhearing a serious crime in progress, particularly a murder, they were obliged to act. And it seemed that every time they listened in to Tana's calls, a serious crime was underway.

The gang quickly put it together.

In the last conversation captured by the wire, one of Tana's workers had advised him, "You got to get a new jack [phone], man."

After that, the tap went silent. It had been up for only eight days, but it had been an eye-opener. It was little wonder that Baltimore's shooting incidents kept climbing. These guys were working at it full-time. "War," YGG Tay's term, was the right word.

The baby-faced rapper was doing his part to bolster the task force's criminal-conspiracy case. In the video for the song "Errday," he and YGG Dre strutted and waved their arms and sang—the Sandtown extras skulking behind them—pointing guns, wearing masks, and waving fistfuls of hundred-dollar bills.

> On the block like errday
> Totin' Glocks like errday
> Gettin' cash done errday
> I risk my life like errday
> Errday we go get it
> Errday we go get it
> Errday we go get it . . .
> We da reason for the yellow tape
> We play our part in the murder rate . . .
> Whole city know a nigga's name

And if notoriety was the point, being targeted by a federal task force was a plus. It was a seal of authenticity, certified badass status. *Of course* the feds were breathing down their necks! "Errday" was like a thumb in the eye to law enforcement. It said: *Here we are!* The video would eventually draw well over 100,000 views on YouTube.

When he ditched his phone, Tana set the investigation back to square one. The task force would get the new number soon enough from Fat Guy, but another mountain of leg- and paperwork loomed. It was, as Landsman would later put it, "a super hassle."

Despite these setbacks, the lost wiretap, and Brown's murder, the probe progressed and matured. The US Attorney was now solidly behind a RICO prosecution, and early that year the probe was reassigned to two veteran criminal prosecutors, Daniel Gardner and Christopher Romano (Sullivan had transferred and Gwinn had retired). Both were, in contrast, gung ho. Gardner was a reserve army officer, a runner, who kept his thinning hair in crisp military trim. His combative manner delighted the task force detectives. When Sullivan and Gwinn had explained to him why they did not regard some of TTG's murders as eligible for the RICO case, Gardner insisted that, in context, *all of them* could be. Romano was older, smaller, more grandfatherly, but shared Gardner's passion. He was nearing retirement after almost forty years as a prosecutor, with sandy white hair that he grew long on the sides and back and combed over his bald dome. He sported a wide, bushy white mustache, curled up at both ends, which made him resemble, to Neptune, the cartoon banker on the Monopoly box. Romano had been working criminal cases for so long that he assumed, usually correctly, that he knew more about the process than the detectives and from time to time became so didactic that their eyes would roll. But in argument, he was salty and concise. He endeared himself to Neptune early on when he snapped at a staffer who referred to TTG as "a drug case."

"No, fuck that!" he said. "We're going after these guys for the murders!"

FBI supervisor Swindell had worried that the April takedown of Shongo Owens, in particular, would dry up the gang's drug supply and possibly put them out of business, but Tana and his crew missed not a beat. Blue Black (Deandre Smith), Denmo, YGG Tay, and Milk picked up the slack. With so much money to be made, there were always people willing to shoulder the risk.

Soon after the wire on Tana's phone was lost, the task force obtained another on his brother's, and while Rell talked slowly, he talked a lot. Since Tana had clearly tossed his phone to avoid investigators, they were eventually awarded a "roving" wiretap for him, which eliminated the need to start from scratch every time he changed phones. All that was needed was the new number, which Fat Guy promptly supplied.

Still, the case consumed months of tedious effort. Rarely do accounts of police work capture the hours, days, weeks, and months of routine and often seemingly wasted effort. Establishing the drug dealing was the first step. This would prove that TTG was an ongoing criminal enterprise, and since the heroin, coke, and weed the crew sold was imported across state lines, placed the crime firmly in federal jurisdiction. Some of that evidence was already in hand. For years Landsman had been busting key members of the crew for selling drugs. There was also the connection unearthed in the Pedestal Gardens probe. But since TTG's operation was relatively small, experienced agents and detectives had to return to the kind of street work they had done at the outset of their careers, observing, photographing, and setting up "controlled" undercover buys, like the one Fat Guy had made with Tana in November. Cooperating sources had to be recruited for undercover drug buys who knew the neighborhood and would not be suspect. An assortment of these were convinced to help in return for consideration on pending charges. They were outfitted with video- and audio-recording devices and monitored remotely by agents. Given money for a purchase, they would return with the drugs. In early January, Fat Guy had set up another deal with Tana, asking for a larger quantity of heroin. Two other sources completed the transaction with Tana at the nearby Mondawmin Mall, coming away with fifty grams.

Many hours were spent watching and recording, often through video binoculars. In April, Fat Guy was able to point the team to a vacant, 1315 Harlem Avenue, just two blocks west of where Tana and Rell had grown up and just a half block from Harlem Square Park. The three-story row house stood at the east end of a row, with an empty lot next door. The house was a ruin, covered with gray Formstone stained by the dirt of ages. Here was where, according to Guy, Tana and Rell stashed drugs and weapons. There was a CitiWatch camera mounted to a light pole directly in front, part of the broad municipal effort to put eyes on troubled locations, but it was predictably broken. When the detectives sought to have it fixed, they were rebuffed. The city, they were told, had no funds for repairs—even though the task force offered to pay. This meant going back to Landsman's old tactics, positioning agents throughout the neighborhood in shifts to keep watch. Even Swindell took shifts.

The team documented Tana and Rell routinely doing business, meeting with customers, selling, moving in and out of the vacant. The empty house was searched on April 8. The agents found a pound of marijuana and a 9mm handgun hidden in the ceiling. Their wiretaps caught Rell discussing the raid as it happened. He arranged for a gang member to go in after the agents left to take pictures of the areas searched and to discover what had been found.

The wiretaps were a steady source of useful intel. There was daily chatter about the business, the need for resupply, for delivering drugs to the busy corners. Once in a while there was something better. In early March, the wire recorded a rich and revealing conversation between Rell and Denmo. It was like striking gold.

At thirty, Dennis Pulley was an older, more established player in The Game. His lifestyle proclaimed his income. Unlike the street players, who thrived on violence and reputation and were constantly on the move, staying with girlfriends, dodging the police and rival gunmen, Denmo cultivated the image of a respectable businessman. He had an apartment at the swank 26 South Calvert Street building, a tall, narrow structure with a stately ornate concrete facade that was just a short walk from the attractions of the Inner Harbor. His was a two-story unit that he shared with his girlfriend and child. While most of the intercepts were so dense with code words and obscure slang that they were hard to follow, Denmo spoke plainly. He knew how to accumulate wealth, how to grow a business and to make his earnings work for him, so he was disappointed in Tana and Rell, who hoarded their money, treating every dollar like it might be their last. Here was unrealized potential. This was the subject he took up with Rell on the golden phone intercept.

The younger man had trouble grasping Denmo's financial advice, stumbling over the concept of investing money both to promote success and to earn more.

"What I was trying to explain to you yesterday was, you spend your money, look right," advised Denmo.

"I know what you were saying."

"You couldn't have, 'cause if that were the case that would be in your mind, that should be your goal."

". . . I'm trying [to] at least wait till I have enough to do that."

"But listen to me, Rell. The longer you got that four grand sitting in the house, do it make money?"

"Yeah, it's adding up."

"How? You not gaining any interest by your money sitting in that house, all right?"

"Shit, it's adding up."

"How is it adding up? But if at the same time you were to spend your money and cop [buy more drugs] with your money, it's going to add up even faster, right or wrong?"

Rell, not a penetrating thinker, didn't get it. "It's going to add up the same way," he insisted.

"It's *not* going to add up the same way. Listen to what you . . . listen to what you are saying." Here was a man with tens of thousands invested in mutual funds trying to convey the basics of capital utilization to a child. Rell's thickheadedness frustrated Denmo but drew them deeper and deeper into a description of TTG's business. Rell spelled out exactly how much money he was taking in, where he was selling, and even exactly how he was cutting the product. But talk of investing his earnings, growing the business, was futile. As their supplier, Denmo had an interest in seeing them move more product, but he also seemed to be sincerely trying to mentor the youths. Rell, the call made clear, was more inclined to follow the advice of his younger brother, who was even more cautious about money than he was.

"You can't listen to Tanner," said Denmo. "Tanner not going to spend his own money."

"I don't be listening to no Tanner."

"He not trying to spend his own money. That's my son, I love him to death, but he ain't trying to spend no money."

Denmo tried to explain that if Rell and Tana upped their game along Pennsylvania Avenue, where "all the big sales" came from, he would cut off their competitors. If they did that, "You getting all that money. And that how you . . . control the market, you hear what I'm saying? If I cut back on hitting [selling to] niggas, all the money going to come to you. You feel what I'm saying? . . . We control what the fuck is going on."

The conversation would prove very helpful to prosecutors. Talk like this was highly suggestive, but not proof of criminal dealing. No one hearing this dialogue would mistake the nature of their business, but they were careful not to mention by name heroin or cocaine or fentanyl or any of their other products. Talk like this was highly suggestive, but not proof of criminal dealing. Proving that they were selling drugs was harder than might be imagined. Because gang members spoke only obscurely about quantity and quality and used only coded slang for their product—"vicks" or "haze" or "sour diesel" all referred to marijuana. The only way to know for sure what was being sold was to set up controlled buys and then send the product to a lab.

More often than not, the rotating shifts of surveillance produced nothing. The agents faced the same problems Landsman had years earlier. It was hard to stay hidden. Many a surveillance outing was cut short. Evidence accumulated incrementally. The individual moments they captured were often fairly insignificant, but each was a brick in the wall. By the time they were ready to indict, the wall would be complete and unassailable. At trial, all the gang's defense lawyers would simply concede that their clients were selling drugs. But this was not all the task force was after.

Documenting the drug business effectively demonstrated how closely Tana and Rell and the others worked to commit crimes. What the task force was ultimately after was collective responsibility for the murders.

Landsman's presence on the team continued to pay dividends. His sources were impeccable: Fat Guy, Pony Head (Jan Gray), and then, out of the blue, Rah (Ronnie Johnson). The three helped to decode wiretap intercepts, sort out gang relationships, and fill in what their targets avoided saying directly. Fat Guy had been present (and wounded) for the kidnapping and murder of Nut (Jamie Hilton-Bey) and had witnessed the killing of Bub (Brandon Littlejohn), so he nailed down two solid murder charges. Rah's participation in the kidnapping-murder buttressed that charge. And like Fat Guy, Rah proved to be an eager undercover operative. Outfitted with a camera inside a key fob—which made for some dizzying video—he mingled with gang members on the street, chatting them up, buying drugs, working his way in. With his long history of wrongdoing and his BGF rank, he was trusted implicitly.

And, as it happened, the gang shared his beef with Ced (Cedric Catchings). The murder of Rah's buddy Slow Down (Larelle Wallace) had drawn them into the same Blue Black–Ced blood feud, which was less about drugs than revenge and reputation. It would rumble through the summer of 2016. Even though neither Rah nor Blue Black had been bosom buddies with Tana or Rell, the amounts offered for Ced's demise had enlisted the Sandtown crew's enthusiastic participation.

Meanwhile, Rah himself remained a target. He was considered to be in such danger that friends stopped him on the street to warn him. Carrying a gun himself, especially with his new handlers watching, was out of the question, so he recruited a bodyguard. He had to abandon his own pursuit of Ced but was free to tag along with Tana as he hunted. With or without Rah, the crew's pursuit of Ced was tailor-made for the task force. It would be one thing to tell a jury that TTG was a killing machine but far better to show the gang actually at work, stalking human prey. The pursuit of Ced and his friend Thug (Antonio Addison) was made to order.

Tana took a call from Timrod on April 14—a Ced sighting.

"Ced and Thug, right there by his grandma's house," said Timrod.

"Oh, here I come, here I come," said Tana, excitedly. "Keep your eyes on them."

The gang came together quickly and in force. Blue Black, armed with an assault rifle, got in a blue Honda with Tana and a young crew member named Darrell Carroll, who would later provide a detailed account in court. Rell and Man-Man (Brandon Bazemore) were in a silver Honda Odyssey van. A third car with gunmen followed them. Tana made a stop to run up a narrow alley and retrieve a .40 caliber handgun.

"It's my bitch," he said, showing off the weapon to the others when he returned. "I wore a lot of niggas out with this bitch."

On the way they learned that Ced had gone to a barbershop in East Baltimore. The task force, hearing Timrod's call, summoned patrol cars to intercept them.

Rell and Tana were linked via videophone as they raced east, planning out their next moves. Tana and Blue Black would pull up to the barbershop, jump out, and, as Rell put it, "throw shot," and "wear him out." Carroll was to move into the driver's seat and pull out when they returned. To set the mood, Tana cranked up the music in the car, the rapper Blac Youngsta, who had just released a new album called *Young & Reckless*. A typical lyric went:

> *Catch a body. Catch a body.*
> *Last time I checked*
> *I wasn't scared of nobody.*
> *Broobroobroobow boom boom boom.*
> *Ima load up now,*
> *Ima hit him with the shot . . .*

Carroll must have made a face, because Tana glanced at him in the rearview mirror and asked, "Y'all ain't down with this? This is new shit!" As he looked back, he saw a police car with its lights flashing. He sped up, turning down McCulloh Street and again at West Preston, leaving the police car behind. He turned right on Myrtle Avenue near the low-rise McCulloh Homes and pulled the car under some trees, just in case a police helicopter moved overhead. Tana told them to leave the guns in the car.

But Blue Black was not going to give up his assault rifle and eyed Tana's silver .40 cal.

"You don't want it?" said Blue Black. "Give it to me. I'll take the motherfucker."

Tana hung on to his gun. They walked away toward the McCulloh Homes, a collection of three-story red-brick apartment buildings, where a friend told them that "Timeout," the police, were nearby. The three hopped a fence and separated. One of the crew's neighborhood watchers heard an alert on police radio and called Rell.

"Listen, listen to me," the man said. "Yo, I heard y'all was on the scanner all day. I didn't know it was y'all until just now. . . . Somebody tellin' on y'all. They know. It just came across the scanner. Something happened on Eutaw, Eutaw and Lafayette. They said something about a four-door blue car, a Honda, and a silver Odyssey, and a white, either an Acura or a Honda. They was talking about them three cars. They said the cars had guns in 'em."

"Yeah," said Rell.

"Right, so listen. So like five minutes ago, it gets came [sic] across the scanner just now. They got GPS on that silver Odyssey. Whoever got a silver Odyssey, they got GPS on it, yo."

That described Rell's car—the task force was monitoring his phone.

"They sayin' something about a house they watchin' . . . on Harlem."

Man-Man then spotted Landsman on Calhoun Street. He called Rell.

"Yeah, that probably was Landsman."

"Yeah, white nigga. You talkin' 'bout Mario."

Darrell Carroll was arrested as he drove away from the scene in his own car. He was stopped and charged with driving without a license.

That day's pursuit of Ced had been short-circuited, by design, but the hunt continued. Less than two weeks later, Rell received another morning call from Timrod.

"Guess who down Lexington Terrace, son?" he said.

"Huh?"

"Down Lexington Terrace right now, son."

"You sayin' who?"

"Ced."

"Where at?"

"Right here, on Fremont."

"Where he sittin'? Right there?"

"He walkin' down the street. He must be out here with these niggas."

". . . Yo, see if he go into somebody's house," said Rell.

But Ced stayed outside. Minutes later, Rell called Timrod back, checking to see if Ced was still there. He was.

"Oh, God damn. Well, I'm ready to try and call somebody. Where he on, Fremont and Fayette?"

"Yeah."

"Where, on the corner?"

"He out there. You ain't gonna miss him."

But the task force once again summoned a patrol car, aborting the hit.

So Ced had a guardian angel, which, ironically, would prove ruinous for Rah. The feud finally caught up with him on May 24, as he emerged from a neighborhood convenience store with his girlfriend and bodyguard. Rah was pulling away in his car when two gunmen appeared on the sidewalk wearing masks. They fired about twenty rounds in all, eight of which hit Rah. His bodyguard stood by on the sidewalk and watched.

One round broke Rah's finger. Seven hit his left leg, which swelled to triple its normal size and would require extensive surgical repair.

When Rah's name popped up as victim in the subsequent police report, Landsman called Neptune. They found Rah in the shock trauma ward, spaced out on painkillers. He greeted them with a broad smile. Neptune visited again the next day, accompanied by the city detectives assigned to investigate the shooting.

"I'm going to talk to him," Neptune told the others. "He's my source. This guy is going to get relocated in several months, if he cooperates. He's going to tell you who shot him. But you cannot disclose that he's the one who identified the shooters until I've moved him."

Rah named Ced as one of the shooters. He didn't know who the other one was. Ced was charged and arrested. Even though he was not named as a witness, Rah was relocated. The attack had not happened because he was an informant, but it had dramatically proved what he had told Landsman—there were people gunning for him. He was shipped out to far western Maryland, to Cumberland, first to a hospital and eventually to a hotel. Surrounded by green mountains and completely out of his element, Rah found a familiar refuge in his painkillers. High, in a full-leg cast, he began again hobbling with a walker, once more in rehab. He felt lucky to be alive.

And he wasn't done helping the task force.

During those months in 2016, it was increasingly clear that the gang knew it was being targeted by the feds and did not seem unduly concerned. Its members had been hearing for years about the various Baltimore-federal partnerships to combat drugs and violence— Project Exile, Operation Ceasefire, BFED, Safe Streets. Each of these hopeful initiatives had kicked off with fanfare, making headlines and allowing local pols to claim they were doing something about the bloodletting, but through it all TTG had prospered—boasting all the way. Still, some of the old heads, like Denmo, sensed danger.

He had more to lose. After his friends Blue Black and Shongo Owens were busted, he considered leaving town. With the feds now circling Tana, the haughty young gang leader's behavior was concerning. Despite his unfailing affability and good manners, Tana's body count had inflated not only his rep but his ego. Denmo was not blind to this.

When Tana heard that his supplier was thinking about moving, he called to tease him, hinting that Denmo might be considering getting out of the business in a different way, by striking a deal with law enforcement.

"Yo, what is this I'm hearing, you talkin' 'bout, you start to think about turning yourself in?" Tana said. His tone was playful, but there was an implied threat. Cooperation was tantamount to a death sentence.

"Man, I'm trying to get this shit over with," said Denmo. "I can't get it right on the real."

"All right, just leave me the apartment then," said Tana.

"Yo, hold on, you just woke me up out my nap. Hold on."

"Yeah, you funny as shit."

". . . Ima wait until my lease is up . . . put my shit in storage." He mentioned New York as a possible destination.

Tana said, "All right. When your lease up?"

"October. . . . I don't know, like, I wasn't sayin' immediately. It was a thought, you know what I'm saying?"

"You said it was a thought. But then you gonna change your fuckin' mind."

"Nah. I gotta get this shit out the way. Nigga needs some real money. I'm here takin' a nap now, still stressed out. I just spent $10,000 already this month. On bills."

Then Tana bragged about holding up a group of youngsters on the street. He took $1,700 from them and a collection of new iPhones.

"You gotta stop doin' dumb shit, son," said Denmo.

"Nah, it wasn't no dumb shit."

Denmo asked why he had done it.

"Man, these niggas don't know who the fuck I am."

"You so caught up in wantin' a nigga to know who you is, that shit."

"Nah. Nah. They get disrespectful."

"Lil niggas actin' real goofy."

"Yeah, they gettin' disrespectful out here."

Denmo was not overly troubled. He even asked Tana to keep one of the iPhones for him. But the growing cockiness worried him. It was extreme even for their world. Denmo warned Rell, "Man, y'all hot. . . . you gotta part from Tana. Tana brings you too much heat."

9

Number One Trigger Puller

*Mark Neptune, left, and Barronette, right,
at Barronette's arrest on August 19, 2016.*

*A naval officer stood on the sand, looking down at Ralph in
wary astonishment. . . .*

"Are there any adults—any grown-ups with you?"

*Dumbly, Ralph shook his head. He turned a half pace on
the sand. A semicircle of little boys, their bodies streaked with
coloured clay, sharp sticks in their hands, were standing on the
beach making no noise at all.*

"Fun and games," said the officer.

—William Golding, *Lord of the Flies*

Despite everything, Valencia Bullock believed that her son
Antonio Addison had righted himself. She called him Tony.
He was a pudgy young man with small features in a wide round face
in which his lips, full but narrow, were pinched, as if he were about to
plant a kiss. In the eyes of his mother, there was nothing about him

to even hint at his street name, Thug. And it was impossible for her to imagine what she'd heard, that some hoodlums were hunting him. Still, it worried her enough to ask him about it.

"It's nothing," he said.

Bullock had never married Tony's father, also named Antonio Addison. He had been in prison for much of the boy's childhood and had another son with the same name by a different woman, which created ceaseless familial confusion. Bullock lived in East Baltimore and had done her best to keep her Tony away from the dangerous Sandtown street life, but much of their family still lived there, cousins, uncles, and both of Tony's grandmothers. Some of them were actively involved in The Game. This exerted a pull on her son that Bullock had not fully overcome. Tony drifted out to the corners after finishing high school and lived more and more at her mother's house.

When he was eighteen, in 2012, the thing she feared most happened. Tony was shot in the head and left on the street to die. He didn't. Surgeons sawed the shattered portion of his skull off and then extracted the bullet from his brain. The excised portion of his cranium was replaced with a metal plate. The wound and radical procedure left him dramatically scarred. The old entry wound was a round lump in the top center of his forehead, and the surgical incision had left a long line up and across his head lengthwise. Recovery from the shooting had been rough, but he had gradually relearned how to walk, eat, and speak, and in time, with a lot of therapy, he was very nearly his old self. There was no hiding the mark at the middle of his forehead, but the long scar was hidden when his hair grew back.

The experience did not drive Tony out of Sandtown, as his mother had hoped. She was aware that he still associated with characters like Ced (Cedric Catchings), but she chose not to read much into it. Everybody in that neighborhood knew people in The Game. Bullock saw hopeful signs. In time she saw her son holding down a demanding job at an Amazon warehouse, working long hours and studying for a commercial driver's license, so that he could step up from retrieving orders to delivering them. She saw a young father trying to help raise the six-year-old daughter who had been born when he was still in high school. She saw him growing up at twenty-two, shouldering his responsibilities, making his way correctly. He'd paid up some old fines for driving infractions and had inquired about the paperwork needed to get a criminal conviction expunged from his record. On Thursday morning, April 25, 2016, he asked her if she'd drive him to the Motor Vehicle Administration (MVA) so he could apply for the commercial license.

Bullock took the day off from her job at a nursing home. Mother and son had a good day together, laughing, talking. Tony bought her lunch. At the MVA he told her that he had recently regained peripheral vision in his left eye, which she'd never known he'd lost. She asked him again about the rumor that people were after him, and he again reassured her. It was just a misunderstanding, even though his friend Pop, Andrew Johnson, had been shot just weeks earlier, allegedly by members of TTG, accused of telling the police about an earlier attempt on his life. Pop, approached by detectives in his hospital bed, refused to say a word. Rumor had it that Tony might be next. He told his mother that his cousin Man-Man (Brandon Bazemore) was tight with the group. He said he was going to ask him to set up a meeting with Tana so he could resolve the matter.

"If you go, don't go by yourself," she said.

In the afternoon she dropped him off at her mother's house and told him she would come back after picking up his brothers from school. When she returned, riding in a car with Antonio Sr., they drove past his mother's house on Carey Street. "Tony's there," he told her. "You want to talk to him?" Bullock said no, she would see him later, when he came back to her mother's house.

That's where she was, sitting outside on the stoop, when a woman stopped and asked for Bullock's mother. She got up to call her to the door when the woman asked, "Are you Tony's mother?"

"Yes."

"There's been a shooting down on Carey Street, and they said it was your son, but I'm not sure."

Bullock walked as fast as she could to Carey Street, so distraught she could hardly breathe. When she arrived, the entire block was cordoned off. She saw shattered glass in her ostensible mother-in-law's front door and, ducking under the yellow tape, saw a wide splash of blood smeared on the floor just inside.

"Miss, you've got to get out of here," said a patrolman.

"I'm looking for my son," she said.

"You gotta get out," he repeated.

Out on the sidewalk a woman asked her, "Are you Tony's mother?"

"Yeah."

"They just took him down in an ambulance. Do you have a ride?"

At the trauma center, doctors told her that her son had still been breathing when he was brought in, but then his heart had stopped. They had revived him, but it had stopped again. He was dead.

Dawnyell Taylor caught the murder. The homicide detective had been on the Baltimore force for sixteen years. Middle-aged, sturdy, smart, and wearily streetwise, she had a smooth, unlined face framed with long, straightened black hair, wide hips and shoulders, and strong arms. She had grown up Black and poor in Baltimore, in a house frequented by drug dealers, whom she remembered as pedophiles who "couldn't keep their hands to themselves." She escaped that world by joining the Marine Corps. She served four years and then enlisted in the army, serving for another nine. During those years she spent time deployed in Somalia and got married. Taylor returned to Baltimore confident, experienced, and self-disciplined, and, with her husband, joined the police force. The very things that would have barred her from the job in years past now made her distinctly qualified for it. After serving a stint in uniform on patrol, her gender, race, and upbringing made her a natural for undercover work, buying drugs on the street, setting up busts. She liked the action, even though she got hurt a few times. Promotions came. She joined the homicide squad not long after Joe Landsman started there.

By the spring of 2016, Taylor was also famous, or infamous, depending on your point of view. She had been the department's lead investigator after Freddie Gray's death, which had so rocked the city the year before and caused seismic changes in the department. But Taylor was no activist reformer. She had reached the opposite conclusion of the district attorney, the medical examiner, and those protesting and rioting. Gray's death was, she believed, a freak accident; Gray was found to have suffered a fatal spinal cord injury while riding in the police van. After her finding was overruled, and the arrested officers had been slapped with a variety of charges, including manslaughter, Taylor's contradictory testimony at their trials was a big reason none were convicted. On the stand, she flatly accused the city's prosecutors and medical examiners of being untruthful, which made her either a quisling in a racist department or a righteous woman who refused to be bullied by political pressure and public opinion. Whichever way you looked at it, Taylor was undeniably neck-deep in Baltimore's troubles and was feeling beat down. Policing in Baltimore just got harder and harder. Not long after the riots stopped, Taylor was called to the scene of a slaying—a middle-aged man shot dead on the street with fifteen bullet casings scattered on the pavement around him. She encountered a stone wall of neighborhood silence. The victim was known to all, had lived on the block his entire life, and yet no one was willing to say that they knew or had seen anything. The man's daughter was there, too, decked out in a "Fuck the Police" T-shirt. Taylor thought, *Sister, we're the only ones here trying to do the right thing by your father!*

All of this was crowding in on her when she was assigned the murder of Antonio Addison Jr.

He had been slain in a hail of bullets from two weapons, struck first on the concrete steps to his grandmother's front door, and then again and again as he stumbled up and into her house. One bullet hit him in the center of his back. The glass of the storm window had been shattered. He had been taken to the trauma center by the time Taylor arrived, but she saw the ugly red smear blackening on the cheerful yellow and orange tiles before his horrified grandmother's TV set.

The victim's family knew who had done it. They had all heard that Tana and Rell were gunning for him, but they were not, at least initially, in a mood to help. Taylor found them not just emotional, which she expected, but hostile. She also encountered the usual disbelief or denial that families displayed whenever a husband or brother or son, caught up in The Game, paid the ultimate price. In their grief they painted a saintly picture of the newly departed. He had been an innocent, tragically and inexplicably struck down. The anger she encountered was mostly directed at her, or the police in general, who were considered useless or worse. Taylor was accustomed to this and to being shown the requisite photos of the victim in cap and gown at a graduation ceremony or posing in shoulder pads with his youth football team or cuddling puppies or his children, nieces, or nephews. That was their Tony.

The naked body on the slab at the morgue told its own story, however—the story not of Tony but of Thug. This story was violent and death-haunted. There was the brutal scar on his forehead and the one across the top of his head from the old shooting. There were the new fatal wounds, raw red holes gouged in his torso and thighs and the one in his back. Etched up his arms, under an ornate crowning tattoo that read "R.I.P.," were tombstones, a pair of praying hands draped with a rosary, and the names of departed friends. The detective had inspected many such bodies of young Black men at the morgue and could often learn things from their tattoos. Teardrops on a face indicated prison time or having killed someone; tombstones with significant dates on them often marked the violent deaths of friends. There were names of girlfriends and children. Sometimes they had birthdates inked on their skin or even partial social security numbers. The tattoos often revealed gang affiliations and home neighborhoods. The story Thug's body told was not that of a perfectly innocent victim.

But whenever she brought this up, the story of Thug, and asked about his role in The Game, his family recoiled. *Why are you smearing his memory? What does that have to do with anything?* It probably had everything to do with his murder, she told them. She argued as gently as she could, explaining that any chance she had of learning about his death depended on them getting real with her about his life.

"Things are going to come out," she said. "If you really don't know, you're going to hear about it eventually anyway. He was involved with these guys."

No matter how much she argued, it was hard to overcome the family's conviction that helping her was dangerous and a waste of time. Even she knew that it was unlikely she'd ever charge anyone, and even less likely that the shooter would face justice. It didn't stop her from trying. Her dogged questions were taken as intrusive and impertinent, as if she were acting out a meaningless ritual, going through the motions. Taylor did care. She'd lost her own brother to a shooting. Her personal and professional contempt was for the dealers and killers who terrorized city neighborhoods. If a gang had done this, she didn't want only Thug's killers—she wanted them all.

And in Valencia Bullock she found a rare ally. Grief and anger emboldened Bullock. She told Taylor about her conversation with Tony earlier that day, about the rumors of him being targeted and by whom. Others in the family, seeing Tony's bereaved mother helping, came around, too. One told her that TTG was angry because Tony had refused to kill someone for them. It was a theory.

The previous year, Taylor had worked the murder of Beezy (Brian Chase), who had been found facedown in dog shit. So she was well acquainted with Tana, Rell, Binkie (John Harrison), and the others. She had questioned Binkie about that killing. He had sat slouched in a chair with his hands in his pockets, wearing a hooded sweatshirt and black knit cap, offering only brief answers in a bored, low growl. Taylor was aware that he had a fearsome reputation, but to her he just looked like a sullen, skinny kid. That case remained open, even though she was sure Binkie and Tana had done it.

The weeks and months after Thug's killing were hard. The Addison-Bullocks were a troubled family to begin with. Relationships were tangled and often hostile. Man-Man, Tony's cousin, was part of the group they suspected of killing him. At a reception after the funeral, which Taylor attended, Antonio Sr. was shot by his son, the other Antonio Jr. A dispute had flared over the funeral arrangements. It was like a bad comedy, or a copyeditor's nightmare. Taylor, who had departed after the funeral ceremony, found herself racing back to the scene to help arrest Antonio Addison for shooting Antonio Addison at the funeral of Antonio Addison.

As weeks and months passed with no resolution, Taylor would find her relationship with the family strained. Each day Tana and Rell were free just confirmed the family's distrust.

But Taylor had been placed in an awkward position. Once she started poking around, she learned of the task force's interest in TTG. Unless she had enough to warrant arresting Tana and Rell on the immediate charge, which she did not—all the information she was getting was second- or third-hand—then it was best to let the task force continue its work. And the task force was taking exactly the approach she preferred, trying to sweep up the whole gang. This was not something she could divulge to the family.

Still, her relationship with Bullock held. Taylor assured her that the law was going to catch up to her son's killers. Soon.

*   *   *

It was murdering season. Shortly before Thug's murder, Tana and Rell and some of the others took a trip to Miami—Tana was pictured in a flotation vest, smiling, swimming with dolphins. On their return, the men went on a spree. Over three or four days in late May, in addition to Thug, two more of Ced's associates were shot dead, Christopher Pennington, known as Magic, and Christopher Jackson. In July, the youngster Tev (Tevin Haygood) was also killed. He was the corner boy who, at Tana's urging, had taken the wild shots at Pony Head (Jan Gray) that missed and the ones at lanky Marquez Jones that did not. The body count ticked up and up. By June the task force could directly link eighteen murders to TTG. In early August, on Lafayette Avenue, it became nineteen, when Tana was linked to the slaying of Dirt, Darius Perkins, brother of the man who had murdered Tev.

Tana and Rell were on top of their world. Pony Head was just a memory. TTG was raking in so much money the crew didn't know what to do with it. Each member had a collection of women. YGG Tay's rap videos were drawing ever bigger audiences. Binkie was a free man again. Markee Brown's murder had torpedoed the case against him for murdering Shotgun (Dominique Harris). Marty (Linton Broughton), who had been locked up after fleeing with Tana during the blizzard, was back on the street, doing his old job supervising the drug corners. On social media the crew posed for pictures together, partying at swank locations throughout the city and across the country—Miami, Atlanta, LA.

The task force toiled away quietly on its RICO case, building it brick by brick. They had the gang wired and infiltrated. Fat Guy (Guy Coffey) was working as a middleman for Denmo (Dennis Pulley) and supplying the phone numbers that kept the wiretaps alive. He also continued to steer them to the places where TTG hid its drugs and guns. As more and more bodies fell, Fat Guy usually had current intel, not only naming the shooters but explaining why, helping to make sense of the mounting madness.

Building a coherent narrative was essential. Federal prosecutors would have to show that these were not just random acts of violence on dangerous streets. There was an ongoing coherent backstory, one that illustrated how closely the gang worked together. In April, Fat Guy alerted the task force to a party that he had attended with most of TTG, a gender-reveal party for an expectant mother at an Eggspectation restaurant in nearby Ellicott City. The party was innocent but useful. The restaurant's front-door camera caught most of the core group sauntering in together: bearded Denmo, in a camouflage jacket talking on the phone; Rell, wearing a blue tracksuit; Tana, with a black jacket over a white T-shirt; Milk (Roger Taylor), in an Orioles shirt and cap; Timrod (Timothy Floyd); Man-Man; Scratch (Darius Singleton) with his sideways baseball cap; and then Fat Guy himself, waddling up the rear, dressed all in black and wearing a shiny necklace. Here was the gang together, illustrating that its members traveled, worked, and played as a group. It was not too much of a stretch, then, to see them killing as a group. The video also showed clearly that Fat Guy was one of them, which would burnish his cred when it came time to testify. Garrulous, funny, charming, and endlessly informative, he would be, the task force detectives had no doubt, their star witness.

And by late summer, Rah (Ronnie Johnson) was back on his feet, walking with a limp and a cane and talking his usual blue streak. He was returned from the mountains of Cumberland, put up in a Baltimore hotel, and kept on a short leash for his own safety. He immediately went back to work. He was good at it, too, entirely authentic and perfectly at ease, fully in his element, even enjoying himself.

On August 4, two cameras inside Rah's car recorded Neptune counting out $200 and handing it over. Rah then phoned Rell to set up a heroin buy. He drove over alone to the rendezvous, where Rell, smiling as always, with his dreads dangling from a baseball cap, climbed in the back seat.

"Is it good shit?" Rah asked.

"I don't know," said Rell, with his lazy laugh. Rah complained that he wasn't going to buy "testers," drugs of uncertain quality handed out as free samples. He wanted "bomb," Rell's best offering. If the product was weak, he complained, it would "fuck up my phone," meaning customers would stop calling him to reorder. Rell climbed out of the car to go fetch the product.

Rah called out to him, "If I beep my horn, that mean the police is out here, yo."

He knew the police were out there, of course, watching and listening. Waiting for Rell to return, alone in the car, he boasted to the camera about his undercover chops: "I keep actin' like I'm so high or somethin' 'cause I don't want him to know what I'm doin'."

Rell returned with twenty-five grams. He was wary and surprisingly perceptive, eyeing a van up the street, in which, in fact, Neptune and other agents were watching and listening.

"That's probably Timeout right there," said Rell, pointing out the van.

"They pulled up just now?" said Rah, who made a good show of being spooked. ". . . Let me get out of here then, yo."

"They be here," said Rell, calmly.

Rah said, "Yeah, let me get out of here then, nigger. Stash my shit." Rell laughed his slow laugh.

Before driving away, Rah called out the window to complain to him: "Why you tell me to meet around that hot motherfucker if you know they be posting up? . . . I'd have been mad as shit [if I] got busted up."

Six days later, Rah bought a larger amount of heroin. The same routine. This time Neptune gave him $850, and Rah made the call. He was clearly into the role, complaining to Rell, "I don't like talking over these phones." He drove to the appointed intersection. Waiting for delivery, he leaned over to the passenger seat and adjusted the camera so whoever stepped in would be neatly framed. This time one of Rell's corner workers made the delivery, twenty-five grams and one hundred pills. With his hands right before the camera, Rah counted out four portions of twenty-five pills, dropping them in plastic baggies. Acting the part of a privileged client, he then phoned Rell to complain that nothing extra had been thrown in. He had expected to be gifted some weed.

"You ain't blessin' me with some extra on this; you was gonna bless me on the grass, right?"

"Yeah."

". . . I just spent eight fifty with you, bro, and you ain't give me an extra pack or nothin'. You feel me?"

Rell said he would "bless" him later.

Each of these encounters was another brick in the wall.

Tana was arrested on Friday night, August 19, coming out of a movie theater with a girlfriend at Arundel Mills, a big shopping complex south of the city.

The RICO case was not ready, but the killing had accelerated so shockingly that delay was no longer an option. Tana would be charged with the one decent local case against him, the 2014 murder of Alfonzo Williams, the young barber who had been shot dead on his front stoop after mildly dressing down Tana for insulting his sisters. It was a state charge, the case assembled by city detective Josh Fuller. Two years earlier, Fuller had helped coax the terrified Gotti (Daniel Purdie), who had been on the steps with Williams, to tell what he had seen. This was the rarest of prosecutorial assets, an eyewitness, but it was far from certain that Gotti, who had wept and shaken with fear in the interview room, would be willing to repeat his story in a courtroom with Tana, his gang, family, and friends all staring bullets at him. There were already indications that he would not. When contacted, he protested that he had suffered a stroke that had left his memory impaired. But given the urgency, the Williams charge would serve. The looming federal indictment would supersede it anyway.

Finding Tana was easy. The task force just tracked his tapped phone. He and his girlfriend were swarmed as they left the theater. Tana just laughed and smiled, showing his gold-capped front teeth. Slender, wearing a tight gray T-shirt and oversize blue jeans cinched across his hips by a wide black belt, he was pliant and insouciant as he was handcuffed. There were a half dozen patrol cars and the city's warrant squad, along with Neptune and Landsman and some of the other task force agents. To Tana it looked like overkill. One of the agents snapped a photo of bearded Neptune in his battered cap, standing behind the new captive with a gleeful smile, pointing at him like an angler displaying his big catch. Tana is looking off camera with a bored little smile, as if to say, *What's the big deal?*

"Man, you all treat me like I was John Dillinger," he said. He was bemused, even cheerful, perhaps even more so when he was told the charge. This was no federal case. It was just a state charge. He had been hauled in and questioned about it years earlier. It was old news. Worst case, he'd stand trial before a local jury, local judge, and serve a term in the state pen.

That was worst case. With a good lawyer, it might never come to trial. And TTG still had countermoves. Witnesses might be discouraged or eliminated. Look at Binkie. Seven months earlier he'd killed Shotgun in broad daylight before witnesses. Now he was free.

Over the next weeks and months, the task force and city police found reasons to round up nearly all of Tana's crew. Rell was picked up on October 27. He was arrested in his car near one of his corners and then sat for one of the least helpful interviews in history. His left arm in a cast and sling from what he said was a dirt-bike accident, he hunched forward in the metal chair in the homicide squad's interview room, his long braids dangling from a under a new flat-brimmed baseball cap. He had his usual smile. In contrast with Tana, who was quick-witted and smooth, Rell was comically slow both in speech and, by all appearances, in thought. Either that or he was playing them. It was, after all, wise of him to offer little. Conducting the interview were Neptune and FBI agent Mark James. Both had listened to Rell's phone calls for months. The way he talked was so distinctive—his voice rarely rising above a mumble, punctuated always with his lazy little laugh—that it amused them. He had a way of saying "Yeaa-aaah" that was so drawn out that the agents had adopted it as a bit. They would interject a long "Yeaa-aaah" in their own conversations and then crack up. So it was amusing to hear him do it in person. They could almost see the wheels turning slowly in his head before each response.

All Rell faced at that point was a gun charge, stemming from the search of his Harlem Avenue stash house in April. They knew he had been fully aware of the raid and what they had found, and that he had sent someone back to inspect the damage, because they had overheard him talking about it as it happened.

"Do you remember—I think it was April—thirteen hundred Harlem—we went into a house, into a vacant and recovered some weed and a gun?"

"Do I remember that?" asked Rell.

"Are you aware of that?"

"No."

"So you're not familiar with an incident where at thirteen hundred Harlem, we pull up in a black Impala, your boy Landsman was out there rooting around through the vacant?"

"No."

"You don't remember that *at all*? You weren't around, you didn't see us?"

"I don't even know what you talkin' about here," Rell said, with his little laugh. "Landsman was involved?"

"Definitely involved. Let's talk about another one."

"Another one?" Rell laughed again, so entertained that he bent over, chuckling quietly.

"What happened to your boy Thug?" asked Neptune.

"I don't know," said Rell, still chuckling.

"Do you know his real name?"

"Yeah. Anton, Anthony, I don't know. What the fuck?"

"Antonio."

Then came the long, low, drawn-out "Yeaa-aaah."

"Do you know his last name?"

"Uh-uh."

Neptune asked if he knew Thug's cousin, Man-Man, who had been arrested earlier.

"Yeaa-aaah."

"Where's Man-Man now?"

"I don't know," said Rell, laughing.

"What do you mean you don't know? Have you seen him?"

"No, I ain't seen him," laughing.

"What do you mean you 'ain't seen him'? Is he in jail?"

"I don't know."

"Do you remember when Thug got shot?"

"You say, do I remember when?"

"Yes."

"Uh-uh."

"You are aware that he's dead, right?"

"Yeah, I remember," laughing.

"When did you first find out he was dead?"

"Probably like, I don't know. I just remember when I saw the polices out, coming past. I don't know."

"Where were you at the time?"

"At the time? Down Harlem Avenue."

". . . Who were you with?"

"I was by myself."

"So this is the one time this entire summer when you're the only person on Harlem Avenue?"

"I'm always by myself."

On and on it went. Neptune pressed on.

"Have I seen you in that blue Honda before?"

This engendered a long discussion concerning whether or not Rell had ever been in the blue Honda he had been driving when he was arrested that day. Neptune tried to instruct him how to answer.

"Well, if you asked me, Detective Neptune, have I ever seen you in that blue car before? No. The answer is no. A hundred percent no because I've never been in that car. So, when I ask you, have I ever seen you in that car?"

"Yeah, I don't know if you saw me in the car, even if I been in it."

"So you've been in the car?"

"You *know* I've been in the car."

Rell didn't know anybody, hadn't spoken to anybody, or, if he had, he didn't know who they were. He didn't know where the $475 in his pocket came from.

"So, you just find money? You're the luckiest guy in West Baltimore?"

"Yeaa-aaah," he said, at which point the detectives could not help laughing, too.

Rell never stopped chuckling and grinning. His opacity was a game, denying knowing things they all knew he knew—indeed, that *he knew* they knew he knew. Neptune did get Rell to say that he had been living at his girlfriend's house, 2307 Avalon Avenue. This would prove useful.

Shortly before Rell's arrest, he had inadvertently given the task force a gift. Rah, wearing a wire and a camera, had met with him on a sunny late summer afternoon at one of his open-air drug locations. Rah asked Rell for advice about setting up his own retail drug shop, and Rell, in a departure from his usual mumblings, was full of detailed counsel, describing for the camera exactly how it was done.

He schooled Rah in how to cut the heroin.

"It's got to be quinine. . . . The quinine is in blocks. You just, three blocks you scrape and mix that."

Rell also mentioned using "benita," said to be a form of "baby laxative," which among other ingredients was used to concoct a highly unpredictable and dangerous heroin blend that on the streets was called "Scramble."

"If you buy five grams, you put it *on a three* [mix in three grams of quinine and benita], you gonna damn near triple your money," said Rell. He explained that earnings would depend on whether the adulterated product was sealed in a small gelcap or large one, called a "Double O."

"I make, like, seventeen hundred, Double O," said Rell.

"Off ten grams?"

"Yeah, putting it *on a three.*"

Rah asked what his minimum daily earnings were. Rell said they regularly sold $4,000 before noon and the same amount again in the afternoon and evening—$8,000 per day, *minimum.* Later, he told Rah that at one point he and Tana were pulling in $50,000 per week, moving about a half kilo every two weeks.

But danger always lurked. Rell repeatedly looked over his shoulder.

"If Landsman see me," said Rell, "he's never going to leave."

The rest of the TTG crew was scooped up one by one. Man-Man at a hospital, where he was being treated for a gunshot wound. He briefly escaped from the police transport van and led officers on a chase. He ducked into a vacant, where officers found him hiding in rubble beneath shattered sheets of drywall, coated with white dust. Marty, Timrod, and Binkie were all arrested at the usual drug corners without incident. A wiretap that caught Denmo talking to Ali (Brandon Wilson) about gathering weapons to retaliate against someone afforded the opportunity to arrest them and search their homes. The detectives arrested Denmo coming out of his fancy downtown apartment. Ali eluded them for a few days, but he was eventually found at his girlfriend's house, along with $12,000 worth of cocaine and a handgun, which would be shown to have been used in the murders of Magic (Christopher Pennington) and Dirt (Darius Perkins). The arrest of Tash (Taurus Tillman) came at a scheduled visit with his parole officer. The officer locked him in a back room until the task force arrived. Milk remained at large. Less involved in overt criminal activity, his arrest would await the RICO charges.

As Tana was being arrested, he had made fun of the officers for treating him like he was "John Dillinger." He was a fan of the 2009 film *Public Enemies*, which tells the story of the legendary criminal's 1933–34 bank-robbing and killing spree. It ended, as did Dillinger, in a hail of police bullets as he left a Chicago movie theater. Tana considered the show of force at Arundel Mills to be over-the-top, but as far as the feds and city police were concerned, the comparison was apt. Dillinger and his gang had killed ten people; Tana and his crew were suspected of killing twice as many, and their drug business earned far more money than Dillinger ever did robbing banks. To them, Tana's bust was a big deal, a huge success for the beleaguered department. Five days after he was cuffed, the city's police commissioner, Kevin Davis, held a press conference, flanked by the commanders of his homicide and investigation divisions. He gave only passing credit to the federal task force, which was still lying low, crediting the arrest primarily to his own men.

"Today we stand before you to announce the arrest of Baltimore's number one trigger puller, Montana Malik Barronette," he said, spelling the last name for reporters. "[He] has been Baltimore's number one trigger puller for some time now. He was arrested over the weekend and charged with first-degree murder, handgun violations, and other related charges. Barronette is an absolute poster child for what a repeat offender is in Baltimore City. We are certain he has been involved in numerous acts of violence, to include multiple shootings and multiple murders."

He described the immediate charge, the killing of Alfonzo Williams, and linked Tana with BGF, characterizing TTG as "a bubble within BGF," which was not true. Davis also said that Tana and his crew had "terrorized" Sandtown, which was.

"We aren't finished with Barronette," he said. "We are still following up on numerous, numerous cases that we believe Barronette is responsible for. Remember his name. You'll hear it again very soon. Baltimore citizens today are safer with Barronette off the streets."

The commissioner noted that citizens had come forward to identify him as Williams's killer, and urged others, "who might have been afraid, absolutely petrified in fact, knowing that Barronette was still on the streets," to come forward now. "He's off the streets, and he's not coming back." He gave contact information.

Sean Miller, chief of the city's investigation division, said that Tana was responsible for "more than a dozen" killings and shootings and robberies, "minimally," and had long topped the list of the most dangerous criminals in the city.

"He's a bad, bad, evil guy," said Miller, "and he's no longer on the streets of Baltimore, and it took a lot of detectives a lot of work, a lot of consultation with prosecutors, state and federal, to get to this point today. . . . Barronette is very good at his craft, and his craft is killing."

Davis added that it took a determined probe, "into every aspect of his life, the lives of his associates, their habits, where they frequent, and we had to pull it all together to make a case. . . . It's a very strong case." Alluding to the pending RICO charges: "We're confident that we will be standing before you in the very near future to talk again about Montana Barronette."

A reporter asked how many other killers in the city compared with him.

"Unfortunately, he doesn't stand alone," said Miller, "but there is only one Montana Barronette in the city, and he's now locked up. He has differentiated himself because of the number of murders and non-fatal shootings that we believe he's been involved in."

To an entirely different audience, the press conference did something Davis did not intend. Labeling Tana Baltimore's "number one trigger puller" effectively enshrined him, for all time, in the Ghetto Star Hall of Fame.

10

Gotta Take It on the Chin

Montana Barronette's 2016 mug shot.

The mind is its own place, and in itself
Can make a Heav'n of Hell, a Hell of Heav'n.
　　　　　　　—Satan, in John Milton's *Paradise Lost*

Tana was still nonchalant early Saturday morning, hours after his arrest. He had been taken to a homicide squad interview room up in the gray-stone police headquarters at the east edge of downtown. He had been there before, or in a room just like it, a bare space with blank white walls furnished with a table that had a single metal chair on one side for the interviewee and two chairs for the questioners, both of mustard-colored plastic, one directly opposite and another to the side. This was not how Tana had expected to be ending his night, but he was still smiling. Relaxed. Congenial. He bantered happily with Neptune before the session began, reminiscing like old friends about a cop they had both known.

"White guy; he got a funny name, started with an E or an F," said Tana. "It was a dumb-ass name," laughing. "Shit. He was aw-right."

"When was the last time you saw him out there?" asked Neptune.

"When Brandon Littlejohn was around."

". . . They change lieutenants around here so often," said Neptune. "He didn't get you out there."

"He didn't get Brandon Littlejohn either."

"*Someone* got Brandon Littlejohn."

Tana chuckled. "They did, didn't they?"

Neptune made a show of placing on the table the contents of Tana's pockets, including a thick roll of bills, almost $1,000.

"I don't want any questions about where your money went," he said. "You don't have any weed on you?"

"Hell, no," said Tana. "I don't even smoke."

After sitting quietly for a few minutes, waiting, Tana said, "It's cold in this fucking room. I'm shaking like a motherfucker."

No one offered him a sweater. For Tana, so far, this would all have seemed familiar and predictable. He had no reason to dread this interview. Cops had been circling him for months; they were bound to haul him in at some point. He and his crew had been careful. Guns were shared, so no one of them could be directly linked to a shooting. Potential witnesses were cowed. Phones were regularly ditched. None of his crew would snitch. They were tight. The cops would lean on him, try to make him think they knew more than they did, that they had him nailed, but if past experience was a guide, they would either be bluffing or exaggerating. The correct response would be to remain calm, chat with them but give them nothing. He had every reason to assume he'd be free again in no time.

For Neptune and Landsman, the moment was huge, one they had been working toward for well over a year—and for Landsman, far longer. After watching and listening all that time to the coded phone conversations, and having only glib little exchanges with Tana now and then on the sidewalk, here was their chance to talk seriously and to level with him. Let him know what he was really up against and gauge his response. They were deeply curious about him. Who did he think he was? How did he see himself? How did he *feel*? Or, perhaps, a better way of putting it: *What could he have been thinking?* Nearly twenty murders, and those were just the ones they knew of. Clearly, he was smart. Did he feel any remorse about all the lives taken? All those healthy young Black bodies lifeless on slabs in the morgue, lives ended in mid-stride? Did he have a social conscience? Did he fear for his own future? The death penalty? A long empty life behind bars? Any one of these was a potential crack they could pry open, upend his cocky equanimity. If he opened up, Tana could wrap up their whole case and, possibly, help himself, although it was hard to imagine how at this point. No matter what he said, he was definitely going away for a long time. But he was very young. A deal might win him years of freedom in his old age, like the old Baltimore kingpin Peanut King, out there trying to talk kids out of following his example. Landsman, in particular, felt this was his first and likely last shot at getting Tana to admit some of what he had done, perhaps even to explain. All these years the detective had been at war with these gangs, and he still didn't understand them. He wanted a glimpse of how Tana actually saw himself.

Tana had not asked for a lawyer yet. Once he did, that would be it. So they would push for some flicker of conscience or remorse, see if they could elicit either. Then they would try fear—surprise and confront him with his new, harsh reality and see if that would shatter his poise. He could not know what was in store for him. They'd make it clear to him that this arrest was not just about the state murder charge, which, while serious enough, was more like a pretext. The RICO case would fall on him like a mountain. Here, at age twenty-one, he had likely ended his life as a free man.

When Landsman arrived, he was all business. He entered the room brusquely, bearded, wearing a rumpled orange T-shirt, and sat across the table from Tana, bending to fill out a form, pen in hand. Landsman asked Tana to spell his name, as if he didn't know. Tana skipped right to the tricky part of the spelling: "R-R-O-N-E-T-T-E."

Landsman read him his rights, and Tana obligingly initialed the form next to each warning and then signed the sheet to waive his right to an attorney. He was not concerned at all. He filled out another form, jokingly complaining to Landsman, "Now I'm doing your job."

"I've got carpal tunnel," said Landsman.

They were like a trio of longtime pals, reunited, working together. When they finished with the forms, Landsman asked Tana if he wanted a sandwich.

"I don't need no break," said Tana.

But they left him for ten minutes. He placed his head on the table and tried to doze. They brought him fast food and a drink in a big plastic cup and left. Tana ate, then put the wrappers and napkins neatly in the bag, stretched, belched, and, to the empty room, said, "Excuse me."

Before Landsman and Neptune could start, there was the matter of the Alfonzo Williams killing. In came Josh Fuller and senior homicide detective Gordon Carew. Tana's mood altered. The easy camaraderie vanished.

"Montana, man, how you doin'?" said Fuller, sitting across from him. Carew sat off to one side, for the time being just observing.

Tana grew quiet, mumbling and whispering his answers, distinctly unhelpful.

"You still seeing the girl that you were seeing, the one who went to City Harbor?"

Tana grunted negatively, "Uh-uh."

"Who you seeing now, what's her name?"

"Too many of 'em; I forget."

"How about that one who was with you tonight?"

"I didn't get her name. I just took her out."

Tana said he didn't remember the conversation he'd had with Fuller two years ago, when he said he'd spent the night of the murder with a girl at an Inner Harbor hotel.

"It wasn't that long ago. How many times you been up here?"

"Twice."

"You would think it might stick in your head a little bit."

"Uh-uh."

Tana said he did not know his own telephone number.

"How do people call you?" Fuller asked.

"I don't know." He said he didn't talk on phones.

"You know you had two phones with you when they picked you up?"

"I don't know the numbers."

Nor did he know his social security number.

"Do you remember my name?"

Tana said no.

"Fuller. . . . We were talking about the guy who got shot down on Lafayette Street, right? You told us about your day. You remember a little more now? You were with that girl up in City Harbor for her birthday or something? Don't remember any of that?"

"Uh-uh."

"Well, we got your phone. I know you remember I had your phone because you asked me about it every time I saw you in the neighborhood for like a year."

Fuller told him that his old alibi hadn't checked out. Hotel records and cameras gave no sign that he had been there. And on Tana's seized phone was the video he had made of himself, rapping about selling drugs and killing.

". . . Saw some of your artistic work on there. You didn't tell me you rap, man, when you were in here."

Tana smiled. "I don't," he said.

"No? You do a little bit."

"Nah. Must have been somethin' else. I was just talking shit."

Fuller acted startled. "It was some—what's a good word?—*accurate* shit. Some accurate shit. Make a video the day after the murder talking about coming out of an alley and bustin' somebody with the same kind of gun that was used in the case. It don't look good, you know what I mean?"

"Don't know nothin'."

Fuller pointed out that there had been "some turnover" in Tana's group recently, which gave them the opportunity to move forward on some things they had been "sitting on."

"So here's the deal. You are here under arrest for the murder of Alfonzo Williams. OK?"

"Who that?"

"The guy on Lafayette. . . . And I don't believe you don't remember our conversation from the first time. It's not every day that you come down here to homicide. . . . I'd like to talk a little more about what happened that day."

Tana said he no longer remembered.

"I don't believe that."

"It was too far long ago."

"It may be, and it may be a little while back. If it was another day—you know what I mean?—I may believe you. The fact of the matter is, we know the killer. We've known it since twenty fourteen. We've had you identified since twenty fourteen. We just needed a little more to move ahead."

Fuller said that the way they had put the story together "makes you look like a really shitty dude. It doesn't look good."

Tana started to comment.

"Hold on. Hold on for a minute. It doesn't look good. OK? It looks like it was over some real bullshit."

Tana smiled, arms folded, head rolled back, and started to answer. Then Carew interrupted. He had heard enough. He leaned in to say that they were not going to review the entire case with him, that they had enough already to convict him.

"What we need from you, if you wanted to help yourself in this situation, is you tell us what happened, tell us the truth."

Tana started to object, but Carew cut him off.

"Hear me out, because you're in a different position than you've been in before. We don't need anything from you. You are under arrest for the murder."

Tana grinned at him.

"That's not a joke. You've been up to a lot of stuff in a short amount of time, and they [the task force] looked at everything that you've done, and you're a high-priority target along with some other people, because they're going after the violent crime thing. This is gonna be the end of the road for you. They're starting off with this murder here, and things are going to get progressively worse unless you do something that's gonna help yourself. Part of it is cooperating now."

Tana sat with his arms folded, listening intently as Carew explained that Landsman and Neptune had their own cases. They were looking at "special prosecution, enhanced penalties, all that stuff," he said. "The idea is to take everything they can prove, throw it at you, and throw you into jail forever. And this is just the first phase. You've had a good run up until this point, but now all that comes to an end."

Carew said that because Tana had "been in this mix," he could help them clear up a lot of the crime in his neighborhood. "And that might go in your favor. But once the ball gets rolling, both state and the feds are looking at this kind of stuff. Ever since the riots, all the trouble, the feds are in here, they are working with the police department, feds are keeping an eye on the police department. . . . Everybody is interested in this. It's a serious thing. You are at the forefront, and you are looking at a whole lot of crap. And you've got one chance to talk about something now that might help you out."

Tana just smiled.

"I know you're smiling with this, and you're probably not going to buy off on this," the detective continued. "They've got a number of cases on you, not just one, and at the end of it you may never see the light of day in your adult life. You've got one chance, maybe. If you start here by telling us the truth, it might work out differently a little bit along the way. You probably don't believe me, because you've been down here and let go and all that stuff, but that's not what's happening here. . . . It ain't gonna work like you think it is."

"I ain't worried about that," said Tana. "Charge me and send me down." Grinning.

"Did you hear what I said?" asked Carew.

"Come on. I heard what you said."

Tana leaned back in the chair, chuckling. They were boring him.

"All right," said Carew. "I had to give you that opportunity. Just remember that we did." If at any point going forward Tana had a change of heart, "You can reach out through your attorney and contact us if you want to talk about the murder."

"I ain't reaching out," said Tana. "But thank you for the offer."

He was left alone in the room again for more than twenty minutes, yawning, placing his head on the table, trying to sleep. It was now the wee hours of Saturday. He picked up the money roll and pretended to take basketball shots with it, tossing it up high and catching it. Coming in with Landsman, Neptune greeted him at last.

"What's up, man? Did you get a chance to eat?"

"Yeah. That shit fucked up my stomach."

Landsman took the chair across from him. Neptune sat to one side.

"So, they explained why you're under arrest?" asked Neptune.

"Yeah."

"What did they say?"

"A homicide. Lafayette Street."

"How long ago?"

"A couple years back."

Landsman asked him what he thought about it.

"Some bullshit."

Landsman went a different way. He was less interested in any individual case than in loosening Tana up, getting him to talk—and think—more broadly. So he asked him about Sandtown. The detective sat with both arms on the table, looking down, not making eye contact.

"What do you think about out there?"

"What do I think about?"

"That whole area."

"Pretty OK to me."

Landsman lifted his head to meet Tana's eyes. They stared at each other.

"Everything's going great?" the detective finally asked, breaking the silence, and they all laughed.

"You love it out there?" asked Neptune.

"No, I don't love it."

"So, what, in your mind, is the best situation you could be in right now?" Landsman asked. "Is being out there the best situation?"

"I don't know."

Landsman asked him about his childhood. Giving short answers, Tana said he'd grown up with his grandma. He'd graduated from

Edmondson-Westside High. He was planning to begin school to become a tractor-trailer driver next month.

"Look, man, so, how old are you now?" Landsman asked.

"Twenty-one."

"So, you were like eight when I started out there. . . . So she [his grandmother] treated you good and got you all the way through school?"

"Right."

"If you had the opportunity to get out of that area, would you have got out?"

"Hell, yeah."

". . . What stopped you?"

"What stopped me?"

"Yeah. You don't have the type of arrest record that other people have. . . . Why didn't you do it?"

"Why *didn't* I?"

". . . Why did you need to be around that area? Do you think that area has a lot of stuff going on?"

"Not that I know of. Little bit of weed gets sold. That's about it."

"I'm talking about people getting killed that shouldn't," said Landsman.

"Nobody gettin' killed in the area."

Neptune laughed and then said, "Not that it's funny." The statement was, of course, ridiculous. The detectives itemized for him the shootings that had occurred only recently in just a small corner of Sandtown.

"Would you consider that bad?"

Tana smiled. "I don't know," he said.

"What do you mean, you don't know?" asked Neptune.

Tana rolled his head, stretching his neck. He had been sitting for more than an hour. Then he smiled. He was not going to concede the ongoing atrocity of his world. Landsman was now curled back in his chair, one arm draped over his head. He looked tormented. He was searching for some way to break through Tana's bland shell.

"What we're doing here is, we're trying to look into a lot of these murders. Do you get that impression?" Neptune asked.

Tana chuckled. "Yeah," he said, still smiling.

"Why? What makes you think that we are looking into a bunch of murders?"

"'Cause everybody got questioned, and then y'all asking them questions about me."

"Name five people," said Neptune.

"Name five people? Come on, man. I cannot reveal my informants."

All three laughed.

Tana said they had questioned just about everybody in the Western District about him.

"What makes you think that we are coming to the conclusion that you might have something to do with this stuff?" asked Neptune. "People just don't like you?"

"Nah. It's all he-said, she-said. Covering their asses. . . . It's easy. Once your name get out there in one case, people keep throwing you under the bus. It's all right. Put it all on me. I'm cool with it."

"You just happen to be at the center, it's all revolving around you," said Neptune.

"So, why would anybody want to bring your name up?" asked Landsman. "You've been around there your whole life. Everybody loves you. You love it out there. Why the hell would anybody want to put a murder on you?"

"I don't know." He suggested that every time someone was murdered, the cops would ask witnesses if Montana Barronette had done it, planting the idea, giving him a false reputation.

"We don't work like that," said Neptune.

"No?" Tana asked, then smiled broadly, shrugged, and said, "Hell, then, I don't know." He laughed.

The killings he had witnessed, he said, had shocked him. He said he had learned about his friend Tev (Tevin Haygood) being killed while he was vacationing in Miami. He denied being unduly upset by it. "Dumb nigga there, ain't supposed to be out there gambling at six o'clock in the morning."

The detectives knew this was not true. Tana had been murderously angry about Tev's killing. In a car with their source Rah (Ronnie Johnson), he had said, "I'm looking for this guy Dirt," who he believed had shot the youth. He told Rah he was going to kill him. Rah texted the agents from the car, "Tana wants to kill this guy."

"You can't be there," the agents texted back.

Tana did not find him that night, but Dirt (Darius Perkins) was shot dead weeks later. Now, questioned about Tev's death, Tana was the picture of unconcern. He didn't know who had killed him. He wasn't all that interested. Landsman was now leaning forward, elbows on the table, his head in his hands.

"You know Beezy?" he asked. Brian Chase had been killed January 4, 2015. This was a murder they believed Tana had done personally.

"No," said Tana, then corrected himself. "Oh, yeah, I knew Beezy."

"What happened to him?"

"I don't know, they say they found his ass in a yard in dog shit!" Tana said, cackling.

"Who found him?"

"My little man Mouse. . . . Devin. He said, 'Dead person in dog shit in my yard.'"

He said he had been nearby, on Calhoun Street, when it happened, but did not hear gunshots. He saw police cars coming and spoke to Devin, whose comment had cracked him up.

"You started laughing?" asked Neptune.

"Yeah, it was the way he said it."

Landsman asked if he had been upset when he found out it was Beezy.

"No."

"Why not?"

"'Cause I hardly knew him."

The detectives then filled the table before him with twelve large photos of victims. Neptune asked him to remove his elbows from the table to make room.

"You've been busy?" the detective said.

"With what?" Tana asked, smiling.

More laughter all around. It was strange. The truth hung heavily in the air, yet the mood was light. Tana knew he had been shooting people, and the detectives knew it, too, but he wasn't going to admit it and he believed they weren't going to be able to prove it. He was not going to help them.

Landsman had hoped that the photos might produce some emotional response, but all Tana showed was curiosity. The detectives were silent as he scanned them. He admitted to knowing eight of the faces, pointing at one, "I went to school with him," and another, "played football with him in Harlem [Square Park]," and another, "my old substitute teacher's son." Tana looked up blankly. He then gestured, rolling his hands, as if to say, *Come on, already, ask me your questions.* So the detectives reviewed them one by one. Tana had nothing helpful to say about any. Yes, he had often been nearby when they were killed. In each case he was "shocked." He used that word several times, but he did not appear to have been moved by the deaths, neither sad nor alarmed. It was just the way things were. Landsman and Neptune were confronting here the steely nihilism of Sandtown itself. Sudden violent death was a reality Tana had absorbed from childhood. When Neptune said that all these men

had been "gunned down," Tana objected. Tana had words for different kinds of murder. Some of the victims had been "gunned down,"
he said, while others had been "shot." The detectives were confused.
What was the difference?

"You get shot, you just get shot," he explained. In some cases, you
later died. "If you get gunned down, like, you never had a chance." You
dropped dead on the spot.

"To me they're the same thing," said Neptune.

"Probably the same thing, but . . . I'm just sayin'."

They pointed to the picture of Dirt.

"Man, he just got killed the other day," said Tana. He said he had
been nearby when it happened and ran around the corner when he
heard the shots. He saw Dirt on the ground in his death throes. He
imitated the grunts he had made.

"Did you care?" asked Neptune.

"Hell, yeah. He had two sons."

"Were you sad?" asked Landsman. "Don't you think his family
deserves closure?"

"What do you mean?"

"Like, deserves to know who did it? And those people need to be
held accountable?"

"I think everybody's family needs to know that."

"So, whoever killed him, when they get caught, and they go to
court and get convicted, what should their punishment be?"

"I don't know about that."

"Well, you're upset about it, right? I'm asking you. What should
the punishment be?"

"I don't know."

Neptune said that if someone killed one of his friends, he would
want them to receive the death penalty.

"I ain't wishin' death on nobody," said Tana.

Neptune laughed. Tana grinned.

"You're funny, man," Neptune said.

Tana leaned back, stretched his arms high, and then laughed, too.

"Is there anything else that you would like to add about any of these murders that may help with the investigation?" Landsman asked.

"Nah."

They were at an impasse. It had been almost two hours. Landsman pulled all the pictures off the table and put them into a neat stack. He had hoped they might jar Tana a little, but their questions and implied accusations rolled off Tana like water off a waxed windshield. He didn't remember. He didn't know. He wouldn't even say where he had been living—he'd been sleeping with different "females." Didn't know their names. He had a key in his pocket; he wasn't sure what it opened. It was clear they were wasting their time.

It was time to try fear.

"Our job, we work for the city," Neptune said, leaning in. "We look at cases with the same suspect, and we go straight to federal prosecutors. That's our job. What we do is, we present these cases to federal prosecutors about what they consider serial killers. If you are a serial killer in the federal system, you are probably looking at the death penalty, minimum, life. All right? You are a young guy. You are only twenty-one. All right? It's your absolute right to not self-incriminate. All right? That's cool. We're gonna meet again. We're gonna have another conversation. But it's not going to be here. It's not going to be in state court. We're going to have a conversation when you are brought in in a maroon outfit. All right? It's going to be on the fifth floor of the federal building. At that point you are going to be charged with probably four to five murders at least. And that's going to be your chance to help yourself to one day not look at the world through bars. If you do not, you're gonna die in prison."

"Gotta take it on the chin," said Tana.

"Don't take it on the chin," interjected Landsman. "Why you gonna take it on the chin?"

Landsman could not comprehend Tana's attitude. He would wonder for years about whether he had come close to cracking his shell that morning, or if he might have succeeded with some different strategy. But it's unlikely. Tana had set his path years earlier. He neither looked nor acted like a man facing a dilemma. He was clearly smarter than the others in his crew. He was more disciplined. He had the personal charm and poise that make success more likely in any pursuit, and, as Landsman pointed out, he'd even had more chances than most to go down a different road. He wasn't just a victim of circumstance, although his circumstances had certainly steered him in a bad direction. He had chosen to be who he was. He had made that choice fully understanding the consequences. Now, if the reckoning had come—and he was by no means convinced that it had—he was ready. But first, these cops would have to prove it.

Neptune said their case was solid. They didn't arrest people "on a hunch," he said. They had witnesses. Unlike in state cases, they could provide protection for them. They had many.

Tana said, "If they can look at me and say, 'that's who shot that guy,' they'd be lyin'."

Neptune suggested that some of his buddies were not going to accept their fate as stoically as him.

"They're not going to take it on the chin." He said they were going to raise their hands—he raised his hand—"and they are going to tell us everything."

"I know that," said Tana, suddenly serious. "I've seen it every day."

"I wish you would take this opportunity before it gets to that point," said Landsman, "and confess to your involvement and help us to understand why this stuff occurred." He mentioned that the gun discovered in the snow after his crackup in the blizzard had been linked to one of the murders.

Tana now leaned back and said to himself, softly, "Oh, fuck."

"Come on, man," he said to Landsman.

"I know. It all comes home."

Tana was no longer smiling. He sat quietly, his head tilted to one side, listening intently. Here was Landsman's opening, a crack in the shell. He leaned in.

"Look, this is your opportunity. I've been here a long time. I went through your background. You don't have this type of history. You know? You had those opportunities to get out. You could have. And this is your opportunity again. . . . People get breaks. You know? But you need to help us understand why this stuff occurred. This stuff's hard. You know what? I can feel where you're coming from. Eleven-eleven Harlem Avenue. I'm sure your grandmother worked hard, got you through school. That environment is responsible for this, you know? It's not necessarily you. And you can have your opportunity, help people to understand."

He stared at Tana intently. After a moment, Tana just lifted both of his hands, palms toward the ceiling, and raised them, saying softly, "Ain't nothin' I can do."

"I swear, *there is* something you can do," said Landsman.

"What's the longest you ever did in jail?" asked Neptune. "A night?"

"No, not even that," said Tana.

"You're not going to like it."

"I'll adapt."

"You're not going to adapt."

"Look, man, no matter which way you put it to me, I don't know nothin' about these," he said, tapping the pile of photos. "And there ain't nothin' I can help y'all with. No matter the outcome. . . . What you put on me, if I'm found guilty, OK, fuck it."

"Why you want to be like that?" asked Landsman. "Look, you have an opportunity. I mean, Baltimore is a tough place. You have a lot of violence. But look, this is a different situation. People need to have the opportunity to explain and help understand, you know? And then you've got that opportunity where that's, like, giving a lesson. . . . Don't let yourself . . . I've heard that before. I've heard that before. People say 'fuck it,' but you should not say that. You have an opportunity. I mean—"

Now Tana was smiling again. He pointed at Landsman.

"You good."

"No, trust me. Listen to me. I swear to God, I dealt with some situations. . . . There was a guy just sentenced yesterday. Two life sentences. And he said exactly what you said. He's about twenty-five, twenty-six years old. And we wish he could have had the opportunity that you have. There are people like him who aren't getting those two life sentences. Because it's tough to understand on the outside looking in, everybody saying, 'This is fucked up, all these people died,' but it's a tough situation. That's why I've asked you. You grew up in that area. Did you want out? Fuck yeah, you wanted out, right? You went to school. You wanted out, but the environment fucked you over. . . . I swear to God. I see it every day."

"You see it," said Tana, agreeing.

Landsman listed cases from the neighborhood, Tana nodding with recognition, of people serving long prison sentences.

"You're a young man," Landsman insisted. "You don't have to do this." He leaned in over the table and whispered, "I swear, man, I wish you would just tell us. It's hard for me, man, to look at you. You're twenty-one years old. I swear to God."

Tana slowly smiled.

"Man, you belong in Hollywood," he said, grinning.

Landsman lay his head on the table.

"You ought to be an *actor.*" Tana was laughing. He said he would see them in court. "And I'll take it on the chin then. I don't have nothin' to say. If you say I did it, so be it. Got to go to trial."

"I don't want you to, man," said Landsman, lifting his head.

"I'm already facing life," said Tana. "I ain't gonna worry about it. Fuck it! . . . I just gonna go in and work out."

"Don't do it, man," said Landsman, head on the table again. Tana looked down at him, grinning. The detective was emotionally exhausted. He had given it his best shot. He tried to gather himself. He had never been so invested in an interrogation, had never felt so utterly defeated. He believed this had been the only opportunity both for him and for Tana—for him, to break through the young man's cunning reserve and gain some insight; for Tana, to possibly escape a lifetime behind bars. He told his brother later that instead of breaking Tana down, he broke *himself* down. He lost sleep over it.

The interview wasn't over. Neptune asked Tana where, in his twenty-one years, he had been.

"Been to Miami. Been to Cancun. Been to Jamaica. Been to Cali. Been to Orleans." He looked back at Landsman, his head still down. "You talking like I'm Dillinger." Then he mimicked the voice of Johnny Depp in the starring role, drawling nasally, "It's OK, doll."

"Is that what he said?" asked Landsman.

"Nah, it's in the movie. They shot his ass."

"Did that actually happen?"

"What?"

"John Dillinger was killing people, and then he got locked up after going to the movies?" asked Landsman.

"No, he was robbing banks," said Tana.

"He was killing people when he was doing it, too," said Neptune.

"Yeah . . . but me, I'm not a murderer."

"I think you were a murderer," said Neptune. "At some point, you flipped a switch, man. A lot of us honestly think you're a psychopath."

"For real?"

"Yeah. One hundred percent, man. I don't mean to insult you, but."

Tana picked up the photos again, leafing through them one by one, pretending to be a witness, "'I saw Montana Barronette do this.' 'I saw Montana Barronette do that.' They *lyin'*. 'I saw him come out the alley.' They *always* lyin'. I wasn't even in the area." He began tossing the pictures around the table. "I don't know him. I don't know him." He stopped at one and tapped his finger on it. He asked Landsman, "They really say I did him?"

"It's funny you should ask about that one, because there were three people in that. Were you in that alley?"

"No."

Tana asked about another. "What did he do?"

"He got killed," answered Neptune.

"How did he get killed?"

"He got shot down there at Baltimore and Gilmor," said Neptune. "You rolled up in a minivan, masked up, and jumped out."

"How many people was involved?"

"You and Binkie."

Tana laughed loudly and clapped his hands.

"That's good," he said.

He gathered up the sheets and made a neat pile of them and set them down on the table.

"Fuck that," he said. He said he was ready to "go and get some sleep."

"What?" said Neptune.

"You heard me. You're gonna find me guilty for this shit? I don't think you are gonna find me guilty for none of them," he said, once more flipping through the photos. "Unless somebody right there, and you got them by the balls, and they're gonna say, 'I saw him.'"

". . . So you say you've never taken money to kill someone?" Landsman asked.

"No! Not enough money in the world to get me to kill someone. . . . If you had given me that money, I'd have run off with it. I'd have pulled right off and spent it."

Neptune mentioned the rap videos about killing people.

"Man, rappin's about tellin' people what they want to hear," said Tana. "Rappin' about that. . . . You gonna make that stick? Get out of here!" Later he would add that rappers, no doubt thinking of YGG Tay, were "a bunch of phony-assed fools."

He complained again about the sandwich. He was tired. Why had they picked him up late at night? "You couldn't come arrest me in the morning on the corner?"

"Come on, man," he pleaded. "I'm a stand-up guy. If you got me, you got me."

"If we got you, would you say we got you?" asked Neptune.

"Fuck yeah! I'd say, get me a lawyer. . . . I've got to take everything to trial," Tana said, "Because I want a person to sit right there," pointing with Landsman's pencil, "and say, 'I saw him.'"

"There are going to be, like, three people willing to go up there and say that," said Neptune, "because it's going to be in the federal courthouse in front of jurors from, like, Wicomico County."

Tana stopped listening to Neptune and spoke over him, looking at Landsman. He said he could see what their strategy would be in court. They would say he committed eight murders, and then the jury would say, *We can't convict him of eight, so we'll just get him on two.* "That's not fair," he said.

Landsman didn't answer.

"Why don't you just charge all of them with the state?" he asked.

"Charge them all with the state?" asked Landsman.

"Yeah, just drop them on me right now. Get it over with."

"Because then you'll have a chance to win," said Neptune.

"Yeah. You want to cop out."

"I want to win."

"You want to cop out."

Having asserted moral superiority, Tana again relaxed. He was cocky. He boasted that in all the years they had been watching and following him, "Y'all ain't never known where I'm at." He told Landsman that he had spotted him one day and had followed him. He described the van Landsman had been in.

"You've got a good memory," said Landsman, and they started reminiscing again like old friends remembering their cat-and-mouse games.

Neptune came back to how little Tana was going to like being locked up.

"I ain't worried about that," he answered. He said that if they convicted him for a murder, "then the real murderer is going to go free."

Neptune mocked him. "You're not like the Jesus Christ of murderers, bearing the burden of other murderers on your shoulders." Then he added that he hoped they'd get a chance to talk again.

"Hell, no," said Tana. "Ain't no talkin'."

Neptune persisted, suggesting the Tana might consider making a deal to avoid a life sentence.

"Look, it ain't in my blood. It ain't gonna be in my blood. This is how I am."

"What if they put you in a cell with, like, Mike Tyson, and he just beats the shit out of you every day?"

Tana said nothing; he just looked at him, making a hard, menacing face, as if to say, *Let him try.*

Tana urged them to leave him alone, lock him up, let him get some sleep.

"I'm just tryin' to get it over with," he said. "Plead guilty, plead not guilty. Get it over with."

"So you want to get sent down," said Landsman, giving up. He stood up. "They're gonna want to take photos. They take four."

"I can pose," said Tana.

The detectives would never get a chance to interview Tana again, and as bad as the picture they painted for him was, he still had moves to make.

11

Drinking from
a Fire Hose

Mark Neptune, left, and Dan DeLorenzo, right.

Real niggas go to the feds no less than ten
Then start over get in the mix and do it again.
                              —YGG Tay, "August 13th (Intro)"

I t would be more than two years before TTG stood trial. Preparing
for it was a mammoth undertaking. Ten gang members and associates were indicted: Tana, Rell, Binkie (John Harrison), Milk (Roger
Taylor, who wasn't charged until 2017 and who would flee the country immediately), Tash (Taurus Tillman), Denmo (Dennis Pulley),
Man-Man (Brandon Bazemore), Marty (Linton Broughton), Timrod
(Timothy Floyd), and Ali (Brandon Wilson). Only two would plead
guilty, Bazemore and, eventually, Milk (in 2020, after he was appre-
hended in the Dominican Republic). The other eight would stand
trial for ten murders atop a sweeping drug case. The crimes alleged
spanned eight years.

To prepare, audio- and video-surveillance evidence had to be culled from hundreds of hours of recordings, and dozens of witnesses had to be readied. There was so much raw material to sort that Dan Gardner, one of the federal prosecutors who would take the case to trial, likened the task to "drinking from a fire hose." All of it had to be crafted into a narrative coherent enough for jurors to follow.

Gardner and fellow prosecutor Chris Romano would establish first, beyond all doubt, that TTG was a drug-dealing criminal enterprise. While the truth of this was obvious to all, assembling the evidence had taken long months of plodding labor. Neptune, DeLorenzo, and Landsman tackled the mass of audio and video surveillance, combing through it for only the most useful snippets—Gardner asked them to select only "home runs." That alone took months. Presenting the case in court would take many days of testimony. Only then, having proved the RICO statute's criminal conspiracy context, would they tackle their real goal, the murders.

These would be presented one by one. Fewer than half of the victims linked to the gang would be proffered—Bub (Brandon Littlejohn), Nut (Jamie Hilton-Bey), Beezy (Brian Chase), Shotgun (Dominique Harris), Markee Brown, Marquez Jones, Thug (Antonio Addison), and the three gunned down together in July 2015: Lamont Randall, Gerald Thompson, and Jacqueline Parker. These were the murders for which there was hard evidence, such as the eyewitness testimony of Fat Guy (Guy Coffey) or a ballistics match. Because the killings had to be directly related to the drug enterprise, Alfonzo Williams, the big barber gunned down after challenging Tana in public, was left out.

Murders were the heaviest lift. A lot of evidence is typically collected at death scenes, bullet casings, bloody clothing, photos, even furniture, doors, and door frames if they had been struck by bullets. If the victim was killed in a car, that might mean taking parts of the vehicle, whole doors or seats. On-the-scene investigators scooped up everything because they didn't know what might prove important. It was the job of detectives and prosecutors to select which items would become evidence. One of the task force members, inexperienced with such matters, requested from city police *all* of the material gathered for the ten murders. Two full truckloads arrived in Windsor Mill. It took days to weed through and select what would be needed.

To press Binkie's guilt in the murder of Dominique Harris, the prosecutors wanted to introduce the eyewitness testimony of the unfortunate Markee Brown, who had been tracked down and killed two days after giving it. Even though they had not charged TTG with his murder, to allow his grand jury testimony they would have to convince the trial judge that the gang had killed him to silence him. All the witnesses they still had, for both the drug and murder phases, needed to be prepped for trial. Most notably, these were Fat Guy, Rah (Ronnie Johnson), and Pony Head (Jan Gray), whose accounts were extensive, firsthand, and convincing. To these they had added five other Sandtown street dealers, who had agreed to testify in hopes of lighter punishment for their own lesser crimes. All had to be thoroughly debriefed and girded for the onslaught of cross-examination, in which a parade of defense lawyers would take turns trying to rattle them, shake their stories, and shred their integrity and credibility. It took some schooling to withstand this kind of assault. Then there was all the expert testimony, from the city detectives who had worked the murders, ballistics experts, medical examiners, chemists, and so on. Even though these were experienced witnesses, their presentations had to be carefully shaped and rehearsed.

While all of this was happening in 2017, Gardner and Romano faced administrative hurdles within the Department of Justice. Before bringing a RICO case to court, it had to pass muster before the Organized Crime Unit, and the Capital Case Unit had to rule whether *USA v. Montana Barronette et al.*, with its ten murders, warranted the death penalty. Defense lawyers and prosecutors were summoned to

Washington for a hearing on this question, which was like a dress rehearsal for the trial itself. The Capital Case Unit decided against seeking the ultimate penalty.

Death would not be adjudicated in the courtroom, but it would still haunt the case.

Before the actual trial began in September 2018, there were two more tragic reminders of how much was at stake. The first would be a shocking and painful blow to Tana and Rell. The second would be a devastating setback for the prosecution.

And before these, an astonishing blunder.

Exactly 145 days after Commissioner Davis heralded the arrest of Baltimore's "number one trigger puller," assuring those who had been terrorized by him and his crew that Montana Barronette would never again walk the streets of Baltimore, the state of Maryland let him go.

He had been housed for those months at the Baltimore Central Booking and Intake Center, part of a sprawling prison complex just east of the elevated Jones Falls Expressway downtown. It sat on an urban acre of unsurpassed architectural ugliness that had grown up around the old Warden's House, a Dickens-era Gothic gray stone castle that was initially used to confine those captured after fleeing enslavement. The modern additions had all the architectural flair of filing cabinets. The center stored thousands of inmates at various stages of judicial custody, most of them Black—just as in the beginning. Inside the center, Tana lived in spare dorm-like conditions with other inmates awaiting trial. One by one his Sandtown crew members joined him, an ill-advised reunion behind bars. Keeping them together surely worked against the task force's hope of getting them to turn on each other. Only Bazemore (wisely) heeded legal advice to plead guilty, and none would testify against the others.

Tana's murder charge, for killing Alfonzo Williams, was superseded when the task force finally filed its RICO case in late December.

When it was dropped, he could no longer be legally held by Maryland. He was supposed to be transferred directly to federal custody, but that part of the directive got lost in the prison's gears. Tana was summoned to the booking center's release area on Saturday, January 14, 2017.

"You're good to go," the guard in the transit room told him.

"I'm going with the feds?" he asked.

"No, you're free to go."

Ever polite, Tana told her, "You shouldn't be releasing me."

Immune to any advice from an inmate, she processed the order, and the city's number one trigger puller walked free.

He didn't run. He went home. A man facing the rest of his life in prison, given such a miraculous reprieve, might be expected to bolt immediately and melt permanently into the distance. But either Tana never really believed the mountain would fall on him, or he assumed it would take the task force some time to notice his release, or he simply could not imagine—and this seems just as likely—a life for himself outside his neighborhood. Whatever the reason, Sandtown was where he went. He didn't even try to hide. He went to see his friend and former supplier Milk, who had not yet been charged. Milk took him shopping. Outfitted in a stylish black ensemble—a pullover sweater, skinny black jeans, and black boots with raised heels—Tana posed in dark shades for a photo Milk posted on his Instagram page. Everyone in their circle thought that he was locked up, so Tana held his long index finger before pursed lips, urging his followers to keep his freedom secret, even as it was posted for all to see. Milk wrote, "They Going To [Lock] Me up in STYLE," followed by two surprised smiley faces, "#TTGFAM," a cool smiley face wearing shades, and two "100" emojis—there were 144 likes. The reunited friends drove to New York to see a boxing match that evening, the much-hyped featherweight title fight between Gervonta "Tank" Davis, a Baltimore fighter, and José Pedraza at the Barclays Center in New York. Milk posted more pictures of Tana from there.

The task force, in fact, would probably not have noticed, but Fat Guy did. He called Neptune.

"Hey, your boy is out," he said.

"Who?"

"Montana."

"No, he's not," said the detective.

So Guy texted the detectives the pic of Tana and Milk at the fight.

"Are you fucking kidding me?" said Neptune.

Luck cuts both ways. Milk's car had an FBI tracker. At first Neptune feared that Tana would vanish in New York. Milk had friends and contacts there. It's what you would expect a fugitive to do, and when the tracker showed Milk's car returning to Baltimore, they assumed he was alone. But then it stopped at Tana's girlfriend's house in Owings Mills.

Neptune was home with his very pregnant wife, Amy. Her water had just broken. She was a nurse, and this was their third child, so they were not in a rush. Best to wait for contractions to begin before going to the hospital. Sometimes this took hours.

"Amy, we've got to go get this guy," he told her.

"Go ahead," she said. "Go get him."

He and Landsman arrived at the house an hour or so later. They knocked on the door, and the girlfriend answered, wearing a short robe. Upstairs they found Tana, naked and annoyed. He was hastily pulling on his new black boots.

"Damn, man!" he complained, "I didn't even get to do anything yet!"

He surrendered peaceably, with what Neptune would describe as "a stupid little smile on his face."

Tana was taken this time to a prison in DC, and later transferred to one in Warsaw, Virginia, to await trial.

He was there when his younger sister, Booda, Sahantana Williams, paid the ultimate price for her brothers' sins.

Industrious Booda had gone her own way. Her sister Shanika called her a workaholic. While Tana and Rell were making their reputations, and Shanika was home caring for her children, Booda had graduated from high school and was holding down two nursing-assistant jobs. Shunning the ready chance to supplement her pay by selling bags of weed, a family tradition, she instead earned extra money as a hairstylist, which she enjoyed. She would tell her friends, "Girl, let me bip you up!" She had just bought her first car and was about to start a third nursing job, when she accepted a call on April 13, 2018, from a man who said he wanted her to do his sister's hair.

She drove to the appointment in her new car and was shot dead as she stepped out of it. She was twenty-one. Both Shanika and the detectives assigned to the case believed she had been killed to avenge the death of James Blake, one of the homicides for which Tana and TTG were suspected. Blake was one of the two men who had plotted to kidnap Milk and had taken Scratch (Darius Singleton) in error. Both of the sisters, Shanika and Booda, had been warned by friends that they might become targets for revenge, especially after Tana's much-ballyhooed arrest. But what were they to do? Hide?

Booda had paid the threat no mind.

By far the most important prosecution witness was Fat Guy, who had toiled with the task force since Landsman had enlisted him in the summer of 2015. The case could not have been assembled without him. Fat Guy's undercover buys from Tana and the other defendants cemented the drug charges, and his timely production of the gang's ever-changing phone numbers had kept the wiretaps alive. Perhaps most important, he had been a steady source of information about the gang's day-to-day life and had provided a running, detailed backstory for the mayhem. Fat Guy had explained to the task force how TTG had found Markee Brown. Guy had gone before a grand jury in November 2016 to describe, as an eyewitness, the murders of Bub and Nut. He was the one who had alerted Neptune when Tana was let out of jail, and after Booda was killed, he had explained why and by whom. Fat Guy was also well liked. He was such a gregarious, funny, and cheerful man that even the prosecutors, known to take an especially dim view of criminals, had warmed to him.

His testimony in the two early killings was a slam dunk. Unlike Rah, who had jumped out of the van, Fat Guy had witnessed the killing of Nut, so close up he had been struck by one of the bullets. He had also seen the execution of Bub. His account of that killing to the grand jury went like this:

"What happened to Bub?"

"Bub got killed."

"Bub got killed. All right. And how do you know Bub got killed?"

"Because I was there."

"You were there? OK. Well, why don't you tell us about that? First off, who was the—who or how many people were responsible for killing Bub?"

"Rell and Tash," Coffey said.

"Rell and Tash?"

"Yes. . . . They shot him. Well, Tash shot him."

"Tash shot him?"

"Yes."

"And what was Rell's role in that?"

"Rell was trying to get to the joint [gun], but he didn't get time enough before Rell—I mean Tash—came out and shot him."

Fat Guy had told the same story to city police in 2011, right after the murder. He was Bub's friend. They had played dice together. He had also picked Tash out of a photo lineup as the killer. Bub had been murdered because he was suspected of cooperating with the police, which underlined the risk Fat Guy was running. His cooperation was a secret—the testimony was sealed in both cases—so he was understandably alarmed and scared when word leaked. This was several months before the trial.

He texted Neptune a picture of a letter from Tash's lawyer, Richard Bardos, circulating on social media. In the letter, Bardos named Fat Guy as the informant who had led the police to his client.

The letter, which Bardos had mailed to Tash in prison, had been photographed and uploaded. Word spread fast. Before he'd seen Fat Guy's text, Neptune heard from a DEA colleague that his prize informant had been outed, and a $20,000 reward had been offered by YGG Tay for his murder.

Neptune got Fat Guy off the street. He arranged for emergency funds to lodge him in a hotel and began efforts to have him placed in the federal Witness Security Program, which would have assigned him a new name and moved him out of town. Fat Guy's wife balked at first but finally agreed to go with him to Philadelphia, under their own names, where they had family.

But Fat Guy had always been a risk taker. Except for a brief period after the Bardos letter surfaced, he never fully shared the task force's concern. It is not easy to give up your way of life. During those months of preparing the TTG case, Fat Guy had not been obeying the rules. He had been selling drugs. The task force, if it knew, turned a blind eye. He assured Neptune that he would stay away from the drug corners and that he'd move just as soon as the relocation money came through. It's easy to understand why Fat Guy's lapses might have been tolerated; his help was invaluable. What was worse, Fat Guy peddling drugs on street corners, or allowing TTG to continue its reign of terror? He had been admonished, and had more than once agreed to stop, but they could not watch him all day every day. Despite his promises, he had set up a drug shop in South Baltimore, along Washington Boulevard and Sargeant Street, where he had assembled a young crew with no Sandtown connections. He felt safe. He considered himself a better judge of danger than his minders.

That's where things stood in mid-June when Neptune left with Amy on a cruise. They were out of touch until the ship returned to

New York, days later, at which point backlogged text messages began pinging his cell phone. Among them was a photo of Fat Guy, dead. The text that accompanied the photo, from a city homicide detective, asked, *Isn't this your guy Jeggings?*

Neptune was angry and sad. He was angry mostly at Fat Guy. He had been killed near his South Baltimore drug corner. There was even video of his killing, captured by a neighborhood camera. His familiar bulky figure is seen running from the corner and hiding behind a car until a shooter steps up behind him. Why did he go back? Fat Guy had made only one concession to the danger; he had stayed away from the corner until well after midnight. He had been killed in the very early morning hours of June 20.

His death wasn't just tragic, it was a severe setback for Gardner and Romano. It cut out the strongest part of the Nut and Bub cases. On the Nut charge, they still had Rah, but he had not witnessed the shooting. And without Fat Guy, they'd struggle to make the case against Tash on Bub's killing. Deliberately or not, Bardos's letter had effectively undercut the most serious charge against his client. The prosecutors were angry. With this and the murder of Markee Brown, they had lost two foundations of their narrative. It galled them that this gang of Sandtown youths could score two such strategic blows to a major US government prosecution.

In the days before the trial began, the prosecutors worked to convince US District Court judge Catherine Blake, who would preside over the trial, to admit Fat Guy's grand jury testimony into evidence, invoking a doctrine called "forfeiture by wrongdoing." They needed to show that he had been killed to prevent him from testifying. To do so they had to draw a clear line from Bardos's letter. The letter alone was circumstantial at best. Bardos argued that there was no proof that his client had even circulated the letter.

Prosecutor Chris Romano would scornfully counter that reasoning: "He wants the Court to believe essentially this: Someone went into Taurus Tillman's cell, went through all of Taurus Tillman's stuff, found a letter that discussed Brandon Littlejohn's murder, and just gratuitously decided to, A, steal the letter; B, try to black out Mr. Tillman's name; and, C, put that letter out on the street. But Mr. Tillman, he didn't have anything to do with it."

Neptune testified that $20,000 had been offered by YGG Tay for the hit, but this was based on a comment made by an informant on a wiretapped call, which amounted to hearsay. As for the rapper, he told a *Baltimore Sun* reporter that the story was false and denied any link to TTG, which had been featured and celebrated in his videos for years.

The sad fact was that Fat Guy had been dealing drugs on a Baltimore street corner, and that occupation alone was enough to explain his violent end. Judge Blake declined to allow his testimony, pointing out that while the prosecutors might vouch for his veracity, neither she nor the jurors would get the chance to assess it for themselves. Romano demurred from pointing out how convenient that was for TTG.

So two more deaths—Fat Guy and Booda—were added to the unofficial tally as Tana and the crew headed to court. The Game, as always, was played for keeps.

Defendants in the 2016 trial, clockwise from top left: Brandon "Ali" Wilson, Dennis "Denmo" Pulley, John "Binkie" Harrison, Linton "Marty" Boughton, Markee Brown, Taurus "Tash" Tillman, Terrell "Rell" Sivells, Timothy "Timrod" Floyd.

12

What Are We Supposed to Do Now, Clap?

It was a very lurid case to try.

—Dan Gardner

The trial would take twenty-four days, spread over six weeks, from September 18, 2018, until verdicts were pronounced on the last day of October.

Sixty witnesses took the stand, and scores of items were entered as exhibits, including weapons, photos (many of them gruesome), and a long list of audio and video clips. In a RICO prosecution, the idea is less to prove that an individual accused is guilty of a specific crime than to prove that the group shares responsibility for all of the alleged crimes. It helped enormously that the defendants had labeled and promoted themselves as such.

To accommodate crowds of spectators, three prosecutors, and the eight defendants with their lawyers, it was held in the grand ceremonial chamber of the Garmatz US District Courthouse in downtown Baltimore. Capacious but plain, in the bare, monumental style of mid-twentieth-century public architecture, with a pale gray floor and white walls reaching high to a vaulted ceiling with recessed lights, it conveyed grandeur strictly by its size. It featured stadium-style seating for up to a hundred spectators in rows that reached in the rear almost to the soaring ceiling. The gallery would be half-full most days and sometimes swelled beyond capacity—Judge Blake arranged to have the overflow seated in an adjoining room with an audio hookup. The audience gazed down on four rows of two tables, one table for each defendant and his counsel. The gang had enlisted some of the best-known criminal defense lawyers in the city. Tana, Rell, and their co-defendants arrived each day neatly groomed and conservatively clad, wearing clean dress shirts. Tana wore gold-rimmed glasses, which made him look studious, even collegiate.

Across the center aisle was a long table for the three prosecutors from the US Attorney's office, Gardner, Romano, and John Hanley. In contrast to the more relaxed manner of the defendants and their counselors, the prosecutors maintained a strict decorum, sometimes bristling when they were approached too casually. Gardner at one point angrily instructed defense lawyers to stop chatting with him during breaks. When Jenifer Wicks, one of the lawyers representing Binkie (John Harrison), asked if she could bring cupcakes to court the next day to celebrate her client's birthday, Romano had erupted: "What do you mean fucking cupcakes? We're presenting murders that this guy did!" There would be no cupcakes.

Judge Blake, a gray-haired woman in her mid-sixties with thick, dark, expressive eyebrows, presided from the elevated bench. Before her was a court reporter, and to her right was the jury box. Between the bench and the jury was an elevated enclosure for witnesses. The setting was theatrically imposing; one of the witnesses described stepping into it from a long hallway as akin to "stepping out on the field at a football stadium."

The show would be no bland, white-collar federal production. For the defendants it would be the final act of a years-long drama, unfolding before a sympathetic home audience. They had their image to uphold. On its second day, two of the defendants—Binkie and Tash (Taurus Tillman)—got in a scrape with the US Marshals who escorted them each day from prison to courtroom. Objecting to some perceived slight, Binkie had to be subdued with a Taser. He and Tash would spend the rest of the proceedings shackled hand and foot. This was colossally self-defeating; nothing says guilty like being shackled. To cover the chains, the two were given loose gray-brown sweatshirts and instructed to keep their hands in their laps and their feet on the floor beneath their table. The judge moved them to the tables furthest from the jury box. Four days into the trial, lawyers for the two pleaded with the judge to remove the shackles, pointing out that their clients had behaved themselves since the incident. Blake declined.

"I think this has to be looked at in the overall context of this trial," the judge said, "which involves extremely serious charges against all of the defendants, including Mr. Tillman and Mr. Harrison. The fact that there has not been, prior to the fourth day of the trial, which I will say is relatively early on in the trial, an actual assaultive action by either . . . does not give me much comfort."

She warned the defendants that they would be removed from the courtroom permanently if there were any further disturbances.

She had further issues with the crowd—mostly family and friends of the accused. They made for a colorful, rambunctious, and occasionally menacing audience. The judge had to admonish both spectators and defendants to refrain from communicating with each other. A fight broke out in the gallery during jury selection between two of Binkie's girlfriends (both mothers of his children), and then another scuffle erupted on the first day of testimony. Early on, one of the spectators was found to have brought a box cutter into the courtroom hidden in a shoe, which compelled footwear searches for the duration. Furniture from a lounge outside the courtroom was removed after the initials "TTG" were found carved in a table. Some of the defendants, notably Tana, made calls from prison urging a bigger turnout for the days when the task force's collaborators—Pony Head (Jan Gray), Rah (Ronnie Johnson), and others—were scheduled to testify. With two already killed, the tactic was chilling, and very nearly, as we shall see, effective. When these witnesses were in the box, members of the audience, people they knew, would lift their shirts to display gang tattoos. Defendants were seen to mouth death threats. Judge Blake wrestled to balance the need for order with the defendants' right to a public trial.

Despite the severity of their predicament, Tana and Rell, perhaps mindful of the audience, were cool, even cheerful. They greeted Neptune and Landsman with broad smiles, like old friends—they had not seen them for many months. Early on, Tana called across the courtroom, "Hey, Neptune, give us all twenty years, and we can get out of this." After one of Landsman's turns on the stand, Rell teased him, "You looked musty up there." The fact that their entire lives literally hung in the balance seemed not to faze them, Tana living up to his pledge to "take it on the chin."

If the prosecutors' goal was to establish collective guilt, the goal for the defense lawyers was the opposite, to separate their client from the pack. Prosecutors had a mountain of proof, but the parts that pertained to specific defendants were less imposing. As the evidence was presented, bit by bit, day after day, defense lawyers rose not to contest its validity but to show that it did not pertain directly to their client. None would argue that their defendant was completely innocent. When the prosecution finally rested, on day seventeen, its presentation was greeted by the defendants and their legal talent with resounding silence. None of the accused took the stand, and no witness appeared to contradict the great bulk of evidence. Their defense would be presented almost exclusively in closing arguments, where one after another, their lawyers ignored the evidence of collective guilt to push back only on those parts pertaining to their own client. In essence, they were warring with the central logic of the RICO Act, which is firmly established law. As a defense strategy, it was suicidal.

The jurors were from all over Maryland, half of them male, half female; most were middle-aged or older. Gardner did his best to eliminate younger jurors, not on any scientific basis, just with the sense that the mature tended to judge criminal acts more harshly—from his perspective, appropriately. Three jurors were Black, and one was Asian. One of the female jurors was in a wheelchair, which made for an awkward moment when they were all asked to stand to be sworn in. There was a prompt apology.

Judge Blake labored to be fair. Before the trial she had handed the defense a major victory by forbidding mention of the Brown and Coffey murders. Mindful of how jurors might be influenced if they learned that two of the prosecution's key witnesses had been killed, she ruled that evidence linking the deaths to TTG was insufficient. The judge also seemed attentive to her mostly Black audience, which she knew to be sympathetic to the defendants. It filled the rear of the big chamber bearing (mostly) silent witness, exuding a deeply rooted distrust for court proceedings. Blake knew this perhaps better than most. She had presided earlier that year over the trial of Wayne Jenkins and another member of his notorious Gun Trace Task Force, the criminal cops who had victimized the city's Black residents for years. Six other members of the squad had pleaded guilty. She sentenced Jenkins to twenty-five years.

At the opening of the trial, Gardner, with his crisp military manner, offered a summary of what would come: "Ladies and gentlemen, some brands are built on things like hard work, innovation, trust, creativity, things like that. And then there are brands like TTG, which are built on drugs and bullets and the willingness to do what other individuals won't. And that's what this case is about. This case is about TTG, or Trained to Go, and their rise to power in West Baltimore."

He pointed to Tana and Rell, and explained how they had started out as teenage corner boys, or "hitters," and that by 2015 they were running several drug shops, selling to retail customers, and even supplying other dealers. The business drove them to killing, and, "at some point, ladies and gentlemen, they weren't just killing people to protect their business, it became part of their business."

He laid out exactly what the government would present, stressing how cold and deliberate the gang was, noting that Beezy (Brian Chase) had been shot down and left for dead, and then tracked down when he crawled away and finished off. Summing up the evidence to come, he warned that it would try everyone's patience, all the wiretap calls, all the "controlled" drug buys, and cautioned jurors that the testimony of cooperating witnesses would sometimes be raw. They had been recruited from the world of TTG, he said, and if their words and behavior were unsavory, they accurately reflected the gang's world.

"You're going to hear evidence that these individuals, this enterprise, killed people for money," he said. "They killed people to protect their business; they killed people to grow their enterprise; and they killed or tried to kill people to silence them from cooperating with law enforcement witnesses."

Then, one by one, the defense lawyers stood to introduce their clients, none of whom looked especially threatening. These were not the burly, scarred thugs of Hollywood movies; they were lean, slight, and extremely, surprisingly young. Each had, at the beginning of the day's session, pronounced himself "not guilty." Now their counsels went to work. Those representing Tana and Rell claimed that the case against the brothers would be based on nothing but rumors and testimony from witnesses looking only to further their own interests. Binkie's lawyer, Jenifer Wicks, told the jury, "You'll not see any physical evidence that Mr. Harrison committed any violent crime or sold drugs." The case, she said, was based "solely on the words of these cooperators,"

and only words: "'Binkie did this.' 'Binkie said this.' . . . There is no
credible evidence he did anything." She stressed—and would do so
throughout the trial—that Binkie was slow, a victim of lead paint poi-
soning, a "special ed" student in school, someone who "can't read or
write." The lawyer for Denmo (Dennis Pulley) argued that while his
client had been a successful marijuana dealer, he was not dealing hard
drugs and certainly had had no part in murder. This was a tack pursued by several other defense lawyers, some of whom acknowledged
up front that their clients were guilty of dealing drugs.

"It might sound strange," said Christopher Nieto, who represented
Ali (Brandon Wilson). "I'm not standing here saying that my client is
not guilty. OK? He is guilty to some aspects. And for that, we're not
disputing. And there will be no fight on that. . . . The government will
purport to present evidence regarding the alleged sins of others in this
courtroom and ask you to connect Mr. Wilson to that. The evidence is
going to show that you can't do it."

Some argued that their clients had not been involved in criminal
activity at all, that they were being tarred "by association."

Harry Trainor, who represented Timrod (Timothy Floyd), talked
about Sandtown: "It's been around for many years. It's got a rich history. I think it was the birthplace of Thurgood Marshall, the justice
on the Supreme Court [true]. And even stars like Billie Holiday, I
think, was born in that neighborhood [she was born in Philadelphia,
although she had performed in Sandtown]. But over the years, that
neighborhood has gone into some decline. What it's characterized by
now and at the relevant time of this indictment, what it was like, is a
neighborhood with a lot of abandoned houses, boarded-up houses,
very little economic opportunity.

"It's an area—at the relevant time of this indictment, it was an
area where it's not uncommon—in fact, it is common—to see corner drug sales. On any given day at almost any hour, you will see a
group of young guys from the neighborhood sitting on the stoop of

an abandoned house and hustling, I guess you might say. People will come through that neighborhood seeking for—seeking cocaine or other drugs. And these young men in the neighborhood will often compete for a sale. . . . And that's the point, that a lot of what one sees on the streets of Sandtown would be young individual men hustling on the street, catering to the whims of people who come through and want to buy drugs. Timothy Floyd was born into and that is the world he grew up in all of his life."

Trainor said that Floyd worked on the corners like so many others but that he was not part of TTG. "If he was working out there, he was working for Timothy Floyd."

Kicking off the prosecution's case was Mark Neptune. The bald, bearded detective would return again and again in the coming weeks. He explained how wiretap authorizations were obtained and how they were monitored, and then for the next three days played one audio clip after another. Little effort was made to provide context for these selected excerpts, and many seemed mystifyingly banal. The first, for instance, a call to Tana from Marty (Linton Broughton), was from the day before the January 2016 blizzard:

"Yo," said Marty.

"Yo," answered Tana.

"Where you at, son?"

"Right here riding out the way."

"All right. I'm on Harlem, yo."

"All right. I'm about to pull up, baby."

And that was it. The second call was between Tana and an unknown man:

"Yeah?" answered Tana.

"Hey, you still around or are you hunkered down somewhere for the snow?"

"Yeah, I'm around."

"All right. I'm going to be there in about, uh, unless I get hung up in traffic, I'll be there in fifteen minutes or so."

"What you needed?"

"Same thing."

"I got some good-ass shit right now. You know the snow coming. It's worth getting a lot."

"Mmm. All right, let's do, let's do one, one hundred."

"I got you. I'm on lookout."

"Let's do fifteen minutes or so."

"I got you."

They might have been talking about de-icing salt, although "good-ass shit" suggested something more potent. On and on it went. Jurors were given transcripts—it had taken Neptune months to transcribe them all—so they could follow along on the printed page. Here and there were allusions to something being sold, always in coded language, but none seemed especially damning. This between Denmo and Rell:

"Yo," answered Rell.

"Yeah, when you gonna be ready?"

"In a second. You heard me?"

"I'm like, damn."

"I got nine. I'm waiting for one more. You heard me."

"Oh, all right."

A few were more substantive. The ones from Tana's abortive hunt in the blizzard for the men who had robbed his corner boy Mike clearly showed him seeking a weapon and in pursuit, but neither Gardner nor Neptune bothered to explain what was going on. The idea was not to tell a story, or at least not yet, even when the dialogue was suggestive. If the veiled references to drugs and weapons were taken in by the jury, so much the better. The desired effect was cumulative. The calls showed conclusively that these young men worked together closely, coordinating with each other daily, hourly, and sometimes from minute to minute. This was an organization.

Next came proof that what they were selling was drugs. A parade of cops and agents described undercover buys and contraband seized from residences used by the defendants, including bulk supplies of cutting and packaging materials, and gave detailed accounts of the various defendants at work on the corners. Again, the effect from day to day was humdrum but entirely convincing. The items seized in arrests and raids were entered into evidence accompanied by testimony from a dry train of analysts and chemists who verified the substances were heroin, cocaine, marijuana, and other illegal substances.

This was all indisputable. Most of the defense lawyers, like Nieto, had already admitted that their clients sold drugs. But the attorneys nevertheless went to great lengths on cross-examination to probe for the slightest inconsistency or advantage. Hammering away at calm, experienced prosecution witnesses was hard work. Occasionally it turned comical.

Hongde Pan, a Chinese-born chemist employed by city police who spoke English with a strong accent, testified that gelcaps purchased from Tash did in fact contain heroin. This was straightforward science, and Pan had been working in the police lab for sixteen years. Still, he underwent stubbornly determined cross-examination by Richard Bardos, who wished to emphasize just how small the purchase was. By the lawyer's calculation, it amounted to only six-tenths of a gram. He was correct, but getting the chemist to say it proved surprisingly difficult. Pan was steady, polite, and resolutely unhelpful.

"OK. So you're given six clear gelcaps—" Bardos began.

"Just to analyze one of six, not a total, all six, no."

"You analyzed one of them?"

"One of six."

"OK. And all six of the gelcaps together weighed two point three four grams?"

"Two point three four grams, yes. That's gross weight, gross weight."

"So, I think, if I got my notes right, you said you've done over twenty-five thousand tests?"

"Totally, yes."

"OK. And you've tested—you've gotten clear gelcaps with tan powder before?"

"Yes, definitely."

"All right. Would you agree with me that the—a clear gelcap—contains approximately point one grams of heroin, in your experience?"

"What do you say? Say again."

"OK. So you have—you've seen these gelcaps before; correct?"

"Yes."

"And they have heroin in them?"

"Some have; some not."

"Some do; some don't."

"But this one, yes."

"OK. I'm not disagreeing with that. OK? We agree on that."

Bardos regrouped, and then started again: "What I'm saying is, in your experience, the gelcaps that contain heroin—"

"Sometimes."

"Sometimes?"

Judge Blake intervened. "Excuse me, sir," she said to Pan, "It will help if you let him finish the question."

Bardos continued: "For those gelcaps that do contain heroin, would you agree that they usually contain about point one grams of heroin in each gelcap?"

"We didn't do the quantitation test. We don't know how many percent of heroin in it."

"You've never tested the amount of weight in a single gelcap?"

The lawyer was missing the chemist's fine distinction here between mass (the quantity of heroin the sample contained) and weight (how much the sample weighed).

"Let's do it this way," said Bardos. "Gelcaps can be empty or have something in them; right?"

"Yes."

"OK."

At this point, Bardos seemed relieved. Common ground at last.

"These ones, six gelcaps, every one has the tan powder," offered Pan.

"I understand that. What I'm trying to—"

"You say it's empty, but [it's] not empty."

Judge Blake tried to help. "No, no, no, no, he's not—let's think of it as a hypothetical."

"Yes," said Bardos.

"You have—so you got six gelcaps. Each one of them had tan powder in them; correct?"

"Yes."

"OK. You could have an empty gelcap, not in this case—"

"Not in this case."

"Not in this case, but in theory, you could have an empty gelcap; correct?"

"Yes."

"And that might have a specific weight?"

"Yes."

"And then if you had a gelcap with tan powder in it, that might have a larger weight; correct?"

"Yes."

At this point the judge, the prosecutors, and even Bardos's fellow defense counsels were rolling their eyes. One or two motioned for him to wrap it up. The point he was working toward was small, and this was becoming irritating. The purpose of the testimony was not to prove that Tash was selling large amounts in single transactions, but that he, like his co-defendants, was selling small amounts continually. But Bardos had started down this road. It had become a test of wills. He seemed intent on pinning the slippery witness down.

"What I'm trying to find out is, in all of your experience, when you've examined these, that extra weight of heroin is—in a gelcap—is usually about point one grams; right?"

"They always mix other substances, not just the pure heroin."

"All right. So in this case, were there other substances that you found in these gelcaps—in the gelcap you analyzed?"

"I think I have—let me see."

Pan sifted through a file.

"Do you have a different report? You have a lot of reports."

". . . heroin is a major part in this gelcap I analyzed."

"I understand that. And you used approximately point oh six in this single gelcap to do your analysis; correct?"

"Yes."

"All right. Do you know how much was left over from this single gelcap?"

"I didn't analyze one—let me see. . . . I didn't measure the single gelcap's weight, but the total weight is two point three four."

"OK. So if I were to tell you that there has been testimony that there's approximately point one grams of heroin in gelcaps generally, would you agree with that?"

"I cannot say that."

"You don't know that. OK. So let's do this: The gross weight of all six was two point three four?"

"Yes."

"All right."

"We can get to the average."

"You can get an average?"

"Yes."

They went back and forth about that calculation.

"All right," said Bardos. "If you add that up, you get a little under five grams. That's everything, not just the heroin, but the gelcaps, right?"

"Gelcaps and the substances inside of the gelcap."

"Right. And if you add all of that up, you get about five—a little under five grams in this case, correct?"

"Yeah, less than five grams."

"Less than five grams."

"For this, you just plus the six to six."

"I understand. And so you have less than five grams total. That includes the weight of the gelcaps. How many grams are in a kilogram, sir?"

"What?"

"How many grams are in a kilogram?"

"One thousand grams equal one kilogram."

"One thousand grams; right?

"Yes."

"OK, thank you," said Bardos.

The relief in the chamber was palpable. The long math lesson (abridged here) thus concluded, Pan was at last excused.

"Thank you," he said. "I'm free!" He stood up, bowed to the jury, and said, "Good evening to all of you."

This performance at Bardos's expense provoked much laughter, during which lawyers from both sides approached the bench.

"Can I say on the record that that was the single most delightful moment of my entire legal career," said Michael Lawlor, one of Tana's lawyers.

Said the judge, "I'm not going to comment on what that says about your legal career, Mr. Lawlor."

*　*　*

After all the drug evidence, the trial's sixth day began with the testimony of collaborators, young men from Sandtown with their own criminal pasts, well known to the defendants and most in the gallery. They had agreed to turn on their friends. There was Tyree Paige, who was the same age as Tana and had grown up with him and Rell and sold drugs with them. A convicted felon, picked up carrying a gun, he had agreed to cooperate with the task force to avoid a return to prison. Once part of the gang, loosely defined, he was in a position to give authentic and extremely damaging testimony. When his name was announced as a coming witness, there was an audible gasp in the courtroom. Paige was prepared to discuss the July night he had watched Tana, Binkie, Thug (Antonio Addison), and Man-Man (Brandon Bazemore) gear up with weapons and masks for the notorious triple homicide that would happen a few blocks away, leaving Lamont Randall and two others dead on the sidewalk. Paige had heard them boasting about it later and had been with Tana when he collected the $10,000 reward.

Paige had been brought to the courthouse the day prior to his testimony, in case he was called early. One glimpse of the crowded courtroom, however, at the big audience of familiar faces in the gallery, and he lost heart. When he was not called that day, and after hearing the audience gasp at the announcement of his name, he disappeared. Neptune and an Anne Arundel County officer assigned to the task force, Jeremy Tepper, spent a long day cruising Sandtown looking for him in his usual haunts. They eventually spotted him on the sidewalk, and Tepper leapt out and grabbed him. Paige was placed in custody. When delivered to the courtroom, he appeared to be trying to make himself invisible. Head down, mumbling, he avoided looking up at the defendants and the gallery as he reluctantly told his stories.

Pony Head, too, lost heart. The former corner king who had been supplanted by Tana years earlier had been very helpful to the task

force behind the scenes after Landsman had played him the recording of Tana's threat. But when the day of his appearance approached,
he ran. Landsman drove out to the house where Pony Head had been
relocated in Pikesville and was told he had checked himself into a
drug rehab center. This was shrewd, because the center was prevented
by law from even admitting that he was a patient. When Landsman
visited and hit a brick wall, he threatened to return with a court order
authorizing a top-to-bottom search of the facility. The center's staff
relented. He was told, "We're not going to confirm or deny that he is
here, but if he is here, we'll go see if he'll come out." Pony Head sheep-
ishly emerged. When his turn came to testify, to face that gallery of
his old neighborhood friends, he gripped the frame of the door to the
courtroom so hard his fingers had to be pried loose.

Despite this reticence, Pony Head's testimony was compelling.
With his long beard neatly clipped, he made an impressive showing, and when defense lawyers tried to undermine his credibility by
showing that he had been a lifelong criminal, they would effectively
enhance it. Clearly Pony Head knew what he was talking about and
had reason to talk.

He was questioned by Romano, who, with his bushy white mustache and slightly theatrical manner, always commanded the court's
attention. In addressing the judge he would sometimes stammer,
"Um . . . um," as if groping for a way to express something, and then
rip into a startlingly succinct, fully reasoned argument. Occasionally prolix with the detectives, in court he wasted not a word. His
cross-examinations were as crisp as well-crafted scenes, often ending
abruptly, leaving a witness's final words to ring.

"Mr. Gray, do you know someone by the name of Tana?" the prosecutor asked.

"Yes."

"Do you know his real name or his full name?"

"Montana Barronette."

"How long have you known Montana Barronette?"

"All his life."

". . . How long have you known Rell?"

"Basically, the same amount of time."

He said the same about each of the defendants.

"Mr. Gray, do you know or have you heard of TTG?"

"Yeah."

"Do you know what that stands for?"

"Trained to Go."

"What does that mean to you?"

"Trained to kill."

". . . How do you—first off, yes or no simply, do you know people who are members of TTG?"

"Yeah."

"How do you know that?"

"It ain't a secret."

Pony Head described how his own Sandtown drug operation once earned him $10,000 a day, and he described exactly how it worked, from packaging the drugs to selling them.

"Right. Why did you stop selling?" Romano asked. "Were you arrested, or did something else happen?"

"I felt threatened for my life."

"OK. Who threatened you?"

"Tana did."

". . . Did you take the threat seriously?"

"Yes, I did."

Romano returned to his seat, letting those words settle.

Pony Head was not the only cooperator whose criminal past was aggressively dissected by defense lawyers—wisely or unwisely. The theory was that jurors might refuse to believe someone so clearly dishonest or who was guilty of alarming crimes. None presented a target so rich as Rah, Ronnie "Jackass" Johnson.

An announcement that he would appear as a government witness came as a palpable shock to the defendants and gallery. Rah had been a notorious, feared, and respected figure in the neighborhood's criminal ranks, a senior BGF leader whose life had been lived as much in prison as out. Tana phoned family and friends that night asking them to turn out, in hopes of intimidating him. The next day the gallery was full to overflowing. Rah was unfazed. As brazen and colorful as ever, neatly groomed right down to manicured fingernails, he was unapologetic about his past and straightforward about his reasons for turning on the gang. He said he had lived the outlaw life until he could see no way to avoid death or another long trip to prison. He had survived years of drug abuse, very bad decisions, hard time in the worst Maryland jails, and two attempts on his life, both of which had left him badly wounded. It was a miracle he was still alive and upright. He wanted out. After days of audio clips and expert testimony, Rah's turn on the witness stand was riveting and, for TTG, ruinous.

He told his whole story: the tragic shooting as a teen that had permanently paralyzed Tavon Kintchen; how he had joined BGF in prison and risen through its ranks; how he had helped orchestrate violence in prison and on the streets; and how, at a certain point, he had taken to robbing and kidnapping drug dealers. He took the jurors with him into the action as he snatched Nut (Jamie Hilton-Bey) off his front stoop and rode around the city trying to get his family and friends to cough up ransom. He told them about the flying leap from the van that had landed him in the hospital with a concussion, and he named Rell as the gunman who had shot thirteen holes in the victim. The prosecutors backed up his stories with physical evidence from the shot-up van and then segued into Rah's recorded drug purchases from Tana and Rell.

The second of these videoed drug buys featured Rah sliding over to the passenger seat in his car to adjust the camera before his target arrived. This occasioned some scornful laughter from the gallery, and someone called out that he was preparing for his "close-up." Rah was seen playing his role to the hilt in these videos, worrying aloud about a van up the street that he knew contained Neptune and another agent, calling Landsman a "dickhead," and warning his targets about police surveillance.

When the cross-examinations began, Rah was uninsultable. He candidly, even cheerfully, owned up to his past, sometimes drawing fine distinctions to his behavior that would elude most. As defense lawyers enumerated the long list of his criminal acts, Rah answered simply, time and again, "Correct."

Tana's attorney Lawlor asked him how many kidnappings he had done.

"A couple," said Rah.

". . . seven?"

"No."

"So this is such an unimportant thing to you, to shove a gun in somebody's face, take them in a van, tie them up, beat them, call their family, get money or not get money, kill them or not kill them, that you can't even recall how many times you participated in an event like that?"

"Yes."

"OK, well, how about this? Between the time you turned eighteen and the day you sit here, what's your best estimate of the number of kidnappings you participated in?"

"A couple."

Rah denied repeatedly that he had ever killed anyone, although he did admit that he had helped order hits for BGF. There was a

significant distinction—large in his mind—between passing along a
kill order and giving the order himself. On one occasion, he admitted,
he had passed along an order to kill a man nicknamed "Los."

"Yeah, fuck him. Kill him," Rah said he had said. He then told
how he had sat beneath a camera in the pizza shop at the time the hit
was to take place so he would have an alibi.

"Did you eat some pizza while you waited for Los to be killed?"
Lawlor asked scornfully.

"Yeah. I got something to eat."

When it was his turn, Joseph Balter, Rell's lawyer, returned to Rah's
fine distinction between passing along a hit order or making it himself.

"You might have been associated but not directly involved, right?"

"Correct."

"Now, do you draw a bright line, or do you think there's a big distinction between whether you actually pull the trigger or whether you
are just associated with a murder?"

"In the life I live, yeah."

"I'm sorry?" said Balter.

"In the life I was living at the time, yeah, it is a difference."

"There is a difference?" asked Balter, disbelieving.

"Yes."

"So would you say that—for you personally—it would cross a
moral line for you to actually commit a murder?"

"Would it?"

"Would it? Do you have a personal belief—"

"I ain't sure. I ain't do it, so I ain't sure."

Eventually the judge halted this line of questioning, explaining,
"It gets into an argument about his moral code."

Hammered on why he had agreed to cooperate with the feds,
Rah seemed better able than the lawyer to parse his agreement with
prosecutors.

"Is it your understanding if you were ever individually prosecuted with respect to these acts of violence, you might be looking at a sentence of life imprisonment?"

"Yes."

"But you understand that just for telling the truth, you won't have to spend a day in prison; is that correct?"

"No, that wasn't—"

"I thought you said your understanding was if you tell the truth, you will not be prosecuted for anything, correct?"

"Not actually 'not prosecuted,'" Rah explained, patiently. "My words that I'm saying can't be used against me." He was right.

Rah and Pony Head were only two of the former neighbors, friends, and associates of TTG to give damaging testimony. There was Sterling Crowder, Tana's age, who had been selling "Sweet Dreams" with him and Rell in Sandtown since he was thirteen, and who had agreed to cooperate after being convicted of robbery, hoping to reduce his prison time. Crowder's cooperation was less of a surprise. The gang had suspected him after one of its workers, Will Thomas, had been busted immediately after selling him drugs. Tana had warned Crowder that if he had set up Thomas, he would not be able to hide it forever, at some point the case would come to court. Crowder told him, "Man, you find out that I did something like that, like, I feed you myself, for real." Now here he was in the witness box, for real, looking out at Tana and Rell and the others, the focus of hundreds of angry stares, featured in a video setting up a deal with Tana and buying more than a hundred grams of heroin from Timrod.

There was Tana and Rell's old employer Davon Robinson, a decade older than Tana, currently in prison on drug and gun charges. He had known the brothers for most of their lives. He had been close to Bub (Brandon Littlejohn), murdered on the street beside Harlem

Square Park's basketball courts. Robinson gave an extremely detailed account of the inner workings of Tana's drug shops and of TTG's role in various murders.

There was Donte Pauling, the same age as Robinson, who had also known Tana and Rell from childhood. Under questioning, Pauling explained the terms of his cooperation:

"OK. Were you convicted in 2003 for first-degree assault and the use of a handgun during a crime?" Gardner asked.

"Yes."

"Recently were you charged with possession of a firearm by a prohibited person?"

"Yes."

"And have you pled guilty to that offense?"

"Yes."

". . . As part of that case, did you agree to cooperate with law enforcement?"

"Yes."

"And are you currently awaiting sentence on that conviction?"

"Yes."

"When you pled guilty, did you plead guilty with a plea agreement and a cooperation agreement?"

"Yes." Pauling's sentencing guidelines had been reduced from a maximum of twenty-seven years to a maximum of ten.

"What's your understanding of that cooperation agreement?"

"The truth."

"To tell the truth?"

"Yes."

"OK. What happens if you don't tell the truth?"

"I'm fucked."

Pauling had been with Tana and Binkie the night they murdered Beezy (Brian Chase) and had been standing alongside Marquez Jones when the masked Tev (Tevin Haygood) strode up the street and shot him in the face. He gave a second-by-second account of the killing, relating how he dropped his phone in panic and ran, and then returned to retrieve it. His description of Jones's wounds exactly matched what was found in the coroner's report. He told the crowded courtroom that Tana had set up the murder and later had reassured him that Tev had been instructed to shoot no one but Jones. This was valuable inside information, entirely believable, and again, defense efforts to bring out Pauling's own criminal past, his drug and alcohol abuse, likely strengthened his credibility. As prosecutor Romano would say later, "These are not *our* friends, they're *their* friends."

There were others who turned on the gang. Darrell Carroll, imprisoned for drug dealing, who had been in the car when Tana blasted the latest Blac Youngsta rap on their abortive ride to find and kill Ced (Cedric Catchings). There was Darrell Mills, a convicted felon who had witnessed the shooting of Magic (Christopher Pennington), after Denmo's offer of a $10,000 reward. One witness testified from beyond the grave, when Judge Blake allowed, over strenuous defense objections, the grand jury testimony of Markee Brown. He described how Binkie had robbed him and his friend Shotgun (Dominique Harris), and then how Shotgun had been gunned down.

There was Anthony Boyd, a career criminal who had not known any of the TTG crew until, in prison, he found himself in a cell at Maryland's Chesapeake Detention Facility next to Denmo, whom he described as "a very talkative person," something that had already been demonstrated in the wiretap recordings. Boyd said that Denmo had told him that he feared being dragged into a racketeering case with TTG because he had paid a reward to someone named Tana for killing someone named Magic. Denmo explained that Magic had been suspected of stealing weed from him. He also told Boyd about the murder of Thug, in front of his grandmother, and spoke admiringly about how "vicious" Tana was, how he killed "with a smile on his face." Denmo said that Tana had once asked for "a thousand dollars for every head shot in the future." Boyd said he didn't know who Tana was until Tana was placed in a cell on the other side of his own.

"This is the guy I told you about," Boyd said Denmo told him.

Asked about Thug, Boyd said that Tana explained, "The nigga got what he deserved. He thought he was going to get away." As for the shooting, Boyd testified, "[Tana] said the guy was trying to make it into the house. He killed the guy in front of his grandmother, and she was screaming. And he thought it was funny."

Then came, one after another, city homicide detectives and medical examiners who detailed the gang's trail of gore. Perhaps even more powerful than their words were the ghastly color photographs of the dead laid out in the morgue, young, naked, sturdy Black bodies, lifeless, looking up with vacant stares from long metal trays. Bald-headed Nut, eyes mostly shut, mouth hanging open exposing gold-capped front teeth and whitened tongue, thirteen holes in his body. Marquez Jones, with two holes in his face, front teeth shattered, confirming Pauling's memory, shot five times. Bearded Dirty (Lamont Randall), with an odd toothy grin and seventeen holes in his body. Dark-skinned Day-Day (David Moore), mouth askew, with a huge gash across his chin, one of nineteen gunshot wounds. Beezy, with an oddly pensive gaze and a bullet wound at his Adam's apple, one of fourteen. The round figure of Thug, with the scar high on his forehead from the shooting he had survived, and with new fresh holes in his back, arm, and leg from the one he had not. That one came with a picture of the blood pool on the floor of his grandmother's living room. Magic, with his face strangely twisted and mouth slackly open, seven gunshot wounds. Shotgun, with a wispy beard and his mouth hanging open exposing blood-stained teeth, shot eleven times. Jacqueline Parker, whose nakedness somehow caused more consternation in the courtroom than the deep gouges in her chest, some of the eleven bullet holes left by the cascade of fire that one of Tana's crew had boasted, "wore them out." The images made indelible the ugly stories told by the cops and pathologists.

When the prosecution finally closed, the defense countered with only two brief parries.

Tash's hardworking lawyer, Richard Bardos, the one who had mailed the letter that the task force believed got Fat Guy (Guy Coffey) killed, who had hammered away at the chemist Hongde Pan, and who had declined, unlike all the other defense attorneys, to make an opening statement, now rose to argue that his client had been wrongly lumped with this murderous crew. He said Tash had never had an Instagram account with a TTG tag, like the others; that there was no direct evidence he had committed any violent acts; that he had not conspired to sell significant amounts of heroin (per the Pan cross-examination); that his house had never been searched; that, in all the wiretap recordings played over days of the trial, his name had hardly ever come up; and that he had, during the time of investigation, held down not one but two conventional jobs, one at a used furniture store and the other at a Popeyes franchise.

Then Gary Proctor, one of Binkie's lawyers, rose to make a fairly minor point. In an effort to at least partially discredit the testimony of Tyree Paige, who claimed to have watched Binkie and Tana and others arm themselves and drive off on the night of the triple murder, and then to have heard gunfire from blocks away, Proctor put a private investigator on the stand who had stood where the murders happened and sounded an air horn. He had placed an assistant at Paige's location, and she took the stand to say she had not heard the air horn.

"How's your hearing?" he asked her.

"Pretty good."

Romano's cross-examination was one of his classic set pieces. In its entirety:

"Good morning, ma'am," he said.

"Good morning."

"Do you know if fifty-three gunshots from three different guns make the same sound as a blow horn?"

"I do not," she said.

"Thank you, ma'am," said Romano.

The judge told her she could step down.

Closing arguments began the following day. The defense lawyers, again one by one, rose to paint the collaborators as liars and to distance their clients as much as possible from—or to explain away—the damaging evidence in the wiretap calls and recorded drug buys. Once more, again and again, they parsed the mountain of evidence to isolate the portions that dealt with their client alone and tried to show how flimsy those portions were. Each claimed that their client was accused only "by association." This was, of course, the whole point in a RICO case, to prove a criminal conspiracy and then assess guilt by association.

Prosecutor Dan Gardner stood at the trial's end to rebut each point raised by the defenders. In a tour de force of counterargument, he reminded the jury of the clear evidence against each defendant in every particular. He spoke for nearly an hour and a half—at one point the judge even interrupted to gently suggest that he wrap it up.

Concluding at last, Gardner said, "Ladies and gentlemen, the origin of the word 'verdict' is 'verdictus.' It means to speak the truth, and you have the opportunity in this case to speak the truth. . . . The defense in this case has vastly understated the evidence that you have before you. . . . You have direct. You have circumstantial. You have eyewitness. You have confessions, admissions, ballistics, intercepted calls, seized firearms and casings, and crime scenes. And all of that demonstrates that these defendants are responsible for these tragedies. You can speak the truth, ladies and gentlemen. Find them guilty."

As he returned to his seat, Tana called over to him, "What are we supposed to do now, clap?"

There was no applause, but also no confusion. The jury took three days to reach a verdict, no doubt because there was so much evidence to sort, so many defendants to consider, and so many specific counts to weigh. Late in the morning of the last day of October, the jury forewoman delivered the decision. Apart from two stray, relatively minor counts on which the jury members could not agree, all the defendants were found guilty on every major charge.

Romano decided beforehand that as the verdicts were read, he was going to watch Tana. And as "guilty" was pronounced for him, likely sealing his fate for the rest of his life, he smiled.

13

Crabs in a Bucket

Altogether, the Old Bailey, at that date, was a choice illustra-
tion of the precept, that, "Whatever is is right;" an aphorism
that would be as final as it is lazy, did it not include the trou-
blesome consequence, that nothing that ever was, was wrong.
— Charles Dickens, *A Tale of Two Cities*

Pronouncing the fates of the eight convicted members of TTG took place at separate hearings over the first half of 2019, most of them well attended. Reports on each of the convicted were prepared for Judge Blake, applying arcane federal sentencing guidelines, which assigned a numerical value to all the guilty verdicts, weighing the severity of each and certain mitigating factors. The higher the number, the more severe the sentence recommended. A total of forty-three called for the maximum penalty. Tana's total was forty-eight.

Factored into this sum, along with the estimated quantity of drugs sold and murders committed, was evidence of remorse. Not one of the gang members in all the months before and after the trial had uttered a word of genuine contrition. Especially damning for all of them was their boastful behavior in rap videos and on social media. Defense lawyers strained to allay the impact of these things, pointing out their clients' youth, the nature of Sandtown, bad influences, terrible upbringings—including parental abandonment (in some cases) and brain damage (in others)—but the die was cast. These young Black men, born to a bad place, had done what came naturally to them. It was perhaps unsurprising that they didn't feel guilty about it.

At the sentencing of Ali (Brandon Wilson), the talented boxer who, next to Tana, was the gang's youngest, the neighborhood excuse was dismissed contemptuously by Chris Romano: "Well, the dog didn't eat my homework. And living in Sandtown did not make Brandon Wilson a criminal."

Arguably the least culpable, he got twenty-five years.

Marty (Linton Broughton), the efficient field commander who had gone hunting in the blizzard with Tana and had tossed a handgun later linked to the triple murder, thirty years.

Timrod (Timothy Floyd), one of the senior members at twenty-seven, who had made the mistake of selling one hundred grams of heroin to a police informant on camera, thirty years.

Denmo (Dennis Pulley), the old head at age thirty, the would-be financial mentor who tried to coach Rell and Tana from his luxury Inner Harbor apartment, thirty years.

Tash (Taurus Tillman), who had been implicated directly in the killings of Bub (Brandon Littlejohn) and Fat Guy (Guy Coffey)—it was the letter from his attorney that outed the latter—got off relatively lightly. At his sentencing, Romano pointed out that not only had he assaulted a US Marshal during the trial, he had also been involved in two more prison assaults since. He urged that Tash be sentenced to life and sent to a supermax prison. This harsh recommendation drew complaints from the gallery. One onlooker was removed from the courtroom shouting, "Fuck this case and y'all, too!"

Blake sentenced Tash to twenty-five years and ignored Romano's supermax recommendation.

Binkie (John Harrison), the gang's primary hitman, who had been directly linked to the murders of Shotgun (Dominique Harris), the three people killed on July 7, 2015 and Beezy (Brian Chase), was sentenced to two life terms. Harris's family members spoke of the grief and pain of Shotgun's loss. His mother said that Binkie would never have killed him "if he had known him." Binkie, one of only two gang members who chose to speak, contradicted her. In a textbook non-apology apology, he said, "I apologize for what y'all had to go through, but I ain't apologizing for what happened because I'm innocent at the end of the day. And I did know Dominique Harris. The detectives were aware that we played football together. So my name on his murder, that's not cool. So, once again, I apologize for what y'all had to go through, but I'm innocent at the end of the day."

The hearings for Tana and Rell were emotional. The courtroom was packed for both. In the audience for Tana's were the jury forewoman and another juror. It was the only time in his long career that Romano had seen jurors return to hear a sentence pronounced.

Valencia Bullock, the mother of Thug (Antonio Addison), stood up for her murdered son at both sessions, the only family member of their victims who did. Romano told the judge that there were others who had wanted to appear but were too frightened. Bullock spoke movingly and with palpable anger. She described her last day with her son, her discovery that he had been shot, being informed of his death at the hospital, and breaking the news to her seven-year-old granddaughter that night:

"She just fell to her knees. I told her it was Tana. She knows Tana."

The girl had responded, "No, grandma, that's my father's friend."

"I said, no, he killed your father. I told her that was our secret. Don't tell anybody, but if she ever saw him, not to go near him."

Bullock said she was haunted by her son's death every day and continued to visit his grave weekly. She felt the futility of grief in a Baltimore that took little notice of her son's death or the deaths of so many young men whose lives were considered dispensable.

"My son was a good person. I don't care what anybody thinks or anybody feels. My son wasn't just some person on the corner. My son finished high school . . . my son had a job. My son was an involved parent with his daughter. He went to her school. He helped her with her homework. He took her out where they had time together, him and her. He's always been there for her. He's always been a good son, a good brother, a good friend. Loyalty and respect means a lot to my son. . . . I used to sit up there and watch the news before this happened, and I used to just—I didn't know why people were killed, but I felt bad for their families. And then it was me. It's my son. . . . So I just feel like—I feel like Montana Barronette is the devil's child. Nobody could be that evil to do so many murders, hurt so many people, take people away from their families, their children."

She came again to Rell's sentencing, defiantly facing him and the audience filled with his family and friends, urging the judge to impose the maximum penalty.

"On my way here I was so emotional. My heart is racing. My hands are shaking. Think about us and the people that these people keep going out here murdering," she said. "And then," addressing Rell, "you sittin' there hollering about how you didn't have an education, who didn't have this, who didn't have parents. Well, you're an adult now and you have choices to make, and you made them when you murdered my son. I pray to God that they never come home."

Shanika Sivells, Rell's older sister and Tana's half sister, rose at Rell's sentencing to forcefully defend them both. She came so determined to speak that when Rell's lawyer, Joseph Balter, began wrapping up his appeal without mentioning her, she interrupted him.

"I thought you said I was gonna talk today!"

Balter conferred with Rell briefly and then invited Shanika to the witness box, saying, "Your honor, Shanika Sivells."

A slender, pretty young woman armed with a lifetime of indignation, Shanika was polite, but her anger filled the room

"I just came up here to speak on my brother's behalf because me and him been through a lot together. . . . Yes, we been through a lot.

Not normal—a lot of kids that grow up in our city go through stuff like this."

Shanika was hurting and was, perhaps, willfully blind to her brothers' murderous trail. As she saw it, they were the ones wronged. She talked about losing their younger sister, Booda, to a revenge killing, and about how she was now going to lose her brothers to prison. For her, this was not just an emotional blow. At least some responsibility would fall on her to care for the five children her brothers had fathered, and she had two of her own. She was not at all persuaded that she or her brothers deserved this. Her family was the victim of a law enforcement vendetta, she believed, ever since the night cops had raided their Harlem Avenue apartment when she was a little girl. The law had removed Tana's father, Delroy, the target that night, from their lives, leaving them with a hopelessly addicted mother and an overmatched grandmother, all of which had driven them as children to the streets. She said that her grandmother had wanted to speak at the sentencing but was still too terrorized from that long ago raid to attend.

"And, yes, he [Rell] was wrong for the drugs or whatever. But my thing is, he's up here being called an animal and, like, a murderer. My brother's not a murderer. He never been. He—my brother—barely talk. And if you listen to the phone taps and all that, he said three words. All he did was chuckle and laugh. . . . I wish it was something I could do to help him more. And that whatever I might say ain't even going to help him."

She said she had watched the whole trial. She was particularly scornful of the men from her neighborhood, Rah (Ronnie Johnson) and Pony Head (Jan Gray) and the others, who had testified for the government.

"They was lying, hard," she said.

She characterized the government collaborators as "people from his childhood that my brother left alone years ago." They had pretended a relationship with him, "just to get an investigation started over nothin'." They had collaborated out of jealously of her brothers' success and popularity in Sandtown. Shanika evoked an old Maryland analogy: "People in the streets, where we live at, it's like a bucket of crabs, literally. We was the bastard kids in the hood. . . . When we grew up and people seen the respect and love we was gettin' from the neighborhood; they hated that 'cause we was the 'church kids.' So when they seen Terrell gettin' respect, Montana—and mind you, my brother used to get bullied by—what's his name?—[Antonio] Addison and his family years ago when he was a little boy. I was right there, used to watch them beat on my brother. I used to have to fight their cousins and them off of him. All I'm saying is when you see kids like that and then you grow up and we gettin' the respect that they ain't want us to get, it's a lot of hate. It be real in the neighborhood where we live at."

How could they even call TTG a gang?

"They was friends that grew up together . . . some of 'em didn't even sell drugs. Half of 'em went to school and trade school. But they ain't put that up in the trial 'cause they wanted them to look like animals and monsters. These are good—like, they was good boys. They played sports. We tried to do other things other than sell drugs. That's all my brother tried to do."

She noted that Rell and Tana had played organized basketball and baseball and were good at both.

"They went all around the city. I'm just putting light on the shade that they throwing on him [Rell] 'cause he's a good, good person. Like, he—my brother is awesome. Like, both of 'em is. Really, it's just that Montana, the young one with the big head—you feel me?—he grew up on his own. We was all put out at a young age 'cause my grandmother was too stressed to deal with the life that we chose to live. Yes, she tried hard. We went to church all week for years. We was brought up on 'turn the other cheek.' That's why it's hard to sit here and believe that they trying to say that my brother admitted to killing somebody, that he really said that he did this stuff."

Neither brother deserved to be sent away for life. "Terrell don't deserve it. He was locked up half the investigation. He tried to come home and do right by his daughters. That's all my brother was worried about, his kids. These—all these murders they talkin' about—that's just something that they [prosecutors and witnesses] came up with on their own, honestly."

The trial had so inflated her brothers' reputation as killers that every member of their family was marked for revenge, as Booda had been.

"I can't even let my son play with his friends because there are nine-year-olds selling drugs right now. And it's gettin' worse by day. . . . It's gettin' worser and worser and worser, like, whereas, though, my son loves to go outside, and I don't even let him go outside because of the stuff that's on the TV"—alluding to news reports of her brothers' crimes—"everybody thinking that my brothers and them did all this stuff around the city. So now it's like we looked upon as, oh, they need to die too. That's the stuff that my family is going through. My grandmother can't even claim her own sons at work because people will harass her 'cause they think that my brothers and them are coldhearted animals who went around the city killin'. Like, we are victims here too 'cause we know for sure what they did do and what they didn't do."

She expressed regret for the families of those who had been killed, and told the judge, "I promise you that my brothers did not have nothin' to do with that. And at the end of the day, I just want to say, Rell, I love you. I miss you and Tana."

"I love you, too," said Rell.

"And this shit has really been hard for me 'cause it's just me and my little brother and my kids, and I'm the only one that really got to do right for their kids, my kids, and them. And it's hard 'cause it's always been four of us." She talked about Booda's murder.

"She died last year this month because someone decided to set her up and kill her, cold-blooded, for nothin'. And she was a working nurse lady.

"My brother is not no evil, coldhearted person who just come home today or tomorrow and say, 'Oh, I'm going to go kill everybody.' No. He worry about his family. When he call home, they still help me out, and they locked up in jail, and they still get people to come bring me money for me and my kids. Now, if he was so much of a cold-hearted person, why is he locked up still worrying about me and my kids and my family? Coldhearted people don't do that."

She thanked the court for "lettin' me talk. . . . This stuff is just ridiculous."

Judge Blake then sentenced Rell to life plus thirty years.

For Tana's hearing, Romano pulled out all the stops. "His offense is really off the charts," he said.

He talked about watching Tana smile as the verdict was read back in October.

"Now I suppose you could say that smile was one of disbelief, but we all in the courtroom know that it was not. [It showed] a complete lack of conscience, a complete lack of remorse."

Tana's lawyer Michael Lawlor, who must have known how fruitless his words would be, swung big. He indicted everyone. He began by noting that Tana had already been in jail for more than two years, and in that time murder totals for Baltimore had not declined—in both those years the annual total had exceeded three hundred.

"Murder is such a part of the fabric of the city," he said. He pointed out that in Montgomery County, the relatively affluent Washington suburb where he lived, homicide totals for a year were ten times lower than Baltimore's, even though it had a larger population.

"Not only was he born and raised in Baltimore City, but he was born and raised in probably the, or one of the, most violent parts of the city, which is Sandtown," he said. Lawlor then suggested, some-what tenuously, that if their upbringings had been switched, "I'd be in that chair, and he'd be standing here. . . . We live in a world with laws. . . . But I also know that we live in a society that permits what goes on in Baltimore to happen. And when I say 'permits,' I mean we permit it. And I don't say 'they,' I say 'we.' I have blood on my hands. With all due respect, you have blood on your hands. And Mr. Romano has blood on his hands 'cause this happens in a society where it need not happen. . . . We all well know that if we made the decision as a society to stop this, we could, but we do not have the political forti-tude to do it."

Lawlor said that he did not have the answer. He noted that he had been "an actor in the system" for twenty years and cited a Sandtown case that Judge Blake had adjudicated over thirteen years before. Nothing had changed.

"So the point I'm making, Your Honor, is that there is room for both punishment and an understanding that we failed Mr. Bar-ronette . . . and so many like him. . . . And to me it is perverse to, on the one hand, either ignore that failure or acknowledge it but fail to account for it in the penalty you impose."

He said that Tana was a victim, too.

"He grew up in Baltimore with parents who were not present or were addicted to drugs. He grew up in a place where he would be sell-ing drugs by age thirteen. . . . He had to stop going to funerals 'cause he had been to so many of his friends' funerals that it began to haunt him. While he was incarcerated for this case, his sister was murdered in the same streets. And it would be easy—and I think everybody in this courtroom, save a handful of us, will sigh with relief at the notion that Mr. Barronette should never walk free because he's a danger to society, but that's a fallacy." The killing, Lawlor promised, would not stop.

His request on Tana's behalf was modest. He wanted a sentence that would allow his client, now twenty-three, to go free when he was in his "early seventies."

Judge Blake asked Tana if he would like to say anything, and he said he would. He and everyone else had listened to Valencia Bullock's passionate remarks, when she had called him "the devil's child."

"OK," he said. "Good afternoon. I just want to apologize to Mr. Addison's family, his daughter, his mother, his sister, for all the heartache and pain that they believe I caused. And I just want to say I was—*he* was a good friend, and a good father to his daughter. And I been with him when he was taking and spending time with his daughter and things like that and [I was] giving him advice on keeping his job and staying out of the streets and everything like that. And I just want to apologize to 'em. That's it."

"OK," said the judge, but then Tana went on.

"OK. I just want to thank my loved ones, my family, friends, for coming out and supporting me and just riding this—riding it out with me for as long as they can and just uplifting me when I be feeling times when I just be all over the place and stressin', just thank them. And thank my two lawyers for speakin' for me and fightin' for me every day as well. Thank you."

The judge then heard a plea from his aunt, Dikeshia King, who addressed Romano's comment about Tana's smile.

"Montana Barronette has always smiled, and a lot of his smiling come from hiding his nervousness and scaredness," she said. "He's always been like that. He even smiled when he got—when it was time for him to get in trouble. I just want to let you know that he's being called an animal and, like, a killer, and, like, he's some kind of animal. He's not. . . . Now I'm not saying that what he did was right, but what I'm saying is don't nobody know anything that was going on in his life and in his head at the age of thirteen on up, even when he came as a little boy. They always wanted extra love from people, but we didn't have it. It was only us. So I'm not going to let anybody belittle him."

When all this ended, Judge Blake pronounced his sentence. Acknowledging that Tana's story "was a tragedy on all sides," she pointed out that many who grew up in circumstances akin to his "don't kill people."

"Perhaps at some age Mr. Barronette will understand what he's done and truly feel remorse and sorrow for it. I'm not sure we're there yet."

She gave him two life sentences. It was exactly the penalty Joe Landsman, on the night of Tana's arrest, warned him to expect.

No matter how satisfying to the families of the gang's victims, and to the agents, detectives, and prosecutors directly involved, the successful prosecution of TTG did nothing to change Baltimore's dreadful status quo.

The city continued struggling to simply govern itself. Its new mayor, Catherine Pugh, became embroiled in a scandal that would eventually lead her to resign. The city police would have three different commissioners during Tana's pretrial custody alone, one of whom resigned after being charged with failing to file tax returns, and another—an interim appointment—who decided staying on was not a good career move. The police department will continue to operate under federal oversight until a federal judge concludes that it has fully reformed. That end is not in sight.

After the TTG roundup, the city's homicide rate did not go down, and in Sandtown itself, it actually went up. According to Daniel Webster, director of the Johns Hopkins Center for Gun Violence Prevention and Policy, the murder rate for the five years after TTG was rounded up in 2016 was 50 percent higher than projected. Nonfatal shootings went down by close to the same amount, which had curious but hardly felicitous implications.

Police crackdowns sometimes produce the exact opposite of what they intend. Large-scale drug busts, for instance, designed to sweep crime from targeted neighborhoods, often cause an uptick in violence. Newly vacated drug corners are suddenly up for grabs, and locals with their handguns compete to take over. The reduction in nonfatal shootings, Webster speculated, may show the effect of programs to discourage impulsive gun violence. Participants are counseled in ways to settle disputes without resorting to guns. But that success may at the same time contribute to the increase in fatal shootings. Instead of pulling guns themselves, acting in the heat of the moment, disputants might be paying others—professional killers—to exact revenge.

"So they go after people very differently from something that's more spontaneous," he said. "A couple of guys happen to be strapped and drinking too much, and something happens, and they start firing the guns and people get hit, but they are more likely to survive than a victim of a deliberate hit. Even the trauma surgeons talk about it, too, the number of people coming in with unsurvivable injuries. Clearly these were professional executions."

Sample numbers from just one neighborhood are too small for bold conclusions. Sandtown may just be a stubborn outlier, given how policing there has fallen short, particularly since the Freddie Gray unrest in 2015. There is no doubt that many of those left grieving by TTG's killing spree felt relief and satisfaction when the crew was locked away. And there is broader evidence that selectively targeting a city's deadliest criminals is a better strategy than traditional drug sweeps. Removing the most violent gangs has been shown to correlate with reduced gun violence in New York neighborhoods and has had a similar effect, at least temporarily, in some of Baltimore's. But there was no such outcome in Sandtown after removing TTG and the city's "number one trigger puller." It certainly didn't affect the demand for drugs. As Shanika pointed out, the markets were still open and humming more than two years after her brothers were arrested. So long as buyers keep showing up, somebody will step up to sell.

A sometime Sandtown dealer who goes by the name Fish summed it up neatly to me in the following text:

Short and sweet to the point when they [TTG] got arrested a new crew takes there place so the neighborhood will always remain fucced up bCuz the police don't do shitt btw always remember people do shitt for money and drugs so as long as they are around killing will always be in the mix and that's it.

Meet the new boss, same as the old boss.

So it's easy to see why Shanika interpreted her brothers' downfall as she did. Somebody was going to get rich off the neighborhood drug trade, why not them? Tana and Rell had been pulled down not by outraged citizens but by rival thugs, those they had bested in The Game.

Her familiar analogy was "crabs in a bucket." Most Marylanders have observed the nasty behavior of live blue crabs confined in this way. They writhe and struggle, reaching up and out with claws that can draw blood from careless fingers. Curiously, if one of the captives on the top manages to crawl up and over the rim, the others will grab at its legs and pull it back in. This was how Shanika saw the government witnesses, as fellow outlaws and former friends, who helped destroy her brothers' success. These were not men who had reformed. Some of them had been playing both sides all along, cooperating with the feds while continuing to sell drugs on the street—the balancing act that had ended so badly for Fat Guy. Others, like Rah, having chosen to play, were trying to escape the tragic consequences of their own choices by violating the unwritten code of the streets. They had been motivated by jealousy, she argued, not by civic duty. They had cooperated with the white establishment (white cops, white prosecutors, white judge, and mostly white jury) to help themselves and get back at her brothers. To Shanika this was not some triumph of justice—*This stuff is just ridiculous.* It was the same old story. Crabs in a bucket.

Isabel Wilkerson, in her important book *Caste: The Origins of Our Discontents*, writes:

> Even as those in the lowest caste try to escape the basement, those left behind can tug at the ones trying to rise. Marginalized people across the world, including African Americans, call this phenomenon "crabs in a barrel." Many of the slave rebellions or the later attempts at unionizing African American laborers in the South were thwarted because of this phenomenon, people subverting those who tried to get out, the spies paid with an extra peck of privilege for forewarning the dominant caste of unrest. These behaviors unwittingly work to maintain the hierarchy that those betraying their brethren are seeking to escape.

If you ignore the severe moral failure of Tana's story, there's a Horatio Alger element to it. Growing up, the Barronette-Sivells children were so poor and neglected, they were held in contempt even in "the basement." The Game had offered them an out. It was not a lazy option. Obtaining, cutting, packaging, and selling drugs was real work. It required smarts and dedication. The competition was ferocious, and the risks terrible. And they had triumphed . . . for a time. They worked hard, and they played hard. They provided for their "baby mamas" and growing number of children, helped their sisters and grandmother and their friends. It's no wonder that Shanika was distressed by their downfall. The arrests ended her spell of prosperity. It left her alone with children and no immediate means of support, and it left her *frightened.* A target.

To fully sympathize with her, however, means setting aside horror over the murders, which lies near the heart of the problem. Shanika did this by denying, at least out loud, that her brothers had killed. If she knew better, and she very likely did, she would not be shocked. Hers was less a denial that her brothers killed than a denial that they killed *for no reason*. Deadly violence was, after all, part of The Game. It was accepted. The gang was inured to it, an unalterable fact of life in Sandtown since well before they were born. Tana killed serially but he was not a serial killer in the common sense of the term. He was no lustful lunatic like Jeffrey Dahmer or John Wayne Gacy or Ted Bundy. Nor was he a "psychopath," which was the word Neptune had applied. While morally null, Tana was not mentally ill. He and the rest of his crew were normal teenagers in an aberrant environment, an extreme product of a violent, oppositional subculture, not just trained to go but *bred* to go, or kill.

"If by whatever chance you happen to be born into that particular space in time, violence is all about you, normalized," said Webster, who has studied urban violence in the city for twenty-five years. "Your capacity to do anything about that is incredibly limited, right? As a survival technique, you adopt the same sort of attitudes and behaviors and practices. You find guns, you find pals who are going to stick together. . . . This culture has emerged out of this set of rather dire conditions. It's a sad state that society and the city, in particular, has not created a safe space for them."

Why? Because Baltimore has been unable, and America unwilling, to stop the crisis of Black urban gun violence. While most children growing up in the worst neighborhoods manage to avoid its pull, enough of them do not to color the perception of such places in general. These are the ones who most often lack any of the necessary guide rails. Shanika and her brothers were shoved out to the corners. Their parents had been in The Game. Their mother *instructed* them in it. Drug dealing offered a clear avenue to everything they wanted in life, if they were smart, tough, and worked at it. It may have been bad for the community and bad for the city as a whole, but what could be more American than putting yourself and your family ahead of everything else? The rewards were great. Even the risks were appealing. Embracing "gangsta" life afforded them status, money, sex, and respect they could not find anywhere else. Celebrated in song and video, they were ghetto stars.

All of this underlay Shanika's point about her brothers not being monsters. Indeed, they were the opposite of monsters. In their own community, they were not just normal, they were champions. They were driven to succeed.

Every high school in America has a cohort of students who, after graduating, because of preference or lack of larger ambition, do not head off to college and far-flung careers. They settle instead into their home community and make their living there, taking whatever work or careers they can find. Landsman himself had done it, embracing with his brother and sisters the same work that their father and uncles had done. When Tana left Edmondson-Westside High, he did exactly this. He went to work on the corners. He employed the violence his work seemed to require, against those who *had it coming*. When civilians were killed, like those in the triple murder, it was just unfortunate, they were collateral damage. Sometimes the gang tried to make amends to their families.

A curious fact about TTG: As violent as the gang was, and as beset as it was by Landsman, Neptune, and the rest of the task force, its members never once shot at cops. If anything, they maintained a kind of friendly, competitive attitude toward them. They killed longtime friends suspected of cooperating with the police but not their primary tormentors. It's not because, as some might surmise, they feared harsh retaliation by the authorities. They were already risking the harshest of penalties: They faced death daily. Those slain were *just like them*, often friends who had violated their codes or who landed on the wrong side of a local feud, like the one between Ced (Cedric Catchings) and Blue Black (Deandre Smith). The consequences of those killings, which invited revenge from rivals or those bereaved, were arguably harsher and more immediate than anything law enforcement could threaten. They didn't go after cops because The Game had rules. Tana and Rell

got more caught up in the killing than most, but they were not aberrant. They were not even rebels. They were entirely conventional. They
embraced The Game as they found it. And they prospered.

At least Shanika was thinking about why. The question hardly
came up anywhere else. Beyond the pleas of Lawlor and some of the
other defense attorneys to consider the world that had shaped their
clients, *why* was beyond the scope of the proceedings. Indeed, when
I asked that question of the cops and prosecutors, all of them smart,
dedicated, and highly skilled, I received only sketchy insights, that
TTG had been motivated by money, although they were not getting
rich. They blew most of the money they earned. They had no idea, as
Denmo's frustrated efforts made clear, how to build on their success,
to grow their business or invest. They didn't seem much interested
in it. They had more money than they knew how to spend. It bought
them drinks, drugs, sex, clothes, and tickets to the fights. It bought
them brief, extravagant vacations to the places Tana had listed, Miami,
LA, Cancun, Jamaica, New Orleans.

And they did not see themselves as bad guys. They did not think
what they were doing was wrong. It was necessary—*either you got to be
that, or you ain't.*

Seeing yourself as a good person while doing something evil
depends on a culture with upside-down values. Ambition in a healthy
society works to the benefit of all. In an unhealthy one, especially one
replete with weapons, it becomes a deadly scrum. Sandtown is what it
is because Baltimore made it that way. It is the achievement of a racist
societal effort spanning centuries, and one that may take that long to
unmake.

What is lacking is not answers but will.

Curbing the plague of violence in places like Sandtown calls for
something much bigger even than the huge attempt made by philan-
thropists like James Rouse, organizations like Habitat for Humanity,

or the various federal, state, and local government agencies that tried to remake Sandtown twenty years ago. Many good, dedicated people threw themselves into that mission body and soul. A Christian group started New Song Academy across the street from Gilmor Homes. Some gave up their homes in the comfortable white suburbs and moved into the community. They created a health care program and a jobs program. Journalist Lawrence Lanahan documented this movingly in his book *The Lines Between Us*, telling the stories of two white Christian families at the center. Some are still at it twenty years later but have been beaten down by challenge. After all, Tana grew up as this unfolded. The same drug markets described in David Simon's work at the turn of this century lured Tana in its second decade and remain open for business today.

So what would it take? It would take social engineering on a scale unlike anything America has ever tried, something perhaps equivalent to the social engineering that created Sandtown, a process that spanned centuries. It begins with redress, acknowledging that the racism that created Sandtown still exists, and working to rectify it in every way possible, with reparations, deep institutional reforms, rethinking our criminal justice system, and a direct investment in the lives of poor Black citizens. It would mean attacking the core failing of the country itself. Du Bois believed it might start with schools: "It is the public schools . . . which can be made, outside the homes, the greatest means of training decent self-respecting citizens. . . . I am becoming more and more convinced . . . that the national government must soon step in and aid popular education in some way."

That was in 1903. There may be other ways of attacking the problem, but schools are where society gets directly involved with families in every American community. If the United States committed itself to having the best public schools in the world, concentrating its effort first on those in the greatest need, it would give children in the worst neighborhoods a better chance at a comfortable life. This would, by definition, require a major investment in the country's poorest, Black-est districts. We presently do the opposite. Since public schools are mostly funded by property taxes, the system today guarantees that the wealthiest—read *whitest*—districts have the best-funded schools, and the poorest the worst.

In 2018, the *Baltimore Sun* editorialized, after surveying statewide school rankings: "What is inescapable in looking at the data is the con-clusion that a Maryland child's chances in life are inextricably linked to where he or she grows up. . . . It should come as little surprise that Baltimore City, the site of Maryland's deepest concentration of pov-erty and a place shaped by decades of institutionalized racism in the form of segregation, blockbusting, and redlining, would also have the most low-ranked schools."

In 2019, the year Tana was sentenced, the Nation's Report Card ranked Baltimore's public schools, which are still overwhelmingly attended by Black and minority students, as the third worst among the twenty-one urban school systems surveyed. And within Balti-more, Sandtown's schools rank lowest. Edmondson-Westside High School, Tana's, which is 99 percent Black and 100 percent "economi-cally disadvantaged," remains one of the worst-performing high schools in the city.

In nearby Pennsylvania, in 2021, six local school districts sued the state government for failing to comply with the state constitution's mandate of equal access to high-quality education. Citing deep dis-parities in school funding between affluent districts and poor ones, the lawsuit claimed that reliance on local property taxes to fund schools baked in this imbalance and assured that children in poor Black urban neighborhoods, precisely the kind of students who would need more help to succeed, were instead being systematically short-changed. Lower Merion, a well-to-do, primarily white neighborhood outside Philadelphia, spends more than $31,000 annually per pupil, compared with an inner-city Black district in York, which spends only $18,000 per pupil. This kind of funding imbalance is common in schools throughout the country.

If the Pennsylvania lawsuit succeeds, it might strike at the deeper social roots of the poverty, crime, and violence that plague Black communities countrywide. Improving the schools where improvement is most needed seems like common sense, but is far from politically feasible. Better schools, higher pay for teachers who work in the most troubled areas, counseling and tutoring, job training and placement for students who struggle academically. . . . If America was serious about stopping the crisis of violence in Black urban neighborhoods, it would be a good place to start.

There is also hope in the approach pioneered by David Kennedy. His Operation Ceasefire showed that dramatic progress is possible with a determined holistic approach, identifying those children most at risk of growing up to be victims or killers and then working hard to steer them off that path. It requires focusing a battery of community and government resources on them, reintroducing what Du Bois found lacking in poor Black communities, *the public opinion of one's social caste.* Baltimore has made several attempts to apply that approach in recent years, but always in a half-hearted, poorly funded way. Webster calls the various local Operation Ceasefire campaigns "almost pathetic." In most cases, the police department subverted the program's central logic. Instead of going to work on at-risk youth, the police used the target data to find and arrest them.

"It totally delegitimized the whole idea of the program," said Webster. "I remember talking with the program director from the mayor's office about it, and him sharing some arrest data, and I was astonished, honestly. Immediately with this initiative, arrests in that area just went way, way, way up. And there were no service provisions, there was little community support. The police and State's Attorney's office were saying, we now have a little more data and intel, so we're going to go in and put people behind bars."

Law enforcement has a huge role to play, despite calls for "defunding" police. The most violent neighborhoods cry out for better policing. Too many shooters are never arrested, and too many of those arrested go free. Where justice fails, revenge further fuels the violence. Larger and larger sums are offered for killing people, and, perhaps worse, killing acquires a measure of community approval. Almost as sad as the lives lost or ruined is the celebration of the "gangsta" life in drill music and on social media, which feeds the racist myths that justify white indifference. Gang violence and white indifference are two sides of the same coin. Just as Shanika accepts the violence of her world, so does the privileged white caste that might end it. In the words of my old city editor, *Those people are always killing each other.* Police need to do more than targeting and removing the most violent actors. They need to work with the community, with schools, and with other agencies to intervene earlier with youths like Tana and his gang to head off the tragedies that await them.

There is no forgiving someone like Montana Barronette for the loss of life and tragedy he caused. His arrest and prosecution and sentence were richly justified. Nor does it diminish his culpability to say that he is normal. But his behavior fits a pattern, one that will not be altered by locking him up. As part of a homicide review commission in Baltimore, Webster took a deep look at sixty-five people who were either victims or suspects in murder cases. Of that number, only one had graduated from high school. Many, when they dropped out of school, were already one or two grades behind. They had been obvious problems in city schools for years.

"Many of them had identifiable problems very early in their childhood and schooling years," he said. "And when you ran these cases, basically you just saw system failures, system failures, system failures."

Better schools, and a program like Kennedy's, would spot a boy like Tana long before he picked up a gun. Kurt Palermo, who runs such a program in Baltimore, said Tana's name was at the top of the first list of likely candidates for intervention that he saw when he came to the city—albeit too late. Tana did his part; he stayed in school. But school failed to change him.

Better schools, better local policing, more counseling and community involvement, stronger gun laws, more employment opportunities, programs like Operation Ceasefire, and the specialized, strategic law enforcement practiced by Cliff Swindell's Safe Streets Task Force—this is how the violence in Baltimore and other cities might end. All that is lacking, as Lawlor put it, is political will.

In the years since TTG was taken down, the Maryland US Attorney's office continued selectively targeting violent groups. In 2020 it corralled another homicidal drug gang that called itself NFL, for Normandy, Franklin, and Loudon, streets in the West Baltimore neighborhood of Edmondson Village. Sixteen people were swept up in this indictment. More sophisticated than TTG, it was peddling heroin and fentanyl and committing murder across the entire Mid-Atlantic region. NFL operated almost exclusively by text messages. It expanded its customer base by allowing those unwilling to drive into the worst city neighborhoods to place their orders by text. They would be directed to a pickup spot in a safe, quiet, usually upscale area. The indictment cited nine overdose deaths. Unlike Tana and his crew, NFL rarely bloodied its own hands. It offered bounties for murder, up to $30,000, and paid the killer through a broker—making it extremely hard for the task force to connect the dots. It did so, but as law enforcement grows more innovative, so do the gangs.

Robert K. Hur, the US attorney who presided over the office during the TTG prosecution, has joined the Washington, DC, law firm

Gibson, Dunn & Crutcher. His first assistant Jonathan Lenzner is now the chief of staff for the FBI. Dan Gardner moved from Baltimore to the Justice Department's National Security Division in DC. Chris Romano retired and then returned to the office a short time later as a special assistant.

Romano continued to pursue charges against Tash and Binkie for their scrape with the federal marshals during the trial. When Judge Blake asked, given the lengthy sentences she had already imposed, if pressing those cases wasn't overkill, Romano told her, "You don't get to take a free swing at a US Marshal on my watch." He won convictions of both men in 2020, and each received an additional year, to be served when and if they complete their longer terms.

Joe Landsman retired from the Baltimore Police Department in 2022 after twenty-two years of service and went to work for his wife Christina's real estate company. His departure meant the department was without a Landsman in its ranks for the first time since 1932. Dan DeLorenzo retired from Anne Arundel County's police, moved to South Carolina, and took a police job there. Mark Neptune moved from the FBI Safe Streets Task Force to one with ATF, doing the same kind of work. He took with him some of the unfinished TTG business.

One of those loose ends was Milk (Roger Taylor), who had vanished sometime after buying Tana a new outfit and taking him to the fight in New York City. At twenty-eight, he was older than the other TTG defendants except Denmo. He had saved and invested his money, which he used to facilitate his escape. He adopted the name Tayvon White, complete with false passport, and flew to Colombia, where he had his smile fixed—his incisors had decayed under the gold fronts he wore in Baltimore. Then he'd taken up residence in the Dominican Republic, where he was living a life of leisure. The flaw in his plan was a girlfriend who took occasional trips from Baltimore to visit him. The feds followed her to him, and the Dominican police arrested him in July 2019. Neptune met him at the airport in Baltimore, wearing a big grin and a black T-shirt with the slogan "Got Milk?" on the front. Milk was sentenced to eleven years after pleading guilty to the federal racketeering charges.

Another of the loose ends was the case Dan DeLorenzo had built against rapper Davante Harrison, YGG Tay, the gang's troubadour, who had responded to revelations of his links to TTG by telling a *Baltimore Sun* reporter, "That is completely false. . . . They're going off something they heard on the street? Come on! That just makes it even worse. . . . I don't want people out there thinking I'm into this stuff. They're trying to damage my name. I got record labels trying to sign me."

Mindful of the rapper's alleged role in the death of Fat Guy, Neptune shepherded the case against Harrison into federal court, where he was convicted in August 2021 of drug and weapons charges. He was sentenced to fifteen years. Murder charges were still pending.

In the summer of 2022, Neptune took a job with the Tampa police, where he would be, he said, "starting all over" as a uniformed patrolman.

Scratch (Darius Singleton), the skinny kid with his sideways baseball cap, who the detectives believed was one of those threatening the prosecution's cooperating witnesses, was found dead in Patapsco State Park. He was twenty-seven. Detectives said he walked into the woods and was felled by an overdose of fentanyl. No drugs or paraphernalia were found on him or in his car. His father believes he was murdered, injected with a fatal dose of the drug and left in the park to die.

Pony Head (Jan Gray) is living with his mother outside the city. His days as a corner king are long past. He has a job and helps care for his grandchildren.

He has no regrets about helping put Tana in prison.

"I was hurt," he said, talking about the recording Landsman played for him of the phone conversation between Tana and Rell. "I felt messed up. That's what really helped me to testify against him, because they would try and kill me. If they would've not involved me, I wouldn't have never said nothing about them. I'd have kept everything a secret. But being as though they wanted to kill me, I knew they wasn't my friends no more. There was no sense in protecting them. I was hurt about it."

He is nostalgic about his days of running Sandtown's drug shops.

"I mean, it was fun, you know. It was fun. We just was about making money. Like we really wasn't into that killing and all that. We would fight. I mean, if trouble came through, you know, people would handle their business. But that wasn't our main thing. Our main thing was making money and girls, you know. She was a fun neighborhood until them little kids came up. They made it cruddy and couldn't trust nobody."

Of all those involved in this story, the one with the most remarkable ending may be Rah, Ronnie Johnson, Junior, or Jackass. If ever there was a young man on a dead-end path, it was him. Locked in an adult prison at age sixteen for shooting a man, he joined BGF, embracing it as "a way of life," and over the next twenty years bounced in and out of prison for ever-longer stretches. He became a drug addict, robbed street dealers almost daily, participated in kidnappings, and survived two attempts on his life, severely injured in both. He became a police informant, participating in the extremely dangerous work of infiltrating TTG and helping set up their fall. And in the end, or at least in the end of this story, he had shed his street name, Rah, and was a steady hand on a construction crew well away from Baltimore.

I met him in a public park in rural Maryland, a world away from Sandtown, beside a duck pond on a summer morning. No one seems more amazed to have ended up alive and free than he does. He appeared out of place in such a bucolic setting, a tall, lean man with dreadlocks and tattoos up and down long, muscled arms, gold at the front of his smile. He goes by Ronnie now and is by all accounts a reliable employee. His hands have grown calluses from handling tools. He lives with a girlfriend and says he sees his five children regularly, usually at places midway between his new home and the city. He has not been back to Baltimore in years. His freedom, his survival, is remarkable. He is happy.

"I always wanted to get away from Baltimore, man," he said. "I knew it was dangerous but, like, to me, in Baltimore, that's just like a way of life. You kill or be killed, you know what I mean? Or you had to fit in some type of way to manipulate the system like I did. I never killed nobody in my life, to be honest." He admits that he worked to maintain that rep: "Have all those guys believe something that wasn't there, you know what I mean?"

Calling Landsman in desperation was the first smart move of his life. Until then he felt trapped by circumstances that, he admits, he helped create.

"By the time I realized I wanted out, it was too late," he explained, "because I caught that charge as a juvenile, so from sixteen on I never could get no good job or nothing." He was hired at one point as a security guard and was excited to have found a legitimate way to earn. "They fired me after, like, one hundred and twenty days when my background check came back," he said. It was back, then, to earning on the streets and another long string of arrests.

"I was so tired of bein' in prison," he said. "I was tryin', man, that's what you see right now, I been working for years now. I'm trying. Trying my best."

The last time Johnson returned to Baltimore was in 2017 to testify against Ced, whom he named as one of the two men who shot him the summer before. He was driven back to the city by Neptune and another task force officer and escorted into the courthouse by an armed team.

"We had him in, like, a side room," said Neptune, "and when it was his time to testify, we had someone walk him down, take him into the courtroom, and then, escort him out and get him out of there. We had someone with him at all times. The trial, it was very Baltimore-esque, to say the least. It's very rare in Baltimore that you get a cooperative shooting victim. Most people get shot in Baltimore, they don't care, they say they're going to deal with it themselves. Ronnie was willing. The problem they had was it was pretty much a one-witness case."

Since Ronnie was the only witness, the defense tactic that he would weather in the federal trial worked better in the state courtroom. His sordid past was presented in detail, and it successfully discredited him or, perhaps, convinced the local jury that when Ced shot him, he had it coming.

"I really think that the jury kind of just looked at him, like, you know, he's a piece of crap, he deserved what he got," said Neptune. "So, they found Cedric not guilty."

Ced was released but was shot—literally as he drove away from the prison gate. He survived, and was charged with the murder of Slow Down (Larelle Wallace). He is currently in prison awaiting trial on both state and federal charges.

"This guy needs to go away," said Neptune.

Tana is locked up in US Penitentiary, Pollock, a high-security prison in Louisiana. He has been behind bars, except for his brief jaunt of freedom in early 2017, for more than six years. In 2021 he was stabbed in a prison fight, though not seriously wounded. He is now twenty-seven. Beyond the highly unlikely prospect of his conviction or sentence being overturned on appeal, he has no prospects.

He declined to be interviewed for this book but has written several letters to me.

"I'm from West Baltimore, as you should know," he wrote in April 2020. "I grew up with 4 siblings, a grandmother and an aunt to care for us. My father or mother wasn't around. I played baseball, basketball, and football my entire youth into high school. I graduated from

Edmondson High. Never had a felony charge until now. I love taking trips and dirtbike riding also kids."

He said that he is writing a book about his life, and in a letter some months later he said: "I am definitely one of a story that needs to be heard. It may seem like what can be different about my story than all of the rest of the stories that are told by people who come from a similar background. In my case, a lot."

He was nevertheless reluctant to talk to me, he said, because his appeal is all he has to hope for and discussing anything about his case might damage that chance.

"God dam you isn't no beneficial to me in anyways," he wrote in a third letter, and then drew a picture of a smiling face.

Notes

1 The Game (or, The Greased Path)

Apart from a brief written correspondence, in which Montana outlined to me a few details of his life, most of the information in this chapter about his childhood comes from interviews with his sister Shanika Sivells. The rest is drawn from interviews with Stefanie DeLuca, Dawnyell Taylor, Clint Fuchs, Johnny Rice II, and Kurt Schmoke; and the transcripts of *USA v. Montana Barronette et al.*

1 **Epigraph**: Eldridge Cleaver, *Soul on Ice* (Delta, 1968), 180.

2 **"a living hell"**: Melody Simmons, "Living Hell Lexington Families Must Struggle to Endure," *Baltimore Sun*, January 20, 1993. I spent time with a family in the towers for a series of stories called "Life in the Projects," for the *Baltimore News-American* in 1979.

2 **Sandtown**: Throughout the book, "Sandtown," the traditional community, refers to the neighborhood now formally designated Sandtown-Winchester, and also includes the adjacent Harlem Park.

4 **highest incarceration rate**: Justin Fenton, "Report: Sandtown-Winchester Leads the State in Number of People Incarcerated," *Baltimore Sun*, February 25, 2015.

4 **"The appearance, therefore"**: W. E. B. Du Bois, "Of the Sons of Master and Man," from *The Souls of Black Folk*, in *Writings* (Library of America, 1986), 486. Emphasis added.

5 **much smaller chance**: Eduardo Porter, "Black Workers Stopped Making Progress on Pay. Is It Racism?," *New York Times*, June 28, 2021.

5 **three times more likely**: Ibid.

6 **"virtually all black"**: Harold A. McDougall, *Black Baltimore: A New Theory of Community* (Temple University Press, 1993), 137. McDougall's book tells how grassroots community organization might play a role in revitalizing neighborhoods like Sandtown. Alas, there is scant evidence thirty years later that its promise has been realized.

6 **defeat those odds**: Stefanie DeLuca, Susan Clampet-Lundquist, Kathryn Edin, *Coming of Age in the Other America* (Russell Sage Foundation, 2016). In their study, DeLuca et al. followed 150 Black Baltimore youths born between the late 1980s and early 1990s. They write: "Contrary to the conventional wisdom, getting 'caught up' in 'the game' was far from the norm—by their own accounts, fewer than one in five had been 'in the street' for even a brief time. Instead, a large majority were actually resisting the street, determined to be 'about something else,' and hungry for postsecondary education and careers. Most scorned the drug dealers and other hustlers who dominated the public space of their neighborhood and struggled to model themselves after the nurses, forensic scientists, lawyers . . . or small business owners they hoped to become. The large majority finished high school and went on to college or trade school. Few got addicted to alcohol or drugs. *Eighty percent found work in the formal sector after high school.* And they did so while continuing to struggle against neighborhood risk and the trauma of coming of age in families often plagued by addiction, violence, and financial strife" (xv). Emphasis added.

6 **worst in the state**: Public School Review reports: "The percentage of students achieving proficiency in math is ≤5% (which is lower than the Maryland state average of 38%) for the 2018–19 school year. The percentage of students achieving proficiency in reading/language arts is ≤5% (which is lower than the Maryland state average of 46%) for the 2018–19 school year." Harlem Park Elementary/Middle, Public School Review, accessed July 3, 2022, https://www.publicschoolreview.com/harlem-park-elementary-middle-profile.

8 **tootling down suburban streets**: Shootings are so commonplace in some urban neighborhoods that in Philadelphia, children at day camps partly

sponsored by city police are given training and medical kits to stanch bleeding and provide emergency care to gunshot victims. "Sign of the times: At this Philly day camp, teens learned 'stop the bleed' training for gunshot victims," by Kristen A. Graham, *Philadelphia Inquirer*, July 22, 2022.

8 **Fatalism came naturally**: Jocelyn R. Smith, "Unequal Burden of Loss," *American Journal of Public Health* 105, no. S3 (2015). After interviewing forty young Black men from a violent Baltimore neighborhood, University of Maryland sociologist Smith wrote that the frequency of traumatic loss "crystalized the lethality of neighborhood violence and created a sense of personal vulnerability to violent death." Criminologist Elliott Currie, in *A Peculiar Indifference* (Metropolitan Books, 2020), notes, "They not only lose people close to them, they also lose faith in a secure future—or any future" (61).

9 **citywide rate**: Baltimore Police Department, Crime Stats, 2022, https://www.baltimorepolice.org/crime-stats.

9 **turned their heads**: Dawnyell Taylor, a Black city homicide detective who grew up in the neighborhoods she polices, has a deeper understanding than most. Speaking of the reluctance of witnesses, she cited first their fear of retaliation for "snitching." But even she feels deeply frustrated by the community's reluctance to help, especially after the Freddie Gray riots.

9 **number of murders**: "What We Know about the Increase in U.S. Murders in 2020," John Gramlich, Pew Research Center, October 27, 2021, https://www.pewresearch.org/fact-tank/2021/10/27/what-we-know-about-the-increase-in-u-s-murders-in-2020/.

10 **162,000 Black people**: Currie, *A Peculiar Indifference*, 20–21.

10 **sixteen times**: Ibid., 23.

10 **Amy Goldberg**: Susan Snyder, "Where's the Outrage," *Philadelphia Inquirer*, January 21, 2022.

11 **320 distinct local gangs**: Interview with Clint Fuchs, Assistant US Attorney, Maryland.

11 **"recklessness"**: W. E. B. Du Bois, *The Philadelphia Negro: A Social Study* (University of Pennsylvania Press, 1996), 325. Du Bois writes: "When one group of people suffer all these little differences . . . the result is either discouragement, or bitterness, or over-sensitiveness, or recklessness."

12 **suburban white boys**: Carl Bialik, "Is the Conventional Wisdom Correct in Measuring Hip-Hop Audience?," *Wall Street Journal*, May 5, 2005. Bialik cites a marketing research study in 2004, which found that 70–75 percent of "rap buyers" were white. More recent studies place the percentage closer to 50.

13 **Danger was a big part**: Tom Wolfe, in *The Right Stuff* (Farrar, Straus and Giroux, 1979), notes that the ego of the average test pilot, boosted by regularly tempting death, was "so big it's *breathtaking!*" (39).

13 **cops who busted corner crews**: See Baynard Woods and Brandon Soderberg, *I Got a Monster: The Rise and Fall of America's Most Corrupt Police Squad* (St. Martin's Press, 2020); and Justin Fenton, *We Own This City: A True Story of Crime, Cops, and Corruption* (Random House, 2021), which detail the predations of Baltimore's Gun Trace Task Force.

14 **"How long can a city"**: Du Bois, *The Philadelphia Negro*, 351.

15 **Harvard University researchers**: Raj Chetty and Nathaniel Hendren, "The Impacts of Neighborhoods on Intergenerational Mobility," Harvard University and National Bureau of Economic Research, May 2015—https://scholar.harvard.edu/files/hendren/files/nbhds_paper.pdf—executive summary, 3.

2 Shabangbang Shaboing

This chapter is based on interviews with Jan "Pony Head" Gray and Joe Landsman; and on a recording of the phone call made by Terrell Sivells to Montana Barronette on May 4, 2014.

16 **Epigraph**: Waka Flocka Flame, "TTG," Flockaveli, https://www.youtube.com/watch?v=ZL83BBfBeGY.

21 **met with ridicule**: Joe Landsman.

3 The Fulton Avenue Wall

32 **Epigraph**: Isabel Wilkerson, *Caste: The Origins of Our Discontents* (Random House, 2020).

33 **century before slavery ended**: Matthew E. Crenson, *Baltimore: A Political History* (Johns Hopkins University Press, 2017). Most of the history summarized here is drawn from Crenson's lively and erudite book and also from McDougall's *Black Baltimore*.

33 **"protein factory"**: H. L. Mencken, *Happy Days* (Library of America, 2014), 41.

35 **Lincoln himself**: Abraham Lincoln flirted with the theory, dispatching a government minister, Elisha Oscar Crosby, to Guatemala to scout out a place for "black colonists"; David W. Blight, *Frederick Douglass: Prophet of Freedom* (Simon & Schuster, 2018), 370. In one of the most regrettable moments of his presidency, in what was certainly a moral if not political lapse, Lincoln lectured a group of Black ministers on the notion, telling them, "We should be separated" (371). Du Bois wrote critically of Lincoln's racist thinking but concluded, "I love him not because he was perfect but because he was not and yet triumphed. . . . The world is full of people born hating and despising their fellows. To these I love to say, 'See this man. He was one of you and yet he became Abraham Lincoln.'" *The Crisis*, September 1922.

35 **"a thing in the South"**: Du Bois, *Souls of Black Folk*, 382.

36 **"Negroes Encroaching"**: *The Sun*, October 27, 1909.

36 **Mayor J. Barry Mahool**: Richard Rothstein, "From Ferguson to Baltimore," *Journal of Affordable Housing and Community Development Law*, 2015, as cited in a Loyola University of Maryland project, The Baltimore Story: Learning and Living Racial Justice, https://thebaltimorestory.org.

36 **"Negro removal project"**: Antero Pietila, *Not in My Neighborhood: How Bigotry Shaped a Great American City* (Ivan R. Dee, 2010). Writing about Preston in his book, Pietila notes that the mayor introduced an ordinance to "set aside certain sections of the city, allowing ample room for expansion, to compel the colored people to have homes only in those segregated

areas." He would do this by invoking the city's police powers in order "to protect the health" of white citizens. Blacks needed to be quarantined, he said. "They constitute a menace to the health of the white population" (52).

36 **US Supreme Court ruled**: *Buchanan v. Warley*. The ruling notably did not defend the rights of Black people to live where they wished; it upheld the rights of *property owners* to dispose of their possessions.

37 **"It could have been the Moon"**: Pietila, *Not in My Neighborhood*, 89.

38 **"Fields were cut up"**: Garry Wills, *Nixon Agonistes* (Houghton Mifflin, 1969), 278–79.

39 **Black residents fell**: Pietila, *Not in My Neighborhood*, 211.

39 **Racial zoning was policed**: Ibid., 235.

40 **harvesting bribes**: Agnew was fined a measly $10,000—a fraction of the sums he had collected over the years—and served three years unsupervised probation.

40 **"white noose"**: Pietila, *Not in My Neighborhood*, 222.

42 **ignored the Black half**: I found the situation pretty much the same when I moved to the *Philadelphia Inquirer* in 1979.

42 **moving . . . toward integration**: Dulaney High School fifty years after I graduated was 45 percent minority, and my old neighborhood was no longer all white. Baltimore County as a whole in 2022 was 31 percent Black, and 46 percent minority—Black, Indigenous, Asian, Latino, and Hispanic.

44 **opening day, in 1980**: Ethan McLeod, "What Happened to Baltimore's Harborplace?," *Bloomberg CityLab*, January 16, 2020.

44 **swiped from Cleveland**: Payback for Indianapolis's theft of the city's beloved Colts franchise.

45 **"tall, sterile buildings"**: Wills, *Nixon Agonistes*, 48.

47 **reverse fortunes**: What follows is drawn mostly from Stefanie DeLuca and Peter Rosenblatt, "Sandtown-Winchester—Baltimore's Daring Experiment in Urban Renewal: 20 Years Later, What Are the Lessons Learned?," *Abell Report*, November 2013.

47 **committed activists**: Lawrence Lanahan movingly tells the story of some of them in his book, *The Lines Between Us: Two Families and a Quest to Cross Baltimore's Racial Divide* (New Press, 2019).

48 **drop in the bucket**: James Bock and Joan Jacobson, "Carters to help rehab West Baltimore's Sandtown Habitat program to rebuild homes," *Baltimore Sun*, March 27, 1992.

48 **largely disappointing**: DeLuca and Rosenblatt, "Sandtown-Winchester": "Overall, the picture that emerges from the data underscores the durability of social inequality and the persistence of overlapping social problems in high poverty and racially segregated neighborhoods."

48 **deliberately created**: Wes Moore, in his book *The Other Wes Moore* (Spiegel & Grau, 2011), writes of his experience with the Black townships created by South Africa's apartheid regime: "They were South Africa's 'projects,' areas where despair and hopelessness were not accidental products of the environment, but rather the whole point" (165).

48 **prospered and moved away**: Robert Embry, president of the Abell Foundation, a philanthropy in Baltimore dedicated to improving the quality of city life, and a former assistant secretary of US Housing and Urban Development, explained to me, "The tough thing with these programs is that the people you help, disproportionately, do better and move out of the neighborhood. The number of vacant houses, in fact, increased." He added that the increase might well have been greater, however, without the initiative.

4 Either You Got to Be That, or You Ain't

This chapter is based on interviews with Allise Bridges, Leandra Williams, Josh Fuller, Joe Landsman, Maurice "Peanut" King, and Ronnie "Rah" Johnson; police interview videos of Tana and Daniel "Gotti" Purdie; the social media accounts of TTG members; and transcripts of *USA v. Montana Barronette et al.*

50 **Epigraph**: Forrest Stuart (on lower-class nineteenth-century Parisian novelists), *Ballad of the Bullet* (Princeton University Press, 2020), 6.

53 **star of Baltimore's streets**: This description and account of Peanut's career is based on Tim Prudente, "Peanut King: After 37 Years in Prison, a Giant of Baltimore's Drug Trade Returns to Face His City's Ruins," *Baltimore Sun*, December 5, 2019; and on my interview with King.

54 **street name "Monster"**: Sanyika Shakur (aka Monster, Kody Scott), *Monster: The Autobiography of an L.A. Gang Member* (Grove Press, 1993), 226.

55 **"We're *not* a secret society"**: Susan Faludi, "Ghetto Star," *LA Weekly*, October 6, 1999.

58 **the internet's role**: Séraphin Alava, Divina Frau-Meigs, and Ghayda Hassan, *Youth and Violent Extremism on Social Media: Mapping the Research* (UNESCO, 2017).

64 **"morally charged"**: Stuart, *Ballad of the Bullet*, 6.

65 **"It has amassed"**: Ibid., 31.

65 **"Before this, he was"**: Ibid., 35

66 **"public persona"**: Ibid., 11.

68 **"Man, the nigger down there"**: This is how Ronnie Johnson would later tell the story in court, and in interviews with me.

76 **"in the trap"**: Somewhat similar was slang usage of the word "shit" to mean one's residence. Where one lived in Sandtown was not especially desirable, but it was home.

80 **"At the heart of the code"**: Elijah Anderson, "The Code of the Streets," *The Atlantic*, May 1994.

5 Shit Be Catching Up with Them

This chapter is based on interviews with Robert K. Hur, Jonathan Lenzner, Martin O'Malley, Kurtis Palmero, Cliff Swindell, Mark Neptune, and Joe Landsman; and on transcripts and exhibits of *USA v. Montana Barronette et al.*

82 **Epigraph**: John Seabrook, "Don't Shoot," *New Yorker*, June 15, 2009, quoting criminologist David Kennedy on his experience doing fieldwork in the Watts neighborhood of Los Angeles in the 1980s.

85 **Drug sweeps**: Daniel Webster, Shani A. L. Buggs, Cassandra K. Crifasi, *Estimating the Effects of Law Enforcement and Public Health Interventions Intended to Reduce Gun Violence in Baltimore* (Johns Hopkins Center for Gun Policy and Research and Johns Hopkins Bloomberg School of Public Health, 2018). This study found that sweeping drug arrests actually

increased gun violence, as upstart gangs fought to control the vacated turf. *In contrast, major drug busts, which presumably are more focused on groups connected with gun violence, and more strategic with respect to prosecutions, were followed by six months of shootings at levels 25 percent lower than predicted if there had been no drug bust.*

86 **"The relationship . . . is broken"**: *Investigation of the Baltimore Police Department* (US Department of Justice, Civil Rights Division, August 10, 2016), 157.

87 **independent investigation**: *Anatomy of the Gun Trace Task Force Scandal: Its Origins, Causes, and Consequences*, executive summary (Steptoe & Johnson, January 2022), by the law firm contracted to investigate the squad.

87 **"victimized vulnerable Baltimore residents"**: Ibid., ii.

89 **criminologist David Kennedy**: Most of the descriptions of Kennedy's work are drawn from Seabrook, "Don't Shoot."

90 **Homicides fell 80 percent**: Fox Butterfield, "Killing of Girl, 10, and Increase in Homicides Challenge Boston's Crime-fighting Model," *New York Times*, July 14, 2002.

90 **"like Jesus"**: Seabrook, "Don't Shoot," cites a line that went around the police department in Cincinnati, where presumably most cops considered themselves Christian: "What's some guy who looks like Jesus got to tell us about crime in Cincinnati?"

91 **crime rates fell**: "Reported Violent Crime Rate in the United States from 1990 to 2020," https://www.statista.com/statistics/191219/reported -violent-crime-rate-in-the-usa-since-1990/#:~:text=The%20rate% 20of%20reported%20 violent%20crime%20has%20fallen%20since %20a,committed%20in%20the%20United%20States.

95 **"holler" at Beezy**: Transcripts of *USA v. Montana Barronette et al.*, testimony of Donte Pauling, October 4, 2018.

6 Here Come Landsman

This chapter is based on interviews with Jonathan Lenzner, Robert K. Hur, Martin O'Malley, Joe Landsman, Mark Neptune, Dan DeLorenzo, Cliff

Swindell, Jan "Pony Head" Gray, and Ronnie "Rah" Johnson; and on transcripts of *USA v. Montana Barronette et al.*

102 **Epigraph:** Charles Dickens, *Bleak House* (Penguin Classics, 2003).

112 **"Arrest me!":** Short video of the incident: "Arrest me! I dare you! From Baltimore Maryland," YouTube, posted February 28, 2020, by Kenny Bowman, https://www.youtube.com/watch?v=XxWeGlirsMY.

113 **full sequence of events:** More extensive video of the incident: "Raw: Man Pepper-Sprayed, Detained in Baltimore," YouTube, posted on May 2, 2015, by Associated Press, https://www.youtube.com/watch?v=zkehS8HPRHA.

113 **Lomax later won:** Tim Prudente, "Jury Awards $75,000 to Man Sprayed, Yanked Down by Baltimore Police during Riots," *Baltimore Sun*, January 24, 2018.

7 The Ballad of Ronnie Jackass

This chapter is based on interviews with Ronnie "Rah" Johnson and his parents, Gary Niedermeier, and Joe Landsman; and transcripts of *USA v. Montana Barronette et al.*

128 **Epigraph:** Joseph Heller, *Catch-22* (Simon & Schuster, 1955), 59.

130 **corrupt guards and gangs:** Ann E. Marimow and Peter Hermann, "Guards and Inmates Charged in Widespread Bribery and Smuggling Operation," *Washington Post*, October 5, 2016. The story describes conditions in the prison that had been present for years.

133 **"Don't nobody follow 'em":** Transcripts of *USA v. Montana Barronette et al.*, testimony of Sterling Crowder, September 28, 2018.

8 We Hunting

This chapter is based in interviews with Ronnie "Rah" Johnson, Joe Landsman, Mark Neptune, Cliff Swindell, Dan Gardner, and Chris Romano; and transcripts of *USA v. Montana Barronette et al.*

145 **Epigraph:** Shakur, *Monster*, 226.

154 **weapon he tossed**: Because this weapon, which was later linked to a gang murder, was found by the disgraced Gun Trace Task Force, it could not be used as evidence years later in the TTG trial. Federal prosecutors were enormously relieved that the unit had not found the second weapon or Marty's cell phone, both of which would later be presented as key evidence.

164 **"vicks"**: A "vick" was a bag of marijuana holding seven grams, so named because the NFL quarterback Michael Vick wore the number seven.

9 Number One Trigger Puller

This chapter is based on interviews with Joe Landsman, Mark Neptune, Ronnie "Rah" Johnson, Dan Gardner, and Chris Romano; and transcripts of *USA v. Montana Barronette et al.*

172 **Epigraph**: William Golding, *Lord of the Flies* (Folio Society, Ltd, 2010), 223.

184 **photo of bearded Neptune**: DeLorenzo and Landsman criticized Neptune for this photo. They felt that it was grandstanding and unprofessional, typical of Wayne Jenkins and others in the Gun Trace Task Force, who regularly circulated photos of themselves posing before captured guns and money.

10 Gotta Take It on the Chin

This chapter is based on videos of interviews with Montana Barronette and interviews with Joe Landsman, Mark Neptune, and Josh Fuller.

192 **Epigraph**: John Milton, *Paradise Lost* (Odyssey Press, 1962), 13.

11 Drinking from a Fire Hose

This chapter is based on interviews with Dan Gardner, Chris Romano, Joe Landsman, Mark Neptune, Dan DeLorenzo, and Richard Bardos; and transcripts of *USA v. Montana Barronette et al.*

215 **Epigraph**: "August 13th," YGG Tay, https://www.youtube.com/watch?v=ZBV8cx65vHU.

216 **barber gunned down**: Tana has not been prosecuted for murdering Williams.

224 **Bardos's letter**: Bardos told me that the letter did not actually name Guy Coffey as an informant, but it clearly does. Coffey photographed it—dated October 17, 2017, with Tillman's name and the case number crossed out—and texted it to Neptune as soon as it came to his attention. The prosecutors found Bardos's behavior shocking.

225 **As for the rapper, he told**: Tim Prudente, "Feds Tell Judge Baltimore Rapper YGG Tay Offered $20,000 for the Murder of a Police Informant," *Baltimore Sun*, September 18, 2018.

12 What Are We Supposed to Do Now, Clap?

This chapter is drawn from transcripts of *USA v. Montana Barronette et al.*, and based on interviews with Joe Landsman, Mark Neptune, Chris Romano, Dan Gardner, Jan "Pony Head" Gray, Ronnie "Rah" Johnson, Michael Lawlor, and Richard Bardos.

227 **Epigraph**: Gardner in an interview with the author.

13 Crabs in a Bucket

This chapter is based on transcripts of *USA v. Montana Barronette et al.*, and on interviews with Valencia Bullock, Shanika Sivells, Daniel Webster, "Fish," Jonathan Lenzner, Chris Romano, Dan Gardner, Joe Landsman, Mark Neptune, Dan DeLorenzo, Ronnie "Rah" Johnson, Jan "Pony Head" Gray, and Terrence Singleton (father of Darius, or "Scratch").

254 **Epigraph**: Charles Dickens, *A Tale of Two Cities* (Pure Snow Publishing, 2021), 69.

265 **Removing the most violent gangs**: Aaron Chalfin, Michael LaForest, and Jacob Kaplan, "Can Precision Policing Reduce Gun Violence? Evidence from 'Gang Takedowns' in New York City," *Journal of Policy*

Analysis and Management, 2021. It concludes: "During the last decade, while national homicide rates have remained flat, New York City has experienced a second great crime decline, with gun violence declining by more than 50 percent since 2011. In this paper, we investigate one potential explanation for this dramatic and unexpected improvement in public safety—the New York Police Department's shift to a more surgical form of 'precision policing,' in which law enforcement focuses resources on a small number of individuals who are thought to be the primary drivers of violence."

265 **similar effect, at least temporarily**: Webster, Buggs, and Crifasi, *Estimating the Effects*.

267 **"Even as those in the lowest"**: Isabel Wilkerson, *Caste: The Origins of Our Discontents* (Random House, 2020), 340.

271 **"It is the public schools"**: Du Bois, *The Souls of Black Folk*, 487.

272 **"What is inescapable"**: "Maryland's School Rankings Tell Us What We Already Know—Your Education Depends on Where You Live," *Baltimore Sun*, December 4, 2018.

272 **Nation's Report Card**: Published by the National Assessment of Educational Progress, a congressionally mandated program overseen by the National Center for Educational Statistics. Only Detroit and Cleveland, also overwhelmingly Black, fared worse.

272 **worst-performing**: *U.S. News & World Report*'s school rankings, 2019. Edmondson-Westside ranked sixty-eighth in the list of one hundred Baltimore-area high schools surveyed.

272 **$31,000 annually per pupil**: Maddie Hanna, Kristen Graham, and Craig McCoy, "A landmark case that could change school funding across Pa. is going to trial," *Philadelphia Inquirer*, November 12, 2021.

277 **"That is completely false"**: Prudente, "Feds Tell Judge."

Books

Cleaver, Eldridge. *Soul on Ice*. Delta, 1968.

Crenson, Matthew A. *Baltimore: A Political History*. Johns Hopkins University Press, 2017. Thorough, insightful, and engaging, the best history of the city I have seen.

Currie, Elliott. *A Peculiar Indifference: The Neglected Toll of Violence on Black America*. Metropolitan Books, 2020. A scathing portrait of the ongoing catastrophe in urban Black America and the shameful lack of political interest in stopping it.

DeLuca, Stefanie, Susan Clampet-Lundquist, and Kathryn Edin. *Coming of Age in the Other America*. Russell Sage Foundation, 2016. A painstaking research project looking at the experiences of hundreds of Black Baltimore youths growing up in the city's housing projects.

Du Bois, W. E. B. *The Philadelphia Negro: A Social Study* (1899). University of Pennsylvania Press, 1996. The classic sociological study of Black experience in that city.

———. *Writings*. Library of America, 1986. The classic works of the sociologist, activist, and essayist. It includes *The Souls of Black Folk* (1903), Du Bois's most famous work, and the one I quote from.

Fenton, Justin. *We Own This City: A True Story of Crime, Cops, and Corruption*. Random House, 2021. An account of the Gun Trace Task Force scandal, adapted by David Simon and Ed Burns into an HBO serial of the same name.

Lanahan, Lawrence. *The Lines Between Us: Two Families and a Quest to Cross Baltimore's Racial Divide*. New Press, 2019. A well-reported, moving—sometimes hopeful, sometimes sad—story of two individuals, one white,

the other Black, and their families, who move into Baltimore neighborhoods of the opposite castes, with mixed results.

McDougall, Harold A. *Black Baltimore: A New Theory of Community.* Temple
University Press, 1993. A perhaps overly hopeful look at prospects for
reviving the city's neglected Black communities through local community action; somewhat sad to read three failed decades later.

Moore, Wes. *The Other Wes Moore.* Spiegel & Grau, 2011. A Black Rhodes
scholar from Baltimore contrasts his poor but fortunate upbringing with
that of a man his own age with the same name—a convicted murderer—
illustrating how something as essential as involved, concerned parents
can make a stunning difference in a person's life.

Moore, Wes, with Erica L. Green. *Five Days: The Fiery Reckoning of an American City.* One World, 2020. A vivid account of the 2015 uprising/riot in
Baltimore that followed the killing of Freddie Gray in police custody.

Moynihan, Daniel P. *Miles to Go: A Personal History of Social Policy.* Harvard
University Press, 1996.

Pietila, Antero. *Not in My Neighborhood: How Bigotry Shaped a Great American City.* Ivan R. Dee, 2010. A brilliant, impeccably researched, power-
fully written account of how racism and anti-Semitism drew the map of
Baltimore over a long century of shameful discrimination and exclusion.
An important book by a veteran *Baltimore Sun* reporter.

Shakur, Sanyika (aka Monster, Kody Scott). *Monster: The Autobiography of an
L.A. Gang Member.* Grove Press, 1993. A disturbing, candid, and compelling first-person account by a man who was caught up in the culture of
street violence in Los Angeles.

Stuart, Forrest. *Ballad of the Bullet.* Princeton University Press, 2020. An
original, convincing, and well-written study of how social media platforms have encouraged poor Black youths to engage in murderous violence, and turn their exploits into fame and (in some cases) money, by
celebrating it online in video and song.

Wilkerson, Isabel. *Caste: The Origins of Our Discontents.* Random House,
2020. A sober, brilliant, pellucid exploration of the racist assumptions

that underlie American life, their origins, and their consequences. An important book.

Wills, Garry. *Nixon Agonistes*. Houghton Mifflin, 1969. A classic exploration of the political forces shaping America during the era of Presidents Lyndon Johnson and Richard Nixon. Wills was then living in Baltimore, and much of the reporting in this book is centered in and around the city. I read it first when I was in college, and it has always been a model for me of deep reporting, research, and abstract thought, and an example of how seriously smart writing can be lively, colorful, and completely original.

Woods, Baynard, and Brandon Soderberg. *I Got a Monster: The Rise and Fall of America's Most Corrupt Police Squad*. St. Martin's Press, 2020. A brisk account of Wayne Jenkins and his Gun Trace Task Force policing disaster.

Acknowledgments

First and foremost, this book could not have been written without the enthusiastic help of Joe Landsman, Mark Neptune, and Dan DeLorenzo, who fielded hundreds of questions in person, by phone, by email and text, and who rarely failed to find answers. Landsman and Neptune served for years in the very troubled Baltimore Police Department and demonstrated that even through its much-disparaged recent history, it has fielded many exceptionally capable, honest, and thoroughly decent police. Each read an early version of the manuscript and offered corrections and shades of understanding that made it much better.

My thanks to Matt Bai, who introduced me to Jonathan Lenzner, then first assistant US Attorney in Maryland, and to Robert K. Hur, and all the members of their staff, who made records available and answered my questions over many months. Particular thanks to Chris Romano and Dan Gardner.

I'd also like to thank Montana Barronette and his sister Shanika Sivells. Even though Barronette turned down my repeated interview requests, he asked his sister to help me. Shanika patiently and carefully explained the history of her brothers and their family. Ronnie "Rah" Johnson and Jan "Pony Head" Gray offered important insight into The Game and into the world of Sandtown. I am also grateful to the dozens of Baltimore academics, politicians, and police who offered me their insights and pointed me to the studies and articles cited throughout the text. My son Aaron and his friend Michael

Payton, and my son William (BJ) gave the text an early critical read and offered useful advice.

And, as ever, thanks to Morgan Entrekin and his terrific staff, old friends and new, at Grove Atlantic for their careful editing and expert packaging and marketing of the final product. We have been working together now for nearly a quarter of a century, since the publication of *Black Hawk Down*, and I cannot imagine a writer having a more fruitful, enjoyable relationship with a publishing house.